BANKING ON SMALL BUSINESS

Microfinance in Contemporary Russia

GAIL BUYSKE

CORNELL UNIVERSITY PRESS
ITHACA AND LONDON

First published 2007 by Cornell University Press

Printed in the United States of America

Library of Congress Cataloging-in-Publication Data

Buyske, Gail.
  Banking on small business : microfinance in contemporary Russia / Gail Buyske.
    p. cm.
  Includes bibliographical references and index.
  ISBN 978-0-8014-4578-1 (cloth : alk. paper)
  1. Bank kreditovaniia malogo biznesa. 2. Microfinance—Russia (Federation) 3. Small business—Russia (Federation)—Finance. I. Title.

  HG178.33.R8B88 2007
  332.1'753—dc22

                                        2007005914

Cornell University Press strives to use environmentally responsible suppliers and materials to the fullest extent possible in the publishing of its books. Such materials include vegetable-based, low-VOC inks and acid-free papers that are recycled, totally chlorine-free, or partly composed of nonwood fibers. For further information, visit our website at www.cornellpress.cornell.edu.

Cloth printing   10 9 8 7 6 5 4 3 2 1

To Rick

CONTENTS

TABLES

ACKNOWLEDGMENTS

Although writing a book is a solitary undertaking, I have benefited from so much friendly support and thoughtful feedback that the process rarely seemed lonely.

To start, there are the friends and colleagues who have commented on chapters of this book. Thank you again to Ala Abakumova, Greta Bull, Gudrun Busch, Cathryn Carlsen, Marina Frolova, Ruth Goodwin-Groen, David Hexter, Jenifer Mudd, Reiner Mueller-Hanke, Bryan Nielsen, Sophie Pompea, Ilkka Salonen, Mike Taylor, Dmitry Toulin, Marilou van Golstein Brouwers, and Dennis Vinokourov. I am particularly grateful to Dr. Tatiana Alimova, who commented extensively on chapter 2 and provided much appreciated research assistance. Meg Osius and Cynthia Stone, as well as two anonymous reviewers for Cornell University Press, generously commented on the entire manuscript. Although of course any errors in this book are my own, the feedback from all of these reviewers has been invaluable in encouraging me to rethink and improve the text.

A number of people, in addition to those I listed above, have graciously shared their insights on microfinance, Russian banking, and Russian entrepreneurs. In particular, I thank Paul Asel, Anna Baitenova, Adam Blanco, Sylvie Bossoutrot, James Cook, Christine Loomis, Mikhail Mamuta, George Orlov, Alexander Sharonov, Oleg Shestoperov, Sergey Suchkov, Nick Tesseyman, Richard Turner, and Laurie Weisman. Eric Hansen of the U.S. Russia Center for Entrepreneurship kindly introduced me to several of the entrepreneurs interviewed for the book.

My brother, Steven Buyske, and his wife, Ann Jurecic, shared insights and moral support that were deeply appreciated. And, although he was not directly involved in my work on this book, Kurt Geiger was a key figure in ensuring that the reality of my working in Moscow was even better than my dream.

There are many KMB staff members with whom I had the opportunity to share KMB's highs and lows. Reiner Mueller-Hanke, Christoph Freytag, Ilsur Akhmetshin, and Sergey Suchkov stand out as the original management team who patiently worked with me as I overcame my skepticism about microfinance and evolved into a disciple. I am particularly thankful for being able to work with Reiner Mueller-Hanke, KMB's CEO, from the inception of KMB through the investment by Banca Intesa and to experience first-hand his valuable contribution. Other members of KMB's staff with whom I had the pleasure of working include Victoria Balyuk, Olga Bodnarchuk, Emmanuel Decamps, Suzanne Decker, Natalya Dirks, Elena Kovyrzina, Dmitry Matveev, Elena Semushina, Dmitry Smirnov, Vincenzo Trani, Ferdinand Tuinstra, Olga Varnene, and Natalya Zadorozhnaya.

The KMB board members and board observers who contributed to making KMB's potential a reality over the years are Jacqueline Barendse, Peter Blom, Gudrun Busch, Klaus Hartmann, David Hexter, Rauf Khalaf, Nicholas Ollivant, George Orlov, Stewart Paperin, Sophie Pompea, Mike Taylor, Marilou van Golstein Brouwers, Elizabeth Wallace, and Andreas Zeisler. I was fortunate to be able to work with all of these individuals as well as with the board members nominated by Banca Intesa.

I can't imagine a better editor than Roger Haydon, whose encouragement and advice helped me figure out what story I wanted to tell. Coming from a three-generation Cornell family, with my grandparents having met while students at Cornell and my mother having recently cochaired her fifty-fifth reunion, has made the experience of working with Cornell University Press even more than usually rewarding.

This book never would have happened without the support of my husband, Rick Hibberd, whose pronouncement after his first visit that he would never return to Russia turned out to be wonderfully inaccurate. I couldn't be happier to dedicate this book to him.

ACRONYMS

ARB	Association of Russian Banks
ARCO	Agency for Restructuring of Credit Organizations
ASA	Association for Social Advancement
ATM	Automatic teller machine
BRAC	Bangladesh Rural Advancement Committee
BRI	Bank Rakyat Indonesia
CBR	Central Bank of Russia
CEFIR	Center for Economic and Financial Research at New Economic School
CEO	Chief executive officer
CGAP	Consultative Group to Assist the Poorest
DEG	Deutsche Investitions- und Entwicklungsgesellschaft mbh
EBRD	European Bank for Reconstruction and Development
EU	European Union
FIDP	Financial Institutions Development Program
FIG	Financial industrial group
FINCA	Foundation for International Community Assistance

FORA   Fund Opportunity Russia

GDP   Gross domestic product

GKO   Short term (Russian) government obligation
(*gosudarstvennaya kratkosrochnaya obligatsiya*)

G-7   Group of Seven

IFC   International Finance Corporation

IIC   InterAmerican Investment Corporation

IPC   Internationale Projekt Consult

KfW   Reconstruction Credit Institute (Kreditanstalt fur
Wiederaufban)

KMB   Lending to Small Business (Kreditovaniye Malogo
Biznesa)

MAP   Ministry for Anti-Monopoly Policy and Support of
Entrepreneurship (Ministerstvo Antimonopol'noy politiki
i podershki predprinimatel'stva)

MFI   Microfinance institution

MIX   Microfinance Information eXchange

MSE   Micro- and small enterprise

NBD   Nizhegorodskoy Bankirskiy Dom

NGO   Nongovernmental organization

OI   Opportunity International

OPORA Association of Organizations of Small and Medium-Sized
Enterprises (Obshcherossiyskaya Obshchestvennaya
Organizatsiya Malogo i Srednogo Predprinimaltel'stva)

PPP   Purchasing power parity

PWC   PricewaterhouseCoopers

RPFB   Russian Project Finance Bank

RSBF   Russia Small Business Fund

SBA   Small Business Administration

SEDF   Soros Economic Development Fund

SME   Small and medium-sized enterprise

Tacis   Technical Aid to the Commonwealth of Independent
         States

TUSRIF   The U.S.-Russia Investment Fund

USAID   United States Agency for International Development

USSR   Union of Soviet Socialist Republics

WWB   Women's World Banking

Note on Transliteration

I have transliterated Russian words using the U.S. Board on
Geographic Names system. All translations from Russian are my own.

BANKING ON SMALL BUSINESS

INTRODUCTION

On a hot Moscow day in 1999 I received an unexpected phone call from my colleagues at the European Bank for Reconstruction and Development (EBRD) in London. They were finalizing the creation of the Russian Small Business Credit Bank, KMB Bank, whose mission was to lend to "micro and small enterprises" (MSEs).[1] They needed some Moscow-based bankers to be members of the board of directors: Would I be interested?

My instinctive answer was no. After twenty years in international banking, I considered small entrepreneurs to be high-risk borrowers anywhere in the world, let alone Russia. Furthermore, the successes that my colleagues had already achieved by working with other Russian banks seemed too good to be true; I didn't believe that their track record would last.

My concerns were reinforced by my previous experience with Russia and the Russian banking sector. Having first studied in the Soviet Union in 1975 as a college student, I was subsequently deputy director of the Chase Manhattan Bank's Soviet and Eastern European Division during perestroika, following which I completed a midcareer PhD for which I researched financial-sector development in post-Soviet economies. These experiences further contributed to my skepticism that

---

[1] The name KMB is based on the acronym of the bank's Russian name, Bank Kreditovaniya Malogo Biznesa (Small Business Credit Bank).

any bank in Russia could succeed. In fact, the financial crisis in 1998 had caused losses that still paralyzed Russia's banking system a full year later, at the time that I received this call.

My response? I agreed to join KMB Bank's board of directors for a brief period. That would give my colleagues time to find someone willing to make a longer-term commitment and it would spare me the risks of being involved with their possibly failing venture.

As it turned out, I chaired KMB's board of directors for six years, until majority ownership was purchased by Banca Intesa, Italy's second largest bank, after which I continued as a board member for nine more months. The experience was one of the most fascinating, rewarding, and humbling of my career. It also led to this book, which addresses three themes in development finance that intersect at KMB Bank: the creation of an effective banking system, the development of microfinance, and the growth of entrepreneurship in Russia.

Banking is a much more fundamental element of how an economy works—or doesn't work—than those of us living in mature market economies typically realize. We grow up taking for granted our ability to put our savings into banks, take our money out at automatic teller machines (ATMs), and borrow to finance many of life's key passages, such as a college education, a wedding, or the purchase of a home. My own first experiences with banks were highly favorable, because they always involved getting a lollipop while my mother took care of banking matters.

Although we all have horror stories about banks as well, we're not very good at picturing life without them. But imagine for a moment that you're a new Russian entrepreneur in the early 1990s, just after the Soviet Union has dissolved. You've lost your job; because of the ruble devaluation you have the equivalent of two hundred dollars in savings; and you share a stall at the market in which you sell bootlegged food products.

If you put your savings into the badly regulated banking system, you run a real risk that the bank could fail and you could lose your savings entirely. There is no realistic way to evaluate this risk based on information provided by the banks or other sources of information. There is also no deposit insurance. And, with inflation rates over 1,000 percent, any interest you might earn on a bank deposit would lead to a net loss in purchasing power. On the other hand, if you leave the money at home, you risk its being stolen in an environment in which law and order have become a memory of the past.

What about borrowing to buy a secondhand car to make it easier to get goods from the factory to your stall, since using public transportation limits your inventory to what you can physically carry? That also is out of the question. Banks are not making small loans like the one you need, and, even if they were, you have nothing to provide as collateral. You can't even go out on a limb and draw down your credit card, because there aren't any in Russia in the early 1990s.

Therefore you're stuck being a small-time food seller at a shared stall, unless somehow you can save enough money to buy the car outright.[2] But, because you are forced to use cash for all of your inventory purchases, and everyone around you at the market knows what profits you make and that you keep your money at home, you are always vulnerable. The whole concept of borrowing now to build a better future in which you will be able to repay your loans does not exist.

If you extend your imaginary case to millions of Russians, you can begin to understand why slow economic development and ineffective banking systems often go hand in hand. When millions of small entrepreneurs can't get loans to expand their businesses, a potential motor for economic growth is extinguished.

A similar scene often plays itself out for larger companies, because underdeveloped banking systems typically don't have the expertise to evaluate and take the risk of larger loans. In addition, when lack of confidence in the banking sector is widespread, banks often don't have the resources to make very many larger loans, because there are insufficient deposits.

States sometimes respond to this chicken-and-egg situation by creating their own banks. These banks have access to state funds for lending, and, if the banks provide retail services as well, the implied reliability of state ownership encourages the population to place deposits with these banks.

Ironically, state-owned banks often create more problems of their own. Money attracts politics like honey attracts bears; a state-owned

---

[2] One other option might be the "money lenders" or "loan sharks" that spring up in such circumstances, but they were a particularly unsavory option in the relatively lawless days of the early 1990s.

bank is almost inevitably vulnerable to requests—or demands—to finance pet projects that may or may not be creditworthy. Projects that aren't creditworthy ultimately create losses and weaken the financial condition of the bank. They also deprive other, more creditworthy projects of funding. The fact that potentially profitable and creditworthy projects cannot be financed translates once again into borrowers—and therefore ultimately the economy—not growing as quickly as they could.

Russia provides an unusually dramatic setting for studying the challenges of developing a smoothly functioning banking sector. Building a new banking sector to replace the state-owned banks of the Soviet period was not a matter of starting with a clean slate and implementing the best banking practices from market economies. If that had been the case there would not be much for us to learn; banking principles that worked in London would have worked equally well in Moscow.

Instead, Russia's commercial banks were created in a chaotic political and economic environment, in the shadow of an entrenched ideology that had long opposed banking's focus on profits. Therefore, many revered banking principles seemed irrelevant to Russian bankers. How could you avoid conflicts of interest in your lending practices, for example, when only your closest friends could be trusted as borrowers while society was falling apart?

On the other side of the spectrum, some principles that were imported were adapted beyond recognition in their new environment. The concept of central bank independence, for example, is typically understood as referring to its independence from the executive branch of government. In Russia, however, the critical relationship was between the central bank and the banks that it was supposed to be regulating; this relationship was characterized by a pronounced lack of independence that Western concepts had not had to address.

Finally, our almost subconscious assumption that the role of banks is to lend was severely challenged in Russia, where other opportunities during the 1990s provided at least Russia's largest banks with much more lucrative returns. Grappling with the resulting complexities gives us a much better understanding of what makes a country's banking sector work—or not work.

The frightening scenario of a banking sector that does not work is the one that played itself out in Russia from the perestroika period until the traumatic financial crisis of 1998. It seems grim enough that many of Russia's largest banks had turned their backs on lending in the years preceding the crisis and that the central bank failed to serve as an effective regulator. It got worse, however, when the crisis provided an environment in which the owners of several large banks created new banks to which they transferred their assets, leaving little behind with which to repay the depositors in the original banks. Russia's banking sector not only failed to provide financing, it sapped trust in a society that was still adjusting to the loss of the planned economy.

While the banking sector provided chastening lessons in how badly economic transitions can go wrong, its evolution following the crisis has been equally instructive. The ensuing vacuum of state activity provided an environment in which the surviving banks found themselves with no option but to return to one of the basics of banking—lending. The story of Russian banking also sets the stage for understanding why Russian banks were relatively slow to lend to entrepreneurs. The key point, often overlooked, is that Russian banks were not discriminating against small entrepreneurs; there were so many profitable opportunities before the crisis that lending in general was not a priority.

Although Russia's banking sector is relatively well known for at least its headline characteristics, one topic that has received very little attention is the perspective that Russia provides on the second theme of this book: the global development of microfinance. Microfinance began as a means of making extremely small loans to extremely poor borrowers; one of the first, and best documented, microfinance loans was a $27 loan made to a group of basket weavers in Bangladesh in 1976.[3] Based on the premise that the poor and financially underserved are an unexpectedly reliable class of borrowers when lenders apply the appropriate methodology, the microfinance field was rapidly developing in Asia and South America as the Soviet Union was collapsing. The field has grown so extensively that in 2006 the Nobel Peace Prize was awarded to Muhammad Yunus, who made the loan noted above, and the microfinance bank that he subsequently founded, Grameen Bank.

[3] The story of this loan, which led to the development of Grameen Bank, is told by the bank's founder, Muhammad Yunus, in *Banker to the Poor: Micro-Lending and the Battle against World Poverty* (New York: PublicAffairs, 1999).

Although economic development specialists quickly embraced microfinance, it has been an uphill climb to introduce the concept and methodology in countries that have long histories in commercial banking. Microfinance poses many challenges to the entrenched worldview of the bankers and regulators in these countries, starting with the most basic question: Given that the poor have no money by definition, how can one safely lend to them? As a result, the microfinance movement started largely outside the banking sector, primarily through nongovernmental organizations (NGOs). Much of the more recent story of microfinance development has been the struggle to incorporate microfinance into the mainstream financial sector, or what the microfinance field calls "building inclusive financial sectors."

Russia serves as a significant exception to this process, since it did not have a commercial banking tradition that had a point of view on microfinance. Instead, Russia's commercial banks began to grow as the global understanding of microfinance began to grow, with organizations such as the EBRD introducing microfinance to Russia through the banking sector. Furthermore, microfinance was introduced to Russia as a tool for helping to create new businesses and contribute to economic growth; it did not have an antipoverty "label." Because everyone is interested in growth, microfinance in Russia has always had a broad audience. In fact, with both banks and nonbank microfinance institutions (MFIs) providing services to MSEs, combined with a legal and regulatory environment that is evolving to accommodate the needs of these borrowers, Russia is now a country in the final stages of creating an inclusive financial system.

Although the idea that Russia might be in the forefront of any financial-sector developments might at first seem unlikely, on reflection it is clear that the microfinance methodology corresponded ideally with the situation in Russia in the early 1990s. Designed to address the borrower's lack of a financial track record and standard collateral, microfinance provided the solution to lending in a country where personal loans had been extremely rare and ownership of assets was uncertain in the rapidly changing legal environment. There were also millions of potential microfinance clients, with many Russians on the brink of poverty unless self-employment was able to take the place of their former government-provided jobs.

Russia differed in this regard from the countries in South America and Asia where microfinance first took hold, because it did not have the same entrenched problem of endemically poor and sometimes illiterate populations. Russia faced a very different sort of potential "first generation" poverty, as millions of well-educated people suddenly found themselves without jobs and without a social safety net. The often-told story about discovering that your unlicensed cab driver in Moscow is a PhD physicist is not such a tall tale. As a result, more of the microfinance lending in Russia is focused on the financially underserved than on the long-term poor. In addition, the loan sizes tend to be larger; an overeducated taxi driver has different aspirations and earning capacity than an illiterate weaver.

The lessons to be learned from this different microfinance model—different in how it was introduced to the economy, different in the nature of its core clients—have been largely overlooked by the economic-development field. The tendency is to disregard Russia's experience because loan sizes in Russia are too large to be "real" microfinance loans. However, not only can the microfinance methodology be applied to those with larger borrowing needs that have been ignored by the formal financial sector but economic development is served equally well with a $50 loan or a $500 loan or even a $5,000 loan to an entrepreneur who has never been able to get financing before. In all cases the loan gives the borrower an unprecedented opportunity to develop her or his business.

The emphasis on loan size as a defining characteristic of microfinance has also contributed to the inability of many microfinance specialists and commercial bankers to recognize the natural synergies of their activities. Microfinance lending is frequently labeled as a noncommercial, poverty-alleviating product, whereas small business lending is clearly a commercial product. It's sadly ironic that the "discovery" of microfinance as a poverty-alleviation tool has branded the field in such a way that some microfinance practitioners are suspicious of activities designed to generate profits, while bankers assume that they have nothing in common with those assisting the poor.

I argue in this book that we are missing the bigger picture when we draw dividing lines between types of clients and lending activities. Instead, we should recognize that microfinance and small borrowers are located along a single spectrum, the broad middle of which is characterized by small and shifting gradations. As a result, it is impossible to create a clear and fixed distinction between microfinance and small business borrowers—and therefore between appropriate lending procedures and even types of lenders. Recognizing the existence of this continuum would create a win-win situation for microfinance lenders and bankers. Microfinance lenders would attract more of the commercial participation that is necessary for the field to continue to grow, while commercial banks could tap a new client base. Although cooperation between microfinance lenders and commercial banks is on a positive upward trend, it is still in its early stages. I hope that this book will contribute to accelerating the trend.

KMB Bank illustrates an important part of this story; with a mandate since its founding in 1999 to lend to micro- and small business clients, KMB's experience illustrates the natural synergy between these two types of borrowers. Furthermore, having grown to become one of the largest privately owned MSE banks in the world by the end of 2005, with a loan portfolio of $415 million, KMB provides lessons about institutional development. Although this growth would be an impressive accomplishment under any circumstances, that it happened in Russia's challenging environment makes KMB Bank a particularly compelling story to investigate.

KMB's story is also significant because it is one of the first cases in the world in which an MSE bank founded by donor agencies and socially committed investors has been acquired by a fully commercial investor, with Banca Intesa having acquired majority ownership at the end of 2005. This acquisition provides support for my argument that the natural link between microlending and small business lending is worth serious consideration by commercial banks.

That KMB has found so many borrowers underscores the third theme of this book, the growth of Russian entrepreneurship. Although Russian entrepreneurs are typically considered to be underdeveloped—and the banking sector is often identified as a culprit—I believe that Russian entrepreneurs are substantially more developed and dynamic than is usually appreciated.

This different point of view has important implications for how to encourage the sector's further growth. If one assumes that Russian entrepreneurs are weak and underdeveloped, the logical response is to protect them from the rigors of the market until they are able to stand on their own feet. One common form of such support is subsidized financing, to reduce interest rate costs. Another common form of support is government guarantees designed to encourage banks to lend to what is assumed to be an unreliable client base.

To those who think that Russian entrepreneurs need some form of state protection, I can only say: When is the last time you lived through perestroika, the collapse of your country, a failed putsch, hyperinflation, and a financial crisis that reduced the value of your country's currency by several multiples? Many entrepreneurs understandably failed at some point during this incredible series of events, but those who survived must be among the most resilient in the world.

To be fair to those concerned about the state of Russian entrepreneurs, the official data have often been discouraging at first glance. The standard observation is that Russian entrepreneurs account for 10–12 percent of GDP, compared to over 50 percent in the countries of the European Union. The hand-wringing that typically results, however, fails to take into account the historical perspective. Not only was entrepreneurship in Russia illegal as recently as 1987 but it could actually be punished by execution. Given that disincentive as a starting point, Russian entrepreneurship has developed surprisingly well.

A second, often overlooked point is that the data used to compare Russian entrepreneurs with those of other countries are calculated so differently that the typically used comparisons are actually meaningless. It is instructive that outsiders are often skeptical of Russian data, ranging from the degree of tuberculosis infections to military capacity, because we assume that the real situation is worse than the data reveal. Nevertheless we accept data about Russian small businesses, which correspond to our low expectations, even though the data have been shown to be inaccurate. The fact that Russian policymakers have also based their premises on these faulty data underscores the entrenched assumptions that envelop Russian entrepreneurs.

Finally, although Russian banks are often identified as the guilty party in the perceived underperformance of Russian entrepreneurs, such finger-pointing neglects to take the history of Russian banking-sector development into account. As Russian banks have steadily increased their lending in the years since the 1998 crisis, so have they turned their attention to Russian entrepreneurs. Well-intended efforts to facilitate this financing with various forms of state support run the risk of disrupting a naturally evolving market trend.

Russia's new billionaires often dominate the headlines, but I think that Russia's real entrepreneurs are the millions of unsung Russians who have adapted to the unprecedented challenges of the last two decades to try to build businesses and support their families. These individuals may even someday form the core of Russia's middle class. The story of Russia's banks and its entrepreneurs therefore has potential lessons for many countries around the world.

I begin this story in chapter 1 by providing the global and historical context for the development of microfinance and how it applies to Russia. The following two chapters focus on the emergence of small entrepreneurs and Russia's banking sector in the context of the collapse of the Soviet Union and the often chaotic efforts to restructure Russia's economy from one controlled by the state to one responsive to market forces. These three themes—microfinance, banking-sector development, and Russian entrepreneurs—intersect in chapter 4 with a discussion of KMB Bank, whose experience illustrates the evolution of finance for Russian entrepreneurs while providing more global lessons about the future development of microfinance.

Chapter 1

MICROFINANCE: A GLOBAL OVERVIEW

Financing for low-income borrowers has become an increasingly hot development topic over the past several decades. Such financing leapt into the popular imagination with the much proclaimed success of Grameen Bank in Bangladesh, which was created after its founder, Muhammad Yunus, made a $27 loan to a group of basket weavers in 1976.[1] It has since become headline news, with Yunus and Grameen Bank having been awarded the Nobel Peace Prize in 2006. Much of the attention has understandably focused on microfinance, which, with loan sizes as small as $5–10, and memorable accounts of how such tiny loans have helped borrowers escape from poverty, offers an intuitively appealing way to help poor and low-income populations help themselves. However, it is also important not to overlook the role of small business finance, which can be an equally valuable development tool for entrepreneurs with larger borrowing needs but who also suffer from limited access to finance.

In this chapter I introduce the first of three themes in this book by providing the global and historical context for the extraordinary development of microfinance and how it applies to the case of Russia. I also highlight one of the main challenges facing the field, which is

---

[1] Other early microfinance pioneers include ACCION International, which began its operations in Latin America, and the Self-Employed Women's Association Bank in India. Brigit Helms, *Access for All: Building Inclusive Financial Systems* (World Bank, 2006), 3.

how to continue to grow. Although microfinance lenders have provided loans to over ninety-one million borrowers who would have previously been considered "unbankable," there is still a daunting gap between supply and demand.[2] Today's levels of microfinance lending would have to increase by several multiples close this gap.

Although the only realistic way to do so is with greater commercial bank participation, both bankers and microfinance lenders have been relatively slow to understand the natural synergies between their activities. Encouraging progress is being made in closing the perceptual divide, but there remains a historic residue of focusing more on differences than similarities; microfinance lending is often perceived as a charitable activity, while banks are clearly focused on profits. I argue in this chapter that adopting a different point of view and recognizing the synergies between microfinance and the small business lending of commercial banks is critical to closing the lending gap. This perspective would also reposition microfinance as a tool for contributing to economic growth. Although microfinance's past contributions to economic development have been extraordinarily important, I believe that the future holds even more potential.

What Is Microfinance?

Microfinance is a methodology for providing financial services to poor or financially underserved populations or both. While a narrower definition of microfinance refers specifically to financial services to the poor, in this book I apply a broader definition that includes the financially underserved.[3] An example of this broader definition is provided

---

[2] The Microcredit Summit, one of the largest associations of MFIs, reported that 3,164 of its institutional members had reached over ninety-one million borrowers as of year-end 2004. Over 70 percent of these borrowers were classified as "the poorest of the poor" when they acquired their first loan. The poorest of the poor are defined as "those who are in the bottom half of those living below their nation's poverty line, or any of the 1.2 billion who live on less than US $1 a day adjusted for purchasing power parity (PPP) when they started with a program." Sam Daley-Harris, *State of the Microcredit Summit Campaign Report 2005*, http://www.microcreditsummit.org (accessed January 4, 2006).

[3] Elisabeth Rhyne discusses these two definitions in the introductory chapter to *Mainstreaming Microfinance: How Lending Began, Grew, and Came of Age in Bolivia* (Bloomfield, Conn.: Kumarian Press, 2001).

by Marguerite S. Robinson, an anthropologist known for her extensive microfinance work in Indonesia, who defines microfinance as

> small-scale financial services—primarily credit and savings—provided to people who farm or fish or herd; who operate small enterprises or microenterprises where goods are produced, recycled, repaired or sold; who provide services; who work for wages or commissions; who gain income from renting out small amounts of land, vehicles, draft animals, or machinery and tools; and to other individuals and groups at the local levels of developing countries, both rural and urban.[4]

I find this broader definition of microfinance useful for three reasons. First, as a lending methodology, microfinance works equally well for both groups. Furthermore, in terms of economic development, improving the financial condition of both groups is critically important; there are no data demonstrating that providing financial services to one group or the other makes a greater contribution to a country's well-being.[5] Finally, there is no clear dividing line between the poor and the financially underserved that would make a distinction between them practically meaningful. Although efforts to create these distinctions are often the result of well-meaning efforts to measure results, in my experience they can create more barriers to economic development than is often realized.

I should note, however, that the appropriate definition of microfinance is contested, particularly over the issue of whether microfinance should focus only on the poor, or whether broadening the definition results in "mission drift" in which lenders shift their focus to larger borrowers who are easier to serve and potentially more profitable.

---

[4] Marguerite S. Robinson, *The Microfinance Revolution: Sustainable Finance for the Poor*, vol. 1 (Washington, D.C.: World Bank; and New York: Open Society Institute, 2003), 9.

[5] Although studies have shown that one-person enterprises are less efficient compared to enterprises with two to nine employees, financing is one of the elements that enables one-person enterprises to grow and become more efficient. For efficiency information, see Carl Liedholm and D. C. Mead, "Small-Scale Industries in Developing Countries: Empirical Evidence and Policy Implications," International Development Paper 9, Michigan State University Department of Agricultural Economics, East Lansing, 1987.

Part of this debate is generated by genuine concern about mission drift, while part seems to be generated by an antipathy toward profit considerations by some who work with the poor.

The challenge of defining and identifying a microfinance client further complicates the situation. There is typically substantial overlap between a microenterprise and the activities of a family—or extended family. Therefore, efforts to define a microenterprise based on its income or assets, as well as the impact of lending on this microenterprise, can be quite complicated. As a result, the microfinance field typically makes the assumption that microfinance clients will define themselves; a microfinance borrower will go to the effort necessary to obtain a $100 loan, for example, while a more established and profitable enterprise will not. Loan size has therefore become a proxy for a microenterprise.

Although the reasons for this approach are straightforward, it has inevitably led to the conclusion that borrowers requiring more than a defined loan size are not microenterprises. And, because microfinance initially developed among very poor populations in South America and Asia, microfinance loans are typically thought of as ranging in size from a few dollars up to several thousand dollars. Although the field is moving toward defining microfinance loans relative to a country's economic development, such as gross domestic product (GDP) or gross national income, there remains some sentiment that larger loans, such as those in the urban post-Soviet transition economies, are not "real" microfinance loans.[6]

It is therefore important to clarify at the outset what is and is not different about the microfinance experience in the transition economies, particularly in Russia as the subject of this book. The key difference to date is that the nature of poverty has been different. Whereas microfinance in Latin America and Asia was developed to address the needs of endemically poor and sometimes illiterate populations, Russia did not have the same problem of chronic poverty, because of the emphasis paid to providing minimum social services and education to the entire population during the Soviet period.

---

[6] A rule of thumb cited by the Consultative Group to Assist the Poorest (CGAP) is that a microfinance loan is lower than average GDP per capita. Although this approach allows for some flexibility to reflect the different stages of economic development of different countries, it is still insufficient. CGAP, "Commercial Banks and Microfinance: Evolving Models of Success," Focus Note No. 28, June 2005.

Instead, Russia faced a massive and unexpected unemployment problem, caused by the breakdown of the Soviet state-ownership system. This situation was exacerbated by the dire state of the Russian government's finances, which made it impossible to maintain the previous level of social services and payments. Russians who relied on pension income, or those who were suddenly unemployed and found that there was no unemployment support, were those most at risk of falling into poverty. Many of these people were relatively well educated and had the intellectual resources and motivation to create new sources of income. They also typically had at least some assets, such as housing that had been transferred to them by the state.

The scale of the businesses these individuals were able to create and manage was typically larger than those of their counterparts in other countries, as were their borrowing needs. At least in the early days of microfinance in Russia, most borrowers could be more accurately described as the financially underserved, although potentially on the brink of falling into poverty.[7]

Although the key difference between microfinance borrowers in the transition economies compared to South America and Asia has been the nature of their financial needs and therefore loan size, the more important considerations are the key similarities. Microfinance borrowers in the transition economies operate in the informal sector and suffer from the same lack of access to formal sources of finance as their counterparts elsewhere in the world. Furthermore, although the loan sizes are larger, the methodology for making the loans is the same. Moving away from a counterproductive focus on loan size and thinking more about the similarities and differences of borrower characteristics will enrich our understanding of microfinance and its potential.

The Evolution of Microfinance

Turning to the historical evolution of microfinance, it is not an exaggeration to say that microfinance has revolutionized the field of

---

[7] Now that the collapse of the Soviet system is more than a decade behind us, a more endemic form of poverty is emerging among those that were not able to adjust to the new system and who have been struggling to survive for ten years or longer.

poverty alleviation in developing countries. The success of microfinance is largely the result of two breakthroughs. First, the field has
demonstrated that the poor can be reliable—and even attractive—
borrowers.[8] Second, a growing number of microfinance institutions
have demonstrated that they can be "sustainable," in the sense of at
least covering their costs, and in some cases achieving profitability.[9]

The pivotal breakthrough in microfinance was the discovery that
the poor can be reliable borrowers. The reason is disarmingly simple:
the poor have only one chance to prove themselves.[10] Particularly in
new markets, where only one MFI is operating, a potential borrower—
who typically has never had a formal loan before—has a unique
opportunity to raise his or her living standard. The lack of an effective safety net in many emerging economies makes this opportunity
particularly compelling. In Russia, for example, once a factory worker
loses his or her job in a one-factory town, self-employment is often the
only alternative to living on the street. The opportunity to borrow in
order to make self-employment viable is therefore invaluable.

The innovation that made this discovery possible was the group-
lending model, in which all group members are responsible for the
timely repayment of any loan made to any single member of that
group. This structure single-handedly alleviated the constraints that
had historically made lending to the poor so difficult: the lack of collateral, the lack of a borrowing track record, and the high costs of
making very small loans.

The group-lending structure works around the collateral shortage
problem because the group members take on the fallback repayment
function that collateral typically plays. And, although most group
members do not have a track record at first, their interest in ensuring
that all loans are repaid so that other members can continue to borrow provides sufficient incentive to mitigate the risk of no previous

[8] Although this book emphasizes the relevance of microfinance for both the poor
and the financially underserved, the original breakthroughs in microfinance concerned the financial behavior of the poor; hence the emphasis on the poor as borrowers in this section.

[9] The term *microfinance institution* (MFI) is used broadly to refer to any organization
that provides microfinance.

[10] In Bolivia, however, where consumer lenders attempted to lend to successful
microfinance borrowers, the resulting lending surplus, combined with the inappro-

borrowing history. Group lending also reduces the time and effort that a lender would typically allocate to monitoring a loan's status; because each member of the group bears responsibility for repayment, each one carefully monitors all of the other members.

A second microfinance model is based on lending to individuals, but this model largely evolved after group lending revealed that the poor can be good borrowers and is based on the principles learned from group lending. For example, having learned from group lending about the importance of a borrower's psychological commitment to loan repayment, microfinance lenders are often willing to accept psychologically significant collateral, such as a wedding ring, to enforce the borrower's commitment.

One provocative caveat to the overall picture of microfinance borrowers as very reliable clients was generated by a recent study of sixty-six microfinance projects, of which twenty-five had "substantial government involvement." Of these twenty-five projects, only one produced sustainable results in terms of recovering costs and successful loan repayments.[11] Although the reasons are complex, anecdotal evidence indicates that borrowers worldwide, as well as lenders, tend to take the borrowing process more seriously when it is on fully commercial terms. A government handout seems to generate the same behavior regardless of location.

The second breakthrough in microfinance was the realization that many microentrepreneurs were willing and able to pay interest rates and fees that were at least high enough for the MFIs to cover their costs. Over years of experimentation, including observing the practices of informal sector moneylenders, field practitioners began to understand that microentrepreneurs were sensitive not only to interest rates but to other factors such as overall convenience, which have implicit costs of their own.

MFIs that were able to address these other factors—such as by visiting clients at their place of business, rather than expecting the clients

---

priate methodology of the consumer lenders, caused widespread defaults. See Rhyne, *Mainstreaming Microfinance.*

[11] CGAP, "Aid Effectiveness in Microfinance: Evaluating Microcredit Projects of the World Bank and the United Nations Development Programme," Focus Note No. 35, April 2006.

to travel to the lender's headquarters—typically found that they could charge higher interest rates; one recent study observed that microfinance lenders can charge interest-rate margins that are from two to four times higher than those on corporate loans in the same market.[12] As one Russian microfinance lender noted, "We observe that the most important factor for entrepreneurs today is the speed at which we make loan decisions. The question of the interest rate is secondary for now."[13] The fact that this insight coincided with financial deregulation in a number of countries also contributed to the expansion of microfinance.

This combination of being able to set interest rates and fees sufficiently high and the fact that the borrower base proved to be so reliable led to an unanticipated conclusion: microfinance was potentially a financially viable "business." This realization had a pronounced impact on a field that had developed on the basis of donor funding. If some MFIs were able to cover their costs, and in some cases even make a profit, then they also had the potential to obtain commercial sources of funding. This step would give the MFIs considerably more autonomy in terms of growth and setting strategy; while donor funding was provided with specific conditions attached, typically the only condition attached to commercial funding was timely repayment.

Although this is a vast simplification of a complex process, the net result was that a number of MFIs set out to obtain licenses, either as banks or as regulated nonbanking financial institutions. Not only did this status enable the MFIs to attract commercial loans but, in the case of banks, it also allowed them to raise deposits. The textbook example is BancoSol in Bolivia, which began as the microfinance nongovernmental organization Prodem in the mid-1980s and then converted to a bank in 1992. At year-end 2005, BancoSol had a loan portfolio of over $200 million.[14]

Profitability also introduced a number of issues with which the microfinance field continues to grapple. One way of summarizing the issues is by asking: Is it appropriate to make money by serving the poor?

---

[12] Development Alternatives, "Banking the Underserved: New Opportunities for Commercial Banks," paper commissioned by the Financial Sector Team, Policy Division, Department for International Development, London, April 2005.

[13] Nadya Cherkasova, "Bum nachnyotsya: No cherez 2–3 goda," *Natsional' nyy Bankovskiy* Zhurnal 7 (30), July 2006, http://www.rmcenter.ru (accessed August 15, 2006).

[14] http://www.mixmarket.org (accessed August 9, 2006).

Some would answer that this is not appropriate, while others would say that it is only by making money that microfinance lenders will be able to continue their work once donors and other supporters move their seed financing to other development projects.

Another way to address the question is to differentiate between those microfinance programs that may never be profitable and those that can be. An example of the former is an MFI focused on assisting extremely poor populations with financial as well as other services and training. In many cases it is not reasonable to expect extremely poor clients to cover the costs of this range of services. Another example is an MFI whose operations are too small to achieve the necessary economies of scale, perhaps because of geographic reasons or because the MFI is focused on a small, tightly defined group. When an MFI in a major city in Kazakhstan, for example, was approached by a potential borrower in a village located two hours away by car, the MFI agreed to consider the loan if the borrower could identify four other borrowers. Ultimately the MFI extended loans to three borrowers in the village. It's hard to imagine any circumstances under which three small loans made to borrowers located two hours away could ever generate profits for this MFI. I would argue that the more MFIs can achieve profitability, the more development funding can be used to focus on MFIs whose operations are important but are not profitable by their very nature.

Nevertheless, one clear dilemma raised by profitability is the impact-measurement challenge that I noted earlier. Similarly to loan size, profitability measurements provide simple numbers that are intuitively appealing to anyone trying to find ways to assess an organization's performance. As in the case of loan size, however, profitability can threaten to take on a life of its own at the expense of assessing other elements of an MFI's objectives and defining the desired balance.

The key tangible outcome of the profitability breakthrough was the creation of benchmarks for other MFIs to emulate. One recent study showed that 49 percent of profitable MFIs have achieved profitability within three years, while another 32 percent have done so in less than six years.[15] If an MFI's goals include profitability, this is extremely useful information that can be used to set goals and monitor performance.

---

[15] Adrian Gonzalez and Richard Rosenberg, "State of the Microcredit 'Industry': Outreach, Poverty, and Profitability," presentation at "Access to Finance: Building Inclusive Financial Systems" conference, World Bank, May 20, 2006.

And, while there is no definitive data to measure whether more MFIs are becoming either profitable or sustainable, the same study estimated that 44 percent of borrowers are borrowing from sustainable MFIs. Although these sustainable MFIs, which number in the hundreds, are outnumbered on an absolute basis by the number of MFIs worldwide, which is in the thousands, this "market share" estimate does provide a useful snapshot of the field.

The increased interest in measuring the financial performance of MFIs also helped to focus the attention of the microfinance field on the best evolving practices, which I discuss in the following section.

Microfinance Methodology

Those who have not had direct experience with microfinance often find it difficult to comprehend its success, particularly in the emerging economies in which it is most often utilized. We constantly hear that developing countries suffer from a wide range of problems, including weak banking systems, corrupt business cultures, and imperfect property rights. Under such circumstances, how could some microfinance lenders possibly achieve loan repayment rates of over 99 percent? That question certainly contributed to my skepticism when I was asked to join KMB Bank's board of directors.

The answer to this question lies partly in the characteristics of the developing economies in which microfinance has evolved and partly in the methodology that has been developed by microfinance lenders. Four characteristics of the economic environment are particularly important: the size of the potential client base, the lack of other borrowing alternatives, relatively low staff costs, and the freedom to set interest rates.

Often up to 75 percent of the population in developing economies is self-employed. This is important not only because of the number of potential clients but because of the scope that it provides for microfinance providers to achieve economies of scale.

Second, as I have noted, microfinance can be a lifeline to poor and financially underserved individuals in these economies by providing them a unique opportunity to raise their living standards. The fact that these individuals typically only have one chance to create a financial track record helps to ensure their reliability. By contrast, this characteristic is much less evident in developed economies such as the United States, where the potential microfinance client base has more financial options and a stronger social safety net.

The third characteristic of microfinance in developing economies is that staff costs are relatively low. Not only are salary levels lower relative to those in developed economies but some microfinance providers prefer to hire young people with no banking experience—making salary levels even lower—because staff with prior banking experience can be difficult to retrain.

The fourth important characteristic, and one that does not always exist in developing economies, is that there must not be any interest-rate controls. Microfinance lending has a high cost base, and lenders cannot be constrained in the interest rates and fees that they charge.

With regard to the lending methodology itself, microfinance lending is based on practices that are almost disarmingly simple. Microfinance applies the basic principles of good banking—accurate financial analysis, appropriate loan structure and collateral or collateral substitute, comfort with the borrower's character—but shows how these can be applied to a population that bankers had not realized could be approached in this way.

The eureka moment in my conversion into a microfinance supporter occurred when I realized that microfinance utilizes the same financial analysis principles as corporate finance. I had always assumed that making loans to borrowers who did not have years of audited financial statements was based on using "street smarts" to assess a borrower's character and was therefore almost impossible to second-guess or replicate. Instead, as I discovered at a seminar for Russian microfinance lenders, the heart of microfinance analysis is a borrower's "cash flow," or how much cash is generated by the business.[16] By making this calculation, and estimating future cash flow as well, a lender can determine both the appropriate loan size and loan repayment schedule for a borrower.

---

[16] A cash-flow statement differs from a profit-and-loss statement because profits are an accounting calculation that includes noncash charges such as depreciation. Therefore a business's profit at the end of the year is not the same as its net change in cash at the end of the year. Because loans are repaid with cash, not accounting profits, lenders must analyze the cash-flow statement as well as the profit-and-loss statement.

Although most accounts of the history of microfinance highlight the breakthrough of group lending as a substitute for the use of collateral, I consider the field's adoption of cash flow analysis to be an equally important contribution. While commercial bankers were frozen into inaction by the lack of formal financial information—among other factors—that they typically require from their clients, microfinance lenders rolled up their sleeves and worked with the financial information that was available. They reviewed the borrower's formal financial information, such as tax statements, if there was any; they analyzed the borrower's informal record keeping; they observed how the business functioned, such as how average daily sales compared to inventory levels; they compared the business to that of similar borrowers; and they used all of this information to construct a picture of the borrower's financial condition, including the borrower's cash flow capacity.

While this process can seem quite mysterious for outsiders—in particular, how can one ever be sure one is being shown the real numbers?—it is not that difficult for experienced microfinance lenders. For example, the turnover and profit margin of a kiosk with a certain size and product mix will fall within a definable range. If the potential borrower's financial information does not fall within that range, either the numbers are not genuine or there are exceptions that can be explained. Furthermore, once a potential borrower realizes that the lender really does understand the business and cannot be fooled by numbers that the borrower might show a government inspector, he or she is usually willing to share the real financial information.

Good financial analysis leads naturally to the second aspect of good lending, which is a loan structured to meet the borrower's needs and repayment capacity. Loan structure plays an important role in creating an environment of success for first-time borrowers by ensuring that timely repayment is fully within the borrower's capacity. In addition, loan repayment schedules that require frequent and regular payments help to create borrower discipline. They also serve as a monitoring mechanism for the lender; if a borrower has problems with that very first loan repayment, the lender can respond much more effectively than if all of the principal is due at the end of the loan period and the borrower fails to pay at that point. Microfinance loan repayments can be required from as often as once a day to the more typical once a week or once a month.

A related characteristic of microfinance lending is the principle of "zero default tolerance," according to which the lender responds to overdue payments by contacting the borrower on the very first day of any delays in order to address the problem. By contrast, commercial banks often wait for up to thirty days before taking action on delayed payments. This strict approach both enforces borrower discipline and helps to address problems before they grow out of control.

Although an appropriately structured loan would seem to be an obvious element of good lending, it is less common than one would expect. I have frequently worked with developing-economy banks whose analysis does not give an accurate picture of the borrower's repayment capacity, and whose loan structures do not correspond with the use of the loan proceeds. An example of the latter is the use of a multiyear overdraft loan to finance real estate construction. Overdraft loans should be used to support short-term changes in cash balances, much as we use the overdraft line on our bank accounts, while construction should be financed by a long-term loan that has a "grace period" for the period in which construction is under way and no cash is being generated, followed by regularly scheduled loan repayments. Not only does such a repayment schedule correspond with the cash generated by the project, but it enables the lender to closely monitor the borrower's status. It is not unusual for microfinance lenders to be more skilled lenders than their commercial banking counterparts, precisely because of their focus on loan structure.

Turning to collateral, I noted earlier that successful microlenders are not constrained by standard views of acceptable collateral and are willing to take into account the psychological importance of a range of types of collateral. In the early days of microfinance lending in Russia it was not uncommon for lenders to accept items such as fur coats as collateral. Although the resale value of a secondhand fur coat in Russia is not significant, the desire of the borrower to get the coat back before winter typically is. Such flexibility not only expands the range of potential borrowers but, particularly for emotionally meaningful collateral, can also increase the borrower's personal commitment to timely repayment.

Finally, although character analysis is not the fulcrum of microfinance lending that I had once assumed it to be, it nevertheless plays a role in microfinance as it does in other forms of finance. As in the case of financial analysis, character analysis often requires some innovation, because standard sources of information, such as borrower track records and credit bureaus, usually do not exist. Therefore many successful microfinance programs include a visit to the borrower's home as part of the analytical process, because of the information that such visits can provide about the borrower's standard of living (and how much money might be taken out of the business), possible collateral items, and a general sense of the borrower's personal life.

I always enjoyed asking Russian microfinance lenders how they managed to explain this somewhat unusual analytical procedure to their prospective borrowers, since I would have found it awkward if I were in their position. Those who also found it awkward tried to construct some reason for dropping by while they were in the neighborhood. Others took the approach that, since the borrowers did not know what was a standard banking procedure and what was not, they simply told prospective clients that a home visit was a required part of the process.

In addition to applying the appropriate lending methodology, microfinance lenders have to maximize their efficiency in order to mitigate the small profits that are inevitably generated by small loans. (Although the relative return can be high, because of the willingness of microfinance borrowers to pay high interest rates, the absolute return on a small loan will always be low.) Successful microfinance lenders typically share four characteristics.

First, ongoing efforts are made to decentralize decision making, recognizing that quick loan decisions (same day turnaround is not uncommon) can be critical for small borrowers operating with limited working capital and thin margins. Decentralization also keeps the decision makers close to the borrowers and enables them to respond quickly to changes in borrower or overall market conditions.

In addition, the loan officer's compensation is structured to reward timely repayments, with as much as 50 percent of compensation based on portfolio performance. Compensation can be adjusted as often as every payday, thus providing strong near-term incentives to meet—and exceed—performance guidelines.

It is also in the loan officer's best interests to retain his or clients, since the first loan requires the most effort. Therefore many microfinance programs make an advance commitment to make larger loans in the future to successful borrowers.

Finally, loan officer productivity is continually evaluated, with the intention of finding the appropriate balance between the highest productivity level and the lowest loan losses. Ratios of one hundred and more loans per employee are typical for the most experienced lenders.

Microfinance Today

Although excitement over the fact that microfinance "works" has abated as its successes have been repeated by MFIs all over the world, the field is still characterized by an invigorating dynamism. In this section I provide an overview of the microfinance field today, beginning with developments in the information infrastructure, regulation, and new products.[17] I conclude with a review of the major providers of microfinance, leading into a discussion of the relatively small role played by privately owned commercial banks.

Some of the most important recent developments in microfinance are taking place in the industry's information infrastructure. One example is the ongoing efforts to increase the use of standard performance measurements and the centralization of data. A leader in this field is the Microfinance Information eXchange (MIX), a nonprofit benchmarking association and Web-based information exchange to which its over six hundred members report semiannually.[18] Another comprehensive effort to improve the database on microfinance is the Data Project that was initiated as part of the activities of the United Nations for the Year of Microcredit in 2005.[19]

The emergence of specialized microfinance rating agencies is also playing a role in encouraging transparency in the field and achieving consensus on reporting and performance measurements; as of mid-2006, 240 MFI ratings had been issued through a rating program

[17] More information about developments in microfinance is in Elizabeth Littlefield and Richard Rosenberg, "Microfinance and the Poor: Breaking Down the Walls between Microfinance and Formal Finance," *Finance and Development* 41, no. 2 (June 2004), 38–40.

[18] MIX is supported by CGAP (Consultative Group to Assist the Poorest), the Citigroup Foundation, the Open Society Institute, the Rockdale Foundation, and other private foundations. The MIX website is http://www.mixmarket.org.

[19] http://www.yearofmicrocredit.org (accessed December 30, 2004).

sponsored by the Consultative Group to Assist the Poor (CGAP—a consortium of development agencies working together to expand access to financial services for the poor), the Inter-American Development Bank (IDB), and the European Union.[20] The major international rating agencies have also been turning their attention to microfinance lenders as potential clients.

Finally, concerted efforts are under way to address the complexities of impact measurement and to devise a methodology for measuring poverty that can be applied transparently and consistently.[21]

Significant developments are taking place on the policy and regulatory side as well. A number of regulatory agencies in individual countries are evaluating how best to regulate MFIs, ranging from Uganda, which introduced well-regarded microfinance legislation in 2002, to Kazakhstan, where the issue was under review at the end of 2006. More globally, the Bank for International Settlements (BIS) is evaluating how the Basel principles for banking supervision should apply to microfinance lenders.

Turning to products and services, the recognition that the poor and financially underserved require more than just loans, together with the quest for sustainability, is leading MFIs to introduce a wider range of products. (The shift in the field's name over time from microcredit to microfinance reflects this trend.) Some of these products include insurance, mortgage finance, leasing, and credit cards. MFIs are also exploring ways to increase their delivery capacity by cooperating with organizations that have large distribution networks, such as post offices and retail chains, and by using cell phone text messaging to enable clients to initiate transactions.

Credit scoring is being explored, as well, as a way of increasing productivity, with one of the main challenges being finding the appropriate balance between quantitatively and qualitatively based decision making.[22]

---

[20] Some of the largest rating agencies include MicroRate, based in Washington, D.C.; PlaNet Finance, based in France; Microfinanza, based in Italy; and CRISIL and Micro-Credit Ratings International Limited (M-CRIL), based in India.

[21] A useful review of poverty assessment tools is available at http://www.povertytools.org.

[22] A useful summary of the status of scoring in microfinance is in Mark Schreiner, "Scoring: The Next Breakthrough in Microcredit?" CGAP Occasional Paper No. 7, January 2003.

Funding is a third important area in which the field continues to make progress. One significant trend is to emphasize microentrepreneurs as a possible source of deposits; although the cost of collecting small deposits can be high, using the distribution infrastructure of other organizations is one possible way to lower these costs.[23] It is worth noting that banks in developed economies often generate more income from small business savings than from lending.[24]

Several microfinance organizations have also issued debt in the capital markets. The first major milestone was achieved in July 2002 in Mexico when Financiera Compartamos was the first MFI to issue unsecured debt, with its peso bond worth approximately $20 million. ProCredit, a major investor in MSE banks, raised $54 million on the German bond market in 2005, while in 2006 BlueOrchard Finance issued a $106 million bond, managed by Morgan Stanley, to provide funding to sixty-five MFIs.

Finally, the range of equity funding is expanding as MFIs create track records and start to look beyond donors for more sustainable sources of finance. As of mid-2006 there were over seventy funds targeted at lending to or investing in microfinance providers or both.[25]

The Lending Gap

The topic of funding options and growth leads us to a discussion about the microfinance providers themselves. A summary of information about five of the world's largest microfinance providers that are members of MIX is provided in table 1.1.[26] Although these institutions

---

[23] One study of fifteen credit unions in Latin America provides a useful perspective on the cost issue; credit unions with savings of under $1 million had a savings-expense ratio of 8.43 percent, compared to a 3.26 percent ratio for savings of $1 million to $5 million. Dave C. Richardson, "Going to the Barricades for Microsavings Mobilization: A View of the Real Costs from the Trenches," *MicroBanking Bulletin*, July 2003, 9. The savings-expense ratio is calculated by adding all the direct and indirect expenses associated with deposit taking and then dividing them by the average annual savings outstanding.

[24] Charles B. Wendel, "Ten SME Facts," *SME Weekly*, Financial Institutions Consulting, April 13, 2004, http://www.ficinc.com (accessed April 20, 2004).

[25] http://www.accion.org (accessed September 19, 2006).

[26] Grameen Bank is not included in this table because it does not report its data to MIX. Its loan portfolio as of July 2006 was $456 million. http://www.grameen-info.org (accessed September 13, 2006).

by definition are not representative of the field, they play key roles in creating performance standards for other MFIs to emulate and possibly even exceed.

All five lenders are impressively profitable, using the rule of thumb that an attractive return on assets for a bank is in the range of 2 percent and an attractive return on equity is in the 18–20 percent range. The only lender to fall below this range is Banco Solidario, whose performance is still strong enough to contribute to the overall picture of sound profitability performance for the group.

As is characteristic of the field, two of the lenders, ASA and MiBanco, have notably low past-due loan ratios of approximately 2 percent or under. The past-due loan ratio for BRAC, which is over 5 percent, is on the high side but has declined from 8.33 percent in 2004.

The average loan size for these lenders ranges from a high of $1,349 at Banco Solidario in Ecuador to a low of $61 at ASA in Bangladesh. It is particularly noteworthy that, despite the field's concern over mission drift, four of these five lenders serve the very poor as well as middle-income or small and medium enterprise (SME) clients.[27]

Turning to ownership structures, only two of these five large microfinance providers, MiBanco and Banco Solidario, are privately owned banks. Even these, however are owned by NGOs and socially responsible funds, not by fully commercial investors. This observation brings us to a key unresolved issue in the microfinance field: the relationship between MFI ownership and the gap between demand and supply.

Similarly to the lack of accurate data about the supply of microfinance, there is no agreed upon data about demand. CGAP makes the broad estimate that there are five hundred million active users of loan and savings services among the "poor and near poor" out of a total market of three billion people.[28] If one-half of this unserved market of 2.5 billion people borrowed the $138 that is the average loan size of the MIX's lenders to the "low" end of the market, the total demand would be $172 billion. If instead they borrowed the $804 that is

[27] Although BRAC has a low average-loan size of $65, it lends to larger borrowers through a related company.

[28] CGAP cautions that it makes this estimate on the basis of "highly speculative assumptions." CGAP, "Financial Institutions with a 'Double Bottom Line': Implications for the Future of Microfinance," Occasional Paper No. 8, July 2004.

TABLE 1.1.
Large Microfinance Lenders, 2005

Name and country	Ownership or legal structure	Loan portfolio (000,000)	Average loan	Client base	Past-due loans* (%)	ROE (%)	ROA (%)
BRI (Bank Rakyat Indonesia), Indonesia	State-owned bank (59.5%)	$2,200	$600–$1,000	Middle to low income	4.19	42.2	5.77
BRAC, Bangladesh	NGO (BRAC also owns an SME bank)	$269	$65	Very poor; loans under $300	5.92	18.08	5.49
ASA (Association for Social Advancement), Bangladesh	NGO	$255	$61	Very poor	1.10	29.09	15.25
Banco Solidario, Ecuador	Bank owned by socially responsible funds	$207	$1,349	Poor and underserved MSEs	4.17	17.5	1.42
MiBanco, Peru	Privately owned bank, majority owned by NGO	$207	$1,342	Small and medium; loans up to $100,000	2.04	34.36	6.74

Sources: Data for all banks except BRI are from http://www.mixmarket.org (accessed August 7, 2006). BRI loan portfolio information is as of year-end 2005 and is from http://www.ivpbri.com (accessed August 9, 2006). The other BRI data is from http://www.irbri.com (accessed August 31, 2006) and is for year-end 2004.
   * Over thirty days.

the average loan size for those lending to the "broader" market, total demand would be over $1 trillion.[29] Estimates though these figures are, they clearly are much larger than CGAP's estimates that there are $15 billion in outstanding microloans.[30]

[29] The average loan amounts are taken from the *MicroBanking Bulletin*, August 2005; http://www.mixmbb.org (accessed January 3, 2006).
[30] CGAP, "Foreign Investment in Microfinance: Debt and Equity from Quasi-Commercial Investors," Focus Note No. 25, January 2004.

How could this gap be closed? Of the $15 billion, $14 billion of the funding is domestic and $1 billion is foreign. The domestic funding includes government funding, deposits, and retained earnings, while almost 90 percent of the foreign funding consists of multilateral and bilateral assistance.[31] Not only are these funding sources insufficient but also it is unrealistic to imagine that donors or governments could increase their microfinance activities sufficiently to close the gap.

The only alternative is therefore the private sector. The picture that jumps out from the preceding discussion, however, is that the private sector's microfinance activity continues to be limited. Although the activity of socially committed investors is increasing, even more noteworthy is that privately owned banks continue to play only a limited role.

Banks and Microfinance

Although a theme of this book is that the relationship between microfinance lenders and commercial lenders is inadequate, this relationship is on an encouraging upward trend. This trend has been fortified by the increasingly widespread use of "building inclusive financial sectors," or bringing microfinance into the mainstream, as an important development principle. This concept has been promoted by CGAP, as well as being a featured element of the UN's Year of Microcredit in 2005.[32] There is a difference, however, between the microfinance field adopting a principle and its acceptance by other financial-sector players, particularly commercial banks. Although the trend is positive, there is still a long way to go.

The following discussion groups MFI investors into four categories: donor organizations; socially committed investors; the state; and

[31] It is also estimated that another $5–10 billion has been provided by foreign sources to MFIs over the past five to ten years in the form of grants and subsidized funding, most of which has presumably been utilized. CGAP, "Foreign Investment in Microfinance."

[32] See for example, CGAP, "Commercial Banks and Microfinance"; *Building Inclusive Financial Sectors for Development* (United Nations, 2006); Malcolm Harper and Sukhwinder Singh Arora, eds., *Small Customers, Big Market: Commercial Banks in Microfinance* (Warwickshire, United Kingdom: ITDG, 2005); Helms, *Access for All*; and references to building inclusive financial sectors related to the UN's Year of Microcredit, 2005, http://www.yearofmicrocredit.org.

commercial, profit-oriented investors.[33] Within these four groups, the role of banks owned by commercial investors is particularly important, because they have the existing infrastructure and potential economies of scale to make the greatest impact on closing the microfinance lending gap. Although the increasing activity of commercial banks over the past several years is heartening, the microfinance commitment of the commercial banks mentioned here is well under $10 billion, compared to a potential demand of over $1 trillion. Furthermore, the definition of microfinance used by many commercial lenders includes larger loans than those used to calculate the lending-gap estimate, indicating that the gap is even larger.

Beginning with donor organizations, these investors have played an irreplaceable role in the development of microfinance by providing capital and credibility to the process of converting NGOs to licensed banks as well as by creating greenfield banks. An incomplete list of donor organizations includes the International Finance Corporation (IFC), the private-sector arm of the World Bank; the Inter-American Investment Corporation (IIC), the private-sector arm of the Inter-American Development Bank; the EBRD; and KfW Entwicklungsbank, a German government development organization.

The indisputable advantage of donor investors is their role in supporting projects that are too risky for commercial funding. The microfinance field simply would not have reached its current stage of development, including the growing level of commercial interest, without donor organizations having led the way. Going back to the first NGO transformation of Prodem in 1992, Elisabeth Rhyne of ACCION International, a U.S.-based MFI investor, notes that the IIC played the role of "anchor investor" that helped convince both investors and the banking authorities of the project's feasibility.[34]

Donor funding by design is not permanent. The mission of most donor agencies usually requires them to provide seed financing to help ventures get up and running. Once this has been accomplished, the donors are expected to redeploy their funding to other development operations still at the seed-financing stage.

[33] Although banks owned by cooperative members provide another potential category, I do not address them in this discussion because they do not have the scale of banks owned by the other four types of investors.
[34] Rhyne, *Mainstreaming Microfinance*, 110.

One obvious class of investors to which donors can "exit" without fearing loss of the original mission of their investee banks is socially committed or socially responsible investors. Although these terms can be confusing because they can also be used to describe donor agencies, I use them here to describe organizations that are not government agencies and that have a "double bottom line" of achieving profitability and contributing to social or development objectives. These investors typically do not see their mission as exiting once an investment has proven that it is profitable; given their objectives, there would be no reason for them to exit from an investment that was performing well. Examples of types of socially committed investors include ACCION International, which supports MFIs in a partnership network that includes providing debt and equity finance; Blue-Orchard Finance, a Swiss company that assists financial institutions wishing to invest in the microfinance industry; and the Dutch Triodos Bank, which only finances projects that add "social, environmental and cultural value."[35]

Another sense of the range of socially committed investors is provided by the membership of the Council of Microfinance Equity Funds. As of June 2006 its sixteen members had made total disclosed commitments to microfinance organizations, in both debt and equity, of over $120 million.[36] Although a number of major investors are not members of the council, the commitment of its membership alone gives a sense of the field's potential.

An important trend that has been supported by both donors and socially committed investors is the creation of greenfield banks focused on micro- and other small clients. This approach bypasses the NGO stage and avoids the organizational, cultural, and regulatory challenges associated with converting NGO microfinance lenders into banks. The most prominent example of this approach is the network of nine ProCredit banks (and one finance institution) in the post-Soviet transition economies that are managed by the MSE consulting firm Internationale Projekt Consult (IPC), the firm that also managed KMB Bank during its first four years of operations.[37]

---

[35] http://www.triodos.com (accessed September 25, 2006).

[36] http://www.cmef.com (accessed September 19, 2006).

[37] The banks are located in Georgia, Albania, Kosovo, Ukraine, Romania, Moldova (finance company), Serbia, Bulgaria, Macedonia, and Bosnia-Herzegovina. The finance

These banks also give a sense of the close overlap that can exist between donor agencies and socially committed investors; the banks all have a similar although not exact shareholder structure that typically includes donors such as the EBRD, the IFC, and KfW, as well as ProCredit Holding AG, the investment arm of IPC that serves as a socially committed investor.[38] (Commerzbank, discussed further below, is typically also a shareholder.) As of June 30, 2006, these banks had a total loan portfolio of €1.4 billion, average loan size of €3,863, and loans past due over thirty days of 1.07 percent.[39]

ACCION International provides another example of a specialized microfinance investor with a similar portfolio approach, although not the same experience in creating greenfield banks. As of June 2006 ACCION's investees had outstanding loans of over $1.6 billion and over 2,250,000 borrowers.[40]

Much of the dynamism in the microfinance field is created by the interaction between donor agencies, socially committed investors, and the banks that they support and in a number of cases have created. With donors, specialist microfinance and MSE firms, and other socially committed investors as their shareholders, these banks have evolved rapidly by creating a synergistic relationship between their hands-on experience and the latest thinking in MSE finance. Many investors are shareholders in a number of MSE banks and often play active roles at the board of directors' level, thereby further contributing to a rapid exchange of knowledge between these institutions.

The availability of financing is the primary constraint to the further development of MSE banks owned by socially committed investors; creating greenfield banks is an expensive undertaking. While IPC's rule of thumb is that a MSE bank should be able to break even within three years, expanding beyond breaking even to developing nationwide banking operations is a different scale of operations entirely and

---

institution was not a greenfield operation. ProCredit's entire portfolio of financial intermediaries consists of nineteen entities, including operations in Latin America, the Caribbean, and Africa; these had a total loan portfolio of €1.7 billion as of June 30, 2006. http://www.procredit-holding.com (accessed August 8, 2006).

[38] Formerly, Internationale Micro Investitionen Aktiengesellschaft—IMI.

[39] The MIX data does not include the IPC-managed banks.

[40] Author correspondence, Bruce MacDonald, vice president, communications, ACCION International, September 15, 2006.

requires both time and money. As of year-end 2006 the microfinance field is so popular that there does not seem to be a shortage of funding. Not only are funds being developed to target socially committed retail investors but there is also the example of large individual philanthropists such as Pierre Omidyar, the chairman of eBay, who contributed $100 million to the microfinance field in 2005.[41] ProCredit's success in raising debt may serve as a precursor to raising equity finance that will enable it to continue to expand. The point is that the growth of this type of bank will depend on the growth of this type of socially committed investor.

The third category of bank owner is the state. The prime example is BRI of Indonesia, with a loan portfolio of $2.2 billion. Another example is provided by Banco Estado Microempresa in Chile, with a year-end 2005 microfinance loan portfolio of $396 million.[42]

State-owned banks have two noteworthy advantages in providing MSE finance. The main advantage is an extensive branch network, including in thinly populated or low-income locations that might not be feasible for other types of banks. The second advantage is a double-edged sword that also presents a potential disadvantage: the availability of state funding. While privately owned banks must continually raise capital to fund rapid growth, a state-owned bank is funded by the state budget. If there is a political commitment to MSE finance, the funding can usually be made available. Of course the negative side of state funding is that it can have a political agenda; for example, a state-owned bank can be a useful mechanism for providing loans to the poor and financially underserved in order to generate support before an election. Some microfinance programs have steered clear of this type of problem, while others have not.

A related disadvantage of state-owned banks is that it can be difficult for them to achieve the efficiencies and innovations that characterize the best privately owned banks. State-owned banks often have

---

[41] Omidyar explained his motivation as trying to "accelerate the growth in this sector [microfinance]. . . . We're really hoping that the existence and size of this fund will motivate people in this sector to figure out how to provide those kinds [traditional investments] of returns." Robert D. Hof, "A Major Push for Microphilanthropy," *BusinessWeek* online, November 4, 2005, http://www.businessweek.com (accessed January 3, 2006).

[42] http://www.mixmarket.org (accessed August 8, 2006).

multiple objectives that include encouraging economic development, while privately owned banks are focused on their bottom line. Some state-owned banks also enjoy substantial market share, which, combined with a steady source of funding, can create a corporate culture in which clients are taken for granted. Partly as a result of these factors, there is a global trend toward privatizing state-owned banks.

Two recent cases are of particular interest, because they are both state-owned banks with a microfinance focus that have been sold to commercial investors. One is the Khan Bank of Mongolia, a formerly state-owned agricultural bank that was successfully rehabilitated under an agreement between the government, the World Bank, and the United States Agency for International Development (USAID). Named the "Best Bank in Mongolia" in 2005 by the financial publication *Euromoney*, the bank's loan portfolio as of June 2006 totaled $161 million.[43] The second case is the National Microfinance Bank Ltd., a state-owned microfinance bank in Tanzania with year-end 2004 total assets of $570 million, in which a Rabobank-led consortium acquired 49 percent of the shares in 2005 for $29.4 million.[44] The future focus and performance of these two banks will provide useful information about the role of private investors in microfinance-focused banks.

The fourth category of bank owner is commercial investors with an exclusive focus on profits. This category can be further subdivided into domestically owned private banks and large international banks. It is difficult to obtain information about both types of banks, because they typically do not report to specialized associations such as MIX. Furthermore, the definition of MSE finance varies from one bank to the next. Therefore, the following discussion is intended to provide a sense of the direction of the field and not a comprehensive accounting.

In the category of domestic, privately owned banks with a large microfinance portfolio, ICICI Bank of India is one of the largest.

---

[43] The bank was sold to HS Securities of Tokyo and a Mongolian company, Tavan Bogd. Jay Dyer, J. Peter Morrow, and Robin Young, "The Agricultural Bank of Mongolia," *Scaling Up Poverty Reduction: Case Studies in Microfinance*, case study prepared for "Global Learning Process for Scaling Up Poverty Reduction" conference in Shanghai, sponsored by CGAP and the World Bank, May 25–27, 2004. Recent financial data is from http://www.khanbank.mn (accessed August 8, 2006).

[44] http://www.psrctz.com and http://www.nextbillion.net (accessed September 8, 2006).

ICICI has adopted the service-company model, in which a third party services the microfinance clients but books the loans on the bank's balance sheet, usually for a fee. As of mid-2006 ICICI's rural microfinance loan portfolio had reached almost $540 million and it had plans to increase the portfolio to $2 billion, in part by buying loans from local MFIs or working with local MFIs by servicing their loans.[45]

Large international banks represent a potentially important part of the future of MSE finance. The involvement of these banks typically takes one of four forms: minority equity investments in microfinance banks, providing loans and grants to microfinance intermediaries, the service-company model, and direct lending to microfinance borrowers. Other forms of international bank support for the microfinance field, such as investment-banking transactions and facilitating remittances, are not addressed here, because these are fee-based transactions in which the banks take either minimal risk or none at all. A truer sense of international bank interest in microfinance is gauged by assessing their direct involvement in accepting the risks of the microfinance business.

The German bank Commerzbank has taken a lead in minority equity investments, with an initial investment of approximately $10 million (since increased) in seven of the transition economy banks managed by IPC. Commerzbank is one of the first Western European banks to integrate emerging SMEs with its international network.[46] Rabobank, following in Commerzbank's footsteps, has announced that its Tanzanian acquisition is part of a strategy to develop "rural banks" in fifteen developing countries.[47]

---

[45] "ICICI Bank's Microfinance Strategy: A Big Bank Thinks Small," http://www.microfinancegateway.org/content/article/detail (accessed December 30, 2004) and "India's Banks Are Big on Microfinance," *BusinessWeek* online, August 22, 2006, http://www.businessweek.com (accessed September 13, 2006).

[46] Eckard von Leesen, senior director, Commerzbank, telephone interview with author, February 4, 2004.

[47] Rabobank made the acquisition as part of a strategy to develop "rural banks" in fifteen developing countries. "Rabobank Consortium Acquires Interest in Tanzanian Bank," Primezone, http://www.primezone.com/newsroom/news.html?d=84571 (accessed January 3, 2005). The consortium included three Tanzanian partners: Eximbank, the National Investment Company Limited, and the Tanzania Chambers of Commerce, Industry and Agriculture.

In the second form of microfinance activity, the French bank Société Générale finances microfinance lenders in ten countries. As of the third quarter of 2006 it had committed slightly over $100 million for periods up to five years. A particularly important aspect of Société Générale's lending program is that loans are denominated in local currency. As I discuss in chapter 4, a historic dilemma for international organizations trying to support microfinance lenders is the difficulty of obtaining local currency to lend to these organizations, while lending in dollars or euros creates foreign currency risks for the MFIs and their borrowers. Société Générale has successfully addressed this challenge by using funding raised by its local subsidiaries. Société Générale also intends to invest directly in MFIs and had several projects under review during 2006.[48]

Citigroup has also undertaken a significant MFI lending program, together with the Overseas Private Investment Corporation (OPIC), a U.S. government agency. Citigroup will lend $100 million to MFIs in developing countries, with a $70 million guarantee from OPIC.[49] A different funding approach has been taken by Deutsche Bank, which funds microfinance lenders through legal entities that are distinct from its banking operations; Deutsche Bank does not lend to these organizations directly.[50]

A prominent international example of the service-company model, the third form of microfinance activity, is provided by the Dutch bank ABN Amro. Its Brazilian subsidiary, Banco Real, created a microlending subsidiary—Real Microcredito—which opened its doors in 2002. As of October 2005 Real Microcredito had sourced $4.8 million in

---

[48] Some of this funding is partially supported by risk mitigants, such as government guarantees, but Société Générale's principle is to fund only sustainable MFIs and to utilize these mitigants only as a precautionary measure. Pascale Lacombrade, *Responsable* Microfinance, International Retail Banking Division, Société Générale, telephone interview with author, September 21, 2006.

[49] David Wighton, "Citigroup Plans to Fund Microfinance Programme," *Financial Times*, September 22, 2006, 18.

[50] Deutsche Bank has housed its microfinance activities in the Deutsche Bank Microcredit Development Fund, which was founded to work with private banking clients to provide long-term equity-like debt to microfinance providers. During 2005 the fund also launched a $75 million debt fund, the Global Commercial Microfinance Consortium, to attract socially motivated investors. http://www.cib.db.com/community (accessed January 4, 2006).

loans for Banco Real, consisting of eight thousand borrowers.[51] ABN Amro's other microfinance operations are in India and the United States (Chicago), and it is actively investigating how to continue to expand this business profitably.[52]

One of the largest international banks active in microfinance lending, the fourth form of activity, is the Austrian Raiffeisen Bank. Its subsidiary, Raiffeisen International, manages the bank's subsidiaries in fifteen countries in central and eastern Europe and the former Soviet Union, including the largest foreign bank investments in Russia and Ukraine. As of mid-2006 the bank's microfinance portfolio, with an average loan of about €20,000, was over $1 billion. Raiffeisen's experience provides an intriguing glimpse of the types of contributions that commercial banks can make to the microfinance field; because its microfinance loans are made on the basis of a scoring methodology, it can make loans as small as $1,000 on a profitable basis.[53] While this approach seems to turn many of the lessons of microfinance on their head, it also provides a new perspective.

Another international bank directly engaged in microfinance lending is the Spanish Grupo Santander and its Chilean subsidiary, Banefe. As of September 2005 Banefe's microfinance loan portfolio had reached almost $97 million.[54] A third prominent example is Banca Intesa, whose majority acquisition of KMB Bank is discussed in chapter 4.

---

[51] "International Banks and Their Expanding Role in Microfinance Investing," *MicroCapital*, http://www.microcapital.org (accessed August 8, 2006). Note that ACCION is also a 20 percent investor in Real Microcredito.

An example on a smaller scale is provided by Citibank India's loan agency relationship with Women's Working Forum (WWF), an Indian cooperative bank, in which WWF organizes and manages the loans but Citibank India funds them and takes the credit risk. As of March 2006, nineteen thousand loans had been made, with a value of $1.5 million. Bob Annibale, Citigroup Microfinance Group global director, "A Commercial Strategy for Microfinance," a presentation at the Asia Microfinance Forum, March 21–25, 2006.

[52] Author correspondence, Onno Mulder, senior vice president, ABN Amro, September 15, 2006.

[53] Michael Marshall, vice president, head of SME Banking, Raiffeisen International, telephone interview with author, September 7, 2006.

[54] Frans Paul van der Putten, coordinating author, "A Billion to Gain: A Study on Global Financial Institutions and Microfinance," ING Microfinance Support, Amsterdam, February 2006, 27.

To conclude this section, although bank involvement in microfinance is clearly on a positive upward trend, the numbers alone indicate that the road ahead is a very long one. And, as I noted, the involvement of commercial banks will be critical; the creation of microfinance banks by donors and socially committed investors is an important part of the process, but their potential outreach cannot compare with that of large international banks.

The Commercial Potential of Microfinance

Given the success stories and exciting innovations in microfinance that I have discussed in this chapter, one question looms large: Why has it taken so long to generate commercial interest in filling the microfinance lending gap? Microfinance has a number of characteristics that should be of interest to commercial banks: it provides access to a largely untapped client base; leading practitioners have achieved a positive return on their microfinance operations; there is a well-tested lending methodology; microentrepreneurs have demonstrated their creditworthiness in country after country; and microfinance lenders are learning that their clients can also be a source of funding.

Of course not all microfinance operations will be commercially viable; it is necessary to achieve the correct economies of scale and efficiency levels, as well as apply the appropriate methodology. Furthermore, some types of microfinance activities, such as making extremely small loans to the poorest of the poor or reaching isolated communities, probably never will be commercially viable. Therefore, the point is not that all microfinance lending should be of interest to commercial banks, but that the field as a whole deserves serious consideration.

There is a simple answer to the question posed above: misperceptions. These misperceptions can be seen most clearly by analyzing the difference between microfinance and small business finance. Microfinance has typically been seen as a noncommercial poverty-alleviating product, while small business finance is clearly a commercial product—as can be attested by any of us receiving regular solicitations to acquire small business credit cards. Therefore microfinance has largely been the province of NGOs, while small business finance has been a bank product. I believe that these perceived differences have been greatly overstated.

Four factors are typically accepted as differentiating microfinance and small business finance: (1) the size of the loan and borrower, (2) the degree of the borrower's poverty, (3) the degree of informality or formality of the borrower's business, and (4) the lending methodology.

Beginning with loan and borrower size, although there is a general perception that microloans are "very small" and small business loans are "small," there is no commonly accepted definition of what these terms mean. I have already pointed out the shortcomings of using loan size as a proxy for a borrower definition. This can lead to some confusion, with microfinance loans ranging from a high of approximately $300 in Bangladesh to up to $30,000 in Russia.

Muddying the water even further, however, small and medium enterprises are typically defined according to variables other than loan size. The European Union, for example, defines SMEs according to the number of employees, turnover or balance sheet size, and degree of private ownership.[55] The small business definition in Russia is based on the number of employees, and there is no official definition of a microenterprise. This use of different variables inadvertently confuses any discussion about loan and borrower size as a reliable point of distinction between microfinance and small business finance.

Turning to the second category—the degree of poverty—we might expect a clearer dividing line between micro- and small business borrowers. Once again, however, this clarity does not exist. Individuals in extreme poverty clearly fall into the microfinance arena, but small business finance is frequently used by governments as an economic-development tool to assist those in less extreme poverty or without access to formal financial institutions. Although it would not be correct to say that microfinance and small business finance are identical in their focus on poverty, neither has an exclusive claim to being a poverty-alleviation tool.

The explanation for why clear dividing lines are so hard to find lies in the third of the four variables typically believed to differentiate

---

[55] The European Union establishes financial limits for balance-sheet size and turnover, one of which can be exceeded. Ownership has to be at least 75 percent private. http://www.ec.europa.eu (accessed August 9, 2006).

microborrowers from small business borrowers: the degree of formality or informality of the borrower's business.

The classic microfinance borrower is located squarely in the informal sector of a country's economy. The borrower is self-employed, or, if he or she has employees, they are often relatives or close family friends. The businesses are often not registered and typically strive to minimize taxes. Usually, the borrower's business and personal economic affairs are closely intertwined; cash moves freely between the two, and the borrower's home typically is used for some part of the business, such as for keeping inventory, serving as a storefront, keeping records, and the like.

A small business borrower, by contrast, operates in the formal sector of the economy. In fact, an important aspect of the bank's loan approval process includes analyzing reliable—often audited—financial statements to confirm not only that the company is creditworthy but that there is no risk of tax claims that might arise in the future and threaten loan repayment.

Between these two extreme versions of the typical microborrowers and small business borrowers, however, is a broad intermediate territory. Although some businesses begin life in the formal sector of the economy, with the owner registering the business and paying taxes from day one, other businesses begin as microenterprises and then gradually evolve into small businesses. For those businesses that begin as microenterprises, the term "evolution" is key; only at the very end of the process can one definitively say that a company has moved into the formal sector. The transition process might start because of the need to increase the number of employees. This may result in a shift from relying on family members as employees to bringing in outsiders, with a corresponding increase in the formality of the employer-employee relationship. Or, as the business grows, the entrepreneur's home may become an increasingly unsatisfactory place to do bookkeeping or maintain inventory, particularly if more employees join the company. If the business is extremely successful, the entrepreneur may find that registering at least part of the business and filing tax returns can be less onerous than the constant threat of unregulated reprisals against informal businesses. The key point, however, is that the process is fluid; for example, a borrower might move the business out of his or her home but still have predominantly family employees.

Not only is the degree of formality of a borrower's business not characterized by a clear cutoff point but also the transition from microborrower to small business borrower is one of similar small gradations. Furthermore, particularly in a rapidly changing economy, the lender must also be sensitive to changes in the market and the consequent need to redefine its loan categories. KMB Bank in Russia has changed the size of its microloans four times since it began operations in 1999: from a maximum of $5,000 when the bank began operations to a maximum of $10,000 at the beginning of 2002, to $20,000 in 2004, and $30,000 in 2005. These changes reflect both ongoing attempts to fine-tune the product for the market's needs as well as a continually changing market.

The fact that borrowers shift from being microenterprises to small businesses in small gradations is relevant for the fourth characteristic typically assumed to differentiate microlending and small business lending—the lending methodology. Once again, the assumed differences between these processes are exaggerated. As clients get larger the complexity of their financing requirements typically grows, but the basics of sound lending remain the same: good financial analysis, appropriate loan structure and collateral or collateral substitutes, and comfort with the borrower's character. One of the most significant methodological adjustments is that borrowers with growing businesses that need to finance capital expenditures have to be allowed repayment grace periods to allow the capital expenditure enough time to be able to generate income. Although this requirement conflicts with the microfinance principle that loan repayments should be regular and frequent, it does not pose an insurmountable challenge, particularly for borrowers with long track records. Even the fact that small business lenders use scoring techniques when possible to maximize their decision-making efficiency does not create the rift between microfinance lending and small business lending that is often assumed, because the scoring data is largely based on the same analytical issues.[56]

---

[56] Furthermore, the degree to which these models are used as exclusive decision-making tools, and therefore differentiate micro- and small business finance, tends to be exaggerated; one leading consultant to U.S. small business lenders noted that less than 10 percent of those in an informal pool used scoring as an automatic decision-making tool. Instead, credit scoring tends to be used more as an analytical tool, which

Clearly none of the four variables typically assumed to distinguish microfinance from small business finance—loan size, the borrower's poverty level, the formality of the business, and the lending methodology—differentiates microfinance from small business finance. We can recognize a microenterprise at one end of the spectrum for each variable and a small business at the other, but the territory in-between is large and fluctuating. The only logical conclusion is that the presumed distinctions do not actually exist.

Misperceptions, exacerbated by the different corporate cultures of the lenders, have kept banks and MFIs from understanding each other's business and potential areas of overlap. In some cases banks and MFIs even have misgivings about the other's mission; MFIs sometimes disdain the profit motives of banks, while banks find the performance claims of successful MFIs difficult to believe. Not only have banks and MFIs historically perceived little common ground but their different corporate perspectives made them disinclined to seek any.

Ironically, the economic-development field has helped to perpetuate these misperceptions, with donor agencies and aid organizations frequently assigning microfinance to its own department, separate from enterprise development as well as financial-sector development. Although some of these organizational barriers are coming down, this separation has clearly contributed to the general impression that microfinance is unrelated to these other important fields. Not surprisingly, this impression can be shared by the employees—my microfinance conversations with experienced financial-sector economists are often characterized either by polite disinterest or uninformed but strongly held views.

Active donor-agency involvement in microfinance may also have inadvertently added to the impression that microfinance is a noncommercial undertaking that requires significant donor funding, at least to get started, if not to perpetuate the MFI's activities. This assumption fails to recognize that most new business ventures require substantial funding. Because commercial banks have historically not been interested in microfinance, aid agencies and donors have stepped in to

---

is how it is also being applied in microfinance. Charles B. Wendel, "Ten SME Facts," *SME Weekly*, Financial Institutions Consulting, April 13, 2004, http://www.ficinc.com (accessed April 20, 2004).

create or support other types of lenders. However, for those banks that do enter the microfinance market, their existing lending infrastructure clearly lowers their profitability hurdle compared to MFIs created from the ground up.[57]

My analysis in this chapter—and this book—is designed to encourage banks, microfinance lenders, and development experts to rethink their assumptions about microfinance and small business and to focus on their common ground, rather than their differences. With no clear cutoff point between microenterprises and small business clients, it would make sense for successful small business lenders to explore how much further down the loan-size spectrum they could go if they weren't distracted by artificial definitions of their client base.

Microfinance lenders and donors in turn should rethink their attitude toward large loans and borrowers. Even if their mandate does not allow them to lend to their clients after the clients reach a certain size, it should be a priority to ensure that these borrowers can graduate to a banking relationship. Although the field's growing interest in building inclusive financial sectors is an important step in the right direction, these efforts would have to be greatly accelerated to ensure that microfinance has the funding and the innovations necessary to realize its full economic development potential.

Recognizing these synergies between microfinance and small business lending is important, not only to encourage more commercial lending. Enabling borrowers to graduate more seamlessly to ever-higher loan amounts would also enhance our appreciation of microfinance's potential as a growth tool.

Microfinance: A Tool for Poverty Alleviation and Growth

As I have discussed in this chapter, microfinance evolved from efforts to help poor and low-income individuals find sustainable ways to help themselves. As a result, a key focus of the field's work has been how to even get entrepreneurs onto the borrowing continuum. Crucial as

---

[57] Bear in mind the distinction that I made earlier between MFIs that will always require outside support because of the nature of their business and those that can become profitable.

this objective is, however, it inadvertently takes attention away from microfinance's equally valid potential as a tool for contributing to economic growth by helping entrepreneurs grow and move along that continuum. One important study of this issue concluded that "loan impact rose in direct proportion to the level of borrowers' pre-loan incomes; or, put otherwise, it was relatively smaller if the borrower was close to or below the poverty line."[58]

Although this finding is not directly relevant for those working with the poorest of the poor, it is extremely relevant to commercial lenders whose goal is to help make their clients—and hence themselves—ever more prosperous. For example, studies such as this one might encourage commercial lenders to make loans that were not profitable on a stand-alone basis—that is, lend on the smaller end of the continuum—if they could be confident that enough of the borrowers would grow to a point where the relationships would become profitable. An emphasis on the growth potential of microfinance could therefore bring more lenders to the field.[59]

Another consequence of microfinance's historic focus on serving the poor is that the organizational divide between microfinance and small business lenders has cut off the information flow about borrower growth at the point where it is most needed: What are the factors that enable some borrowers to grow from one category to another? Currently many borrowers have to physically move from one lending organization to another when their borrowing needs outgrow the MFI that helped them get started. As a result, information about the borrower's subsequent development is lost.

Because most SMEs in emerging economies began life as microenterprises, the policy repercussions of this loss of information are not trivial. For example, one survey of seven countries in Africa showed that approximately half of the enterprises with ten to fifty

[58] David Hulme and Paul Mosley, *Finance against Poverty*, vol. 1 (New York: Routledge, 1996), 130.

[59] A similar point is made by Christina Barrineau, chief technical advisor for the International Year of Microcredit 2005, who suggests that economic-development projects should be refocused on wealth creation rather than poverty alleviation. Lauren Kesner, "Redefining Microfinance as a Strategy to Achieve the MDGs: International Year of Microcredit Report Advocates Shift from Poverty Alleviation to Wealth Creation," *Microfinance Matters* 16, September 2005, http://www.yearofmicrocredit.org (accessed January 3, 2006).

employees had started with fewer than five employees.[60] KMB Bank's experience provides equally provocative results, with 59 percent of the borrowers who have had a five-year relationship with the bank having more than doubled their loan size. Policymakers wishing to encourage economic growth would be well advised to analyze whether these figures can be improved: What would it take, for example, to ensure that an even higher proportion of small African enterprises grew to have ten to fifty employees?[61] Lenders who are able to keep pace with the increased borrowing requirements of their clients could help to answer this question; they would also have a commercial motivation to do so.[62]

The poverty label has also contributed to the failure of many policymakers to recognize the role that microfinance—and MSE finance more broadly—could play in financial-sector development. The banking sector in emerging markets worldwide, not only in Russia, is characterized by a common litany of problems: inexperienced bankers, vulnerability to political influence, excessively close ties with large borrowers, and unhealthy concentrations of large loans. Attempts to address these problems often focus on training bankers to make better loans and training supervisors to recognize bad loans and weak banks when they see them. Although this approach enables everyone to see the problem, it does not create a solution, especially in

---

[60] Carl Liedholm and Donald C. Mead, *Small Enterprises and Economic Development: The Dynamics of Micro and Small Enterprises* (New York: Routledge, 1999).

[61] Although a recent World Bank report on the relationship between SMEs (not microenterprises) could not identify—or deny—a causal relationship between SMEs and economic growth, this research was hampered by the lack of data about the informal activity characteristic of this sector (although estimates were made). Furthermore, the results are not completely relevant to the argument I am making because it includes data from both developed and developing countries. I am arguing that a growing MSE sector could help emerging economies accelerate GDP growth, not that a large microenterprise and SME sector has a lasting impact on GDP growth acceleration in a mature market economy. In any case, the World Bank study does conclude that a strong SME sector is characteristic of strong economies. Thorsten Beck, Asli Demirguc-Kunt, and Ross Levine, "Small and Medium Enterprises, Growth, and Poverty: Cross-Country Evidence," World Bank Policy Research Working Paper 3178, December 2003.

[62] Another way in which a poverty focus can inadvertently reduce potential growth is in program design. Take a $1 million program, for example, in which 50 percent of the resources must go to the very poor. Assume for the sake of simplicity that the very poor borrow $50 on average, while the less poor borrow $500. Such a program

countries where the economy is dominated by large state-owned or state-influenced firms that may not even be creditworthy.

MSE finance could be part of the solution to this dilemma. Small entrepreneurs are an untapped client base in many countries, equally accessible to any interested bankers willing to apply the appropriate methodology. Furthermore, they are a diversified client base; the failure of a small client will never threaten a bank's solvency. And small entrepreneurs are not politically aligned, therefore enabling a bank to maintain the type of professional arms-length relationship that can be elusive in some markets. Finally, the keys to successful microfinance and small business lending are the keys to good lending overall. MSE lending arguably provides one of the best training grounds for bankers of all aspirations and, with it, the ultimate strengthening of a country's financial sector. The microfinance field's increasing emphasis on building inclusive financial sectors could benefit not only small borrowers but the financial sector as a whole.

Although microfinance has made an enormous contribution to economic development over the past several decades, its ability to continue to do so requires new commercial partners. Not only would commercial lenders bring more financial resources and their own expertise to the field but a relaxation of the conceptual boundaries between microfinance and small business finance could also help us take a new view that embraces microfinance's potential as a tool for facilitating growth as well as alleviating poverty. I hope that this book will contribute to the recent progress being made in this direction.

In the following chapters of this book I shift from the global context to the story of the development of entrepreneurship in Russia. I also shift from a focus on microfinance to MSE finance more broadly, in order to emphasize the synergies between serving microenterprise

---

would end up lending to ten thousand very poor clients and one thousand less-poor clients. Note that, if the borrowers were in a closed group, simple arithmetic shows that a limited number of the very poor borrowers could graduate to become a less-poor borrower. Therefore, even to the degree that the poverty focus of this hypothetical program might lay the groundwork for growth, the program design makes it impossible for borrowers to pursue growth to its maximum.

and small enterprise clients. While emphasizing the specifics of the Russian case, I discuss how lessons from Russia are relevant to the global development field: particularly the need to understand the dynamics of entrepreneurial growth and financial-sector development in order to design appropriate policies.[63]

[63] As a point of clarification, in this book I use a number of overlapping terms including entrepreneurs, small business, microfinance, MSEs and MSE finance, SMEs and SME finance. I use the terms *entrepreneurs* and *small businesses* interchangeably, whether they refer to one individual or a small business with several hundred employees. I use the terms *MSEs* and *MSE finance* when I am emphasizing the closely related nature of micro- and small businesses and micro- and small business finance. The term *microfinance* is used when I refer specifically to the microfinance field. Finally, I used the terms *SME* and *SME finance* when I am referring to a third- party definition or when I specifically mean to exclude microenterprises or borrowers or both.

Chapter 2

THE GROWTH OF RUSSIAN ENTREPRENEURS

Understanding the relevance of the global development of microfinance to Russia requires understanding the development of Russian entrepreneurship. Although the Russian MSE sector is typically considered to be underdeveloped, and the banking sector is often identified as a culprit, I argue that Russian MSEs are substantially more developed and dynamic than is usually appreciated. This different point of view has important implications for how to encourage the sector's further growth.

The key context for analyzing Russian entrepreneurship is that its history is surprisingly short; private economic activity was introduced only gingerly in the Soviet Union in 1987 and not made fully legal until the end of 1990. Furthermore, legal entrepreneurship came into being as the Soviet Union was collapsing; new Russian entrepreneurs had to cope with one of the most incredible social, economic, and political upheavals of the century. Any assessments of Russian entrepreneurship, including comparisons of Russian small business with that of other countries, miss a crucial point if they do not take these unique—and recent—starting conditions into account.

The history of entrepreneurship in Russia reveals one of the two major reasons why MSE finance has developed relatively slowly. Entrepreneurs were officially criminals in the Soviet Union; this stigma has taken a long time to abate, particularly because the early days of legal entrepreneurship were characterized by considerable gray and black market activity. The second major reason for the low level of Russian MSE finance is addressed in chapter 3, where I discuss the incentives built in to the creation of Russia's commercial banking system.

Analyses of Russian entrepreneurship that lack the appropriate context typically miss the second point made in this chapter, which is that the story of Russian small entrepreneurs is still actively unfolding. Russian entrepreneurs have shown remarkable dynamism over their short history. Although analysis inevitably has to be done at a fixed moment in time, we must remember that this moment is on a time line that will extend far into the future. As just one example, the fact that Russian entrepreneurs have had so little access to financing during their brief existence indicates their still considerable potential to grow.

In contrast to many analyses of the development of small entrepreneurs in Russia, in this chapter I emphasize the positive; this is the third point of this chapter. By understanding the constraints under which entrepreneurs have operated, and the results that they have achieved nonetheless, we can only be impressed by the resilience and dynamism exhibited by this economic group. Viewing the development of Russian entrepreneurship in this light has important implications for policy prescriptions for the future development of Russian entrepreneurs. These prescriptions should emphasize facilitating the ability of entrepreneurs to realize their potential, rather than treating them like a weak child in need of nurturing.

I begin with a discussion of the conditions under which entrepreneurship was introduced during the perestroika period, and in particular the antipathy with which Soviet society viewed private enterprise. I then trace the evolution of Russian entrepreneurs in four stages. The first stage, "perestroika," is the period from 1985 to 1990 and is characterized by the search for new forms of economic association that would be more responsive to market demand than the behemoth state-owned enterprises that were answerable only to their ministries. The perestroika stage spanned an extraordinary period that concluded with the complete legalization of private enterprise by the Russian—not Soviet—government.

The second stage, "initial consolidation," covers the period from 1991 to 1998; it begins with the collapse of the Soviet Union and concludes with the 1998 crisis. The analysis during this stage shifts from the introduction of private enterprise to the development of small privately owned businesses. Despite the continuing economic and political upheavals during this period, small businesses were estimated to account for over 10 percent of GDP on the eve of the 1998 crisis.

The third stage is the financial "crisis," from August 1998 to the end of 1999. Although initially an enormous shock, the crisis ultimately laid the groundwork for a more sustainable approach to economic development in Russia—one based on the painstaking process of step-by-step reform, rather than relying on shock programs or international rescue packages. The resilience of small business in the crisis made it an important protagonist of this new approach.

Finally, the period from 2000 through 2006 is the "mainstream period." One key characteristic of this period is that Russian entrepreneurs began to take responsibility for their own development; they no longer hoped for significant official support. The other key characteristic is that Russian entrepreneurs were finally recognized as an important element of the economy—they became part of the mainstream.

Starting Conditions

Russian entrepreneurs have proven to be so adaptable that it is easy to forget the starkly inimical environment from which they emerged. To understand the radicalness of the innovations introduced during the perestroika period, we should pause to absorb the fact that essentially all private economic activity was a criminal offense in the Soviet Union as recently as 1987. The most prominent form of legal private economic activity for most Soviet citizens was the collective farm markets, where prices were based on supply and demand and farmers could keep the proceeds for goods produced on their individual plots. Although Article 17 of the Soviet Constitution permitted "individual labor activity," the only allowable activity that was well defined was handicrafts. As a result, only a tiny fraction of the Soviet Union's workforce—in the range of 100,000 people—was registered as being engaged in private economic activity at the outset of perestroika.[1]

---

[1] Anthony Jones and William Moskoff, *KO-OPS: The Rebirth of Entrepreneurship in the Soviet Union* (Bloomington: Indiana University Press, 1991), 3.

This official outlawing of any significant form of private economic activity had two important implications—one psychological and one practical—for the subsequent development of entrepreneurship in Russia. The psychological antipathy to entrepreneurship during the Soviet period was profound. Not only was the activity of entrepreneurs illegal but even the concept of private enterprise was difficult for most Soviet citizens to understand in any practical way, having lived their entire lives in a planned, state-run economy, and in most cases having few opportunities to travel and experience firsthand how other economies functioned. This conceptual difficulty can be seen in the perestroika period with the adoption of cooperatives as the first radically new form of business association. Cooperatives incorporated the incentives of private ownership but retained a veneer of socialist principles, because the ownership was collective and all of the owners were also workers. Therefore they provided a safe ideological haven of economic reform for Soviet officials.

Not only was the concept of private economic activity largely foreign but decades of anticapitalist propaganda had created a caricature of private enterprise as a vehicle for the exploitation of workers by owners, as well as one that created enormous risks, ranging from unemployment to the U.S. Depression. Even though more sophisticated Soviet citizens—such as those in the more Western-oriented Baltic republics—rejected the most heavy-handed claims of the propaganda machine, the concept of the unfairness and uncertainties of an economy based on private enterprise was deeply embedded in the national psyche. When combined with the fact that the death penalty could be applied in cases of embezzlement, bribery, and speculation, it is little wonder that entrepreneurship was viewed so suspiciously by the Soviet citizenry. Although corruption was widespread, and the death penalty rarely invoked, the severity of the potential punishment made such "capitalist" activities seem particularly vile. Some of the results of the perestroika innovations only entrenched this negative view.

The outlawing of private economic activity had a practical impact on the development of Russian entrepreneurship as well. Economic activity during the Soviet period was the province of the closely interlinked Communist Party and the state. Essentially all property was owned by the state, and economic activity was directed by the state and the party on the basis of a minutely detailed annual plan. However, not only are plans rarely 100 percent fulfilled as anticipated but the Soviet economic plans were notorious for focusing on industrial production at the expense of consumer products and services. (Although it is only fair to note that, even if the plans had been more consumer oriented, consumer demands are so unpredictable that there still would have been a gap between supply and demand.)

These two inherent shortcomings in the plan—they could not be completely fulfilled as intended and they did not satisfy consumer needs—contributed to the development of an extensive "second" economy.[2] Part of the second economy was engaged in ensuring that the plan could be met; for example, if insufficient fuel allocated to a railroad line meant that a factory manager would not get his raw materials on time, supply specialists at the factory were responsible for figuring out how to solve that problem. Furthermore, the challenge was not just to find the necessary missing item but also to deliver it to the factory and arrange for payment—all in an economy where these transactions were only supposed to occur when sanctioned by the plan.

The other part of the informal economy fed off consumer shortages; if you wanted to avoid the drab clothing available in the state-run stores, there was a way to arrange that as well, as long as you had the contacts, the cash, and whatever form of barter might also be required in exchange.

It should be stressed that achieving these out-of-plan objectives, whether at the level of the factory manager or the individual consumer, required extensive interaction with the official formal economy; the formal economy was the source of the necessary resources as well as having the forbearance to look the other way, if not actively help, those pursuing these other objectives. As economist Gregory Grossman put it memorably, "Given the plethora of administrative superiors, controllers,

---

[2] Gregory Grossman defines the second economy as "the aggregate of economic activities (production, trade, and so on) which meet at least one of the following criteria: (a) they are pursued directly for private gain, whether legally or illegally; (b) they are pursued knowingly in contravention of the law in some significant respect(s), whether for private gain or socialist benefit." Gregory Grossman, "The Second Economy: Boon or Bane for the Reform of the First Economy?" in *Economic Reforms in the Socialist World*, ed. Stanislaw Gomulka, Yong-Chool Ha, and Cae-One Kim (Armonk, N.Y.: M. E. Sharpe, 1989), 79.

inspectors, auditors, law enforcers, party authorities, expediters, and just plain snoopers that beset every economic activity, legal or illegal, in the Soviet Union, anything done out of line requires the buying off of some and often very many people."[3] Grossman further noted that "the public seems to accept petty illegality as a normal and even inevitable part of making one's way in a refractory and shortage-ridden environment."[4] The resulting corruption among party and government officials was well known; Gorbachev's predecessor, Yuri Andropov, had made particularly concerted efforts to combat official corruption, with only limited results.

Although the line is difficult to draw, we must distinguish between two categories of illegal activity. In one category were those who were helping a factory fulfill its plan requirements and who broke the law in order to do so, or someone who wanted to have nicer clothes or to arrange access to a special medical clinic. In the second category were the outright criminal groups that seemed to grow exponentially as law and order in the Soviet Union collapsed. The activities of the latter group, such as extortion and drug trafficking, would be considered illegal in any economic environment. They are relevant to the development of Russian entrepreneurs primarily because of the protection rackets that they created in the late 1980s and early 1990s.

My discussion emphasizes the first category, the players in the second economy and their counterparts in the official economy, because they were among the first to take advantage of the liberalization of the perestroika period; their previous experience in manipulating the planned economy helps to explain some of the ways in which "legal" entrepreneurship initially manifested itself. Furthermore, the rerobing of these second economy specialists in the cloak of legality further antagonized much of society toward the concept of private enterprise. The explosion of outright criminal activity as the Soviet Union dissolved also worsened the attitude of many Russians to what they understood private enterprise to represent, but I will not pursue that theme in this book.

---

[3] Gregory Grossman, "The 'Second Economy' of the USSR," *Problems of Communism* 26, no. 5 (September–October 1977): 25–40.

[4] Grossman, "The 'Second Economy'" of the USSR."

Perestroika, 1985–1990

When Mikhail Gorbachev became general secretary of the Communist Party in 1985, the Soviet economy was suffering from a range of problems often referred to as the *zastoi* (stagnation) characteristic of the Brezhnev years. There were two particularly worrisome manifestations of these problems. One was a decline in economic growth, which had slowed down from 4 percent annually in the early 1970s to 2 percent during the first half of the 1980s. The other was an increasingly visible technology gap with the United States and Western Europe. A major theme in Gorbachev's response to these challenges was to introduce more flexibility into how the economy functioned. One approach was to reduce the state's control over enterprises so that they could be both more responsive to demand and more responsible for their own decisions. The other approach was to allow independent economic activity by entities that were not state owned. The three key laws that implemented these reforms were the Law on Individual Labor Activity, the Law on State Enterprise, and the Law on Cooperatives.

The Law on Individual Labor Activity, adopted in November 1986, was one of the first steps to providing more economic flexibility. The law was intended to encourage more innovation and initiative by expanding on the constitutional right to individual labor activity. (As I noted, individual labor was allowed, but few people utilized the opportunity.) The fact that this law was only intended as a fine-tuning of the planned economy, and not as a significant change, can be seen in the comments of I. I. Gladky, chairman of the USSR State Committee on Labor and Social Questions: "It is perfectly obvious that the measures being taken do not signify a return, in any form whatsoever, to private entrepreneurial activity. . . . the intention is to develop individual enterprise solely on the basis of the personal labor of citizens. . . . In this way, any type of private entrepreneurial activity or exploitation of man by man is ruled out."[5]

Four provisions in the law are important to highlight. First, those who were allowed to participate in individual labor activity were those who were already on the margin of economic activity: housewives,

---

[5] Cited in Jones and Moskoff, *KO-OPS*, 6.

pensioners, the disabled, and students. Those who already had jobs could only participate in individual labor activity in their free time; they were not allowed to leave their state employment to take up individual labor activity on a full-time basis. These limits on those eligible to participate indicate the degree to which this law was intended to make only marginal changes to economic activity. In practice, however, these limits were often ignored.

Second, these individuals were also allowed to form cooperatives, in which ownership would be "collective" and all of the owners would work in the business. The activity of these cooperatives played a major role in the evolution of perestroika.

Third, individuals and cooperatives were provided considerable independence in setting the prices for their products and services. This right was a significant departure from past practice, because prices for the output of state-owned enterprises were set by the plan and not alterable by the enterprises.

Finally, local authorities were given significant powers to implement the law, including expanding the permitted types of activities as required by local conditions and issuing permits. This provision had two critical consequences: it opened the door for official influence on the operations of the cooperatives; and it enabled those local authorities that wished to do so to implement the law much more liberally than had been anticipated, on the grounds of adapting to local conditions.

The response to the Law on Individual Labor Activity was positive but not overwhelming. The number of individuals registered as working independently increased from approximately 100,000 before the law was adopted to 429,000 at the end of 1988, and 723,000 at the end of 1989.[6] By the beginning of 1988 fourteen thousand cooperatives had been registered.[7] Although generating a large change in relative terms, the law did not create a massive shift in employment in a country of about 250 million people.

Operating under the new law entailed a number of challenges that contributed to this measured response. Because the economy was still

---

[6] E. G. Yasin, A. Yu. Chepurenko, V. V. Bueva, eds., "Maloye predprinimatel'stvo v Rossii: Proshloye, nastoyashchee i budushchee" (Moscow: Fund "Liberal Mission," 2003), 20.

[7] Jones and Moskoff, *KO-OPS*, table 2.1, p. 16.

state owned and managed, obtaining raw materials and premises that were not envisaged by the state's economic plan was not a straightforward matter, despite broad attempts in the law to address these issues. Bribes were often used to resolve these challenges. The powers given to local authorities also slowed down the response of some potential entrepreneurs to the new law, because these authorities were able to play favorites in providing approvals. Finally, a number of would-be entrepreneurs, including black marketeers who could legalize their activities under the new law, had doubts about the long-term implications of revealing their private initiative. The Soviet state had a long track record of punishing those who showed such initiative, and a reversal of policy direction could easily occur.

On the other side of the coin, the financial rewards for those who persevered could be considerable, because the primarily consumer-oriented goods and services that were offered had been unavailable for decades and were now being provided in a market with minimal competition and free price setting. Tales of the profits made by some of these first entrepreneurs only worsened public opinion, but the dynamism of these entrepreneurs made an important impression on policymakers.

Following close on the heels of the Law on Individual Labor Activity was the most far-reaching reform of the perestroika period—the July 1987 Law on State-Owned Enterprises. The key innovation in this law was enabling enterprises to function relatively independently provided that they fulfilled state plans. Along with this unprecedented independence came the responsibility for "self-financing" or achieving profitability, and the corresponding threat that enterprises not able to cover their costs would become bankrupt. The law also significantly reduced the previously monolithic authority of the ministries and Gosplan, the state planning agency, over the enterprises. This authority became more general and supervisory, with elected workers' collectives taking over operating control of the enterprises.

In retrospect it is clear that this well-intentioned effort to introduce some market discipline to the activities of the state-owned enterprises was the nail in the coffin of the state-planned economy. The Soviet economy did not have any of the legal, regulatory, or institutional mechanisms in place for enterprises to function according to market terms. Simply as an incomplete list of examples, there was no accounting system to determine the true costs of production; no contract-enforcement mechanisms; no quality control or consumer protection provisions; and, as I discuss in chapter 3, there were no banks with any experience or authority to lend for non–state-authorized purposes. As a result, the Law on State-Owned Enterprises inadvertently led to decreased economic output—at least as officially measured—and gave enterprise managers unprecedented freedoms. The state loosened its control, but there was no market-imposed discipline to take its place.

The third important law of the perestroika period was the Law on Cooperatives, which was adopted in May 1988 and which built on the cooperative activity that had commenced with the Law on Individual Labor Activity. Although the Law on Cooperatives was a significant step toward more liberal economic activity, cooperatives were seen as a legitimately socialist form of enterprise; the cooperative was owned collectively, and all of the owners were also employees.[8] Therefore the bridge to a capitalist form of enterprise, in which an individual owner hired employees and simply collected the profits from their work, was not being crossed.

The Law on Cooperatives had four key elements: previous limitations on a cooperative's sphere of activity and size were removed; anyone was free to work in a cooperative; cooperatives were allowed to form joint ventures with foreign companies; and cooperatives were given the right to open banks.

The new law accelerated the pace of cooperative formation, which grew from 14,100 on January 1, 1988, before the new law was passed, to a peak of 220,000–230,000 by June 1990. As of year-end 1989, reported cooperative output accounted for 4.3 percent of GDP, including a 15.4 percent share of consumer services.[9] Unreported cooperative output was inevitably higher.

A revealing survey of 586 cooperative members in early 1990 shows that liberalizing the regulations for cooperative members had a significant impact on the membership profile. These individuals had clearly been part of the economic mainstream in terms of their training

---

[8] There could be employees who were not owners, but there could not be owners who were not employees.

[9] Jones and Moskoff, *KO-OPS*, 18.

and authority; two-thirds had higher education, 40 percent had held responsible positions in state-owned enterprises, and 57 percent were thirty-six or older. At least based on this survey, the cooperatives were attracting the interest of solid Soviet citizens. It is also instructive that 57.6 percent of the respondents cited realizing their potential as the primary reason for joining a cooperative, while 20.4 percent cited higher income as the primary motivation.[10] Therefore, this first generation of cooperative members included a high proportion of individuals who made a proactive choice to improve their lives.

"For my sister, opening a cooperative was the natural next step."

Lyudmila Beshchekova is the financial officer, partner, and sister of the founder of KVOLL, a company that designs and produces contemporary women's clothing. Dressed in a sophisticated but comfortable-looking knit suit, Beshchekova bustled me through crowded rooms of women at sewing machines, racks of clothing, and one of the company's stores. The young woman who accompanied me to the appointment quickly excused herself to visit the store, where we later found her the proud new owner of two chic suits.

Lyudmila's sister, Tatiana, was one of those pioneering individuals who participated in "individual labor activity" in accordance with Article 17 of the Soviet Constitution. Although she had a day job at a state enterprise, Tatiana spent all of her free time on her true avocation, creating fashionable clothing for women. Tatiana was therefore one of those people for whom starting a cooperative was not the unimaginably daring step that it might seem for some of us but a natural evolution for someone with creative abilities and initiative who had never fit easily into the Soviet mold. As Lyudmila stated matter-of-factly, "For my sister, opening a cooperative was the natural next step."

The first several years of Tatiana's cooperative business went extremely well; consumers were starved for attractive clothing and demand was high. By 1991 Tatiana was able to offer her sister a salary four times greater than what she was earning in a prestigious government position and finally enticed Lyudmila to join the business as the

---

[10] Jones and Moskoff, *KO-OPS*, 27.

financial officer. Financing was available to help the company grow, with Mosbusinessbank providing short-term financing without even requiring collateral.

This situation changed dramatically in 1993. Privatization had created extensive disarray in the retail system, which was exacerbated by the worsening finances of many enterprises. As a result, stores suddenly became unable to buy the company's clothing. For the next three years the company's four owners were forced to spend their weekends at Russia's extensive outdoor markets—one at each market—hawking their products themselves. Over ten years later, as she recounted this experience, Lyudmila's voice reflected the stress and humiliation of those years. The situation was worsened by the increasing demands of Mosbusinessbank, which was presumably responding to the deteriorating economic situation; its new requirements included collateral that KVOLL was unable to provide.

KVOLL enjoyed a year and a half of resumed prosperity as Russia's economy stabilized in 1996, but then it had to endure the 1998 financial crisis. Like all of the entrepreneurs I interviewed for this book, Lyudmila Beshchekova recounted the events of this period in a matter-of-fact way. The situation actually seemed less traumatic than the outdoor market days earlier in the 1990s. As Lyudmila Beshchekova put it, "We had children in school and expenses to cover; we had no alternative but to endure."

Although KVOLL's partners lived from paycheck to paycheck and put any spare money back into the business, the crisis ultimately helped them by making imported clothing inaccessibly expensive to most Russian consumers. By switching to inexpensive synthetic fabrics and searching out the lowest-cost providers, KVOLL was able to lower its prices enough to suit Russian pocketbooks. And, as an example of how many entrepreneurs viewed the crisis as part of a spectrum of ups and downs rather than as a terminal disaster, Tatiana even prevailed over her partners' doubts and convinced them to purchase a factory building outside of Moscow. This additional production capacity has proven to be a valuable addition to KVOLL's growth; as of the end of 2005, KVOLL was selling its clothing from five of its own stores in Moscow and had plans to expand into the regions.

Most of the cooperatives formed under the new law had close ties to state-owned enterprises or official bodies; as of 1989 approximately 80 percent were either located on the premises of a state-owned enterprise or had some form of sponsorship by an official body, such as a local government or state-owned enterprise.[11] Although it is easy to criticize these state ties, we should bear in mind the difficulties at that time of creating a cooperative without some form of official connection. The banking sector had no experience lending to cooperatives, cooperatives only had access to supplies after the state-owned enterprises had taken what they needed to fulfill the plan, and local authorities had the power to approve or deny permits. Furthermore, state-owned enterprises had been given more autonomy and were looking for ways to exercise it. Hence the development of close ties between state-owned enterprises or other official bodies and cooperatives was quite logical.

Unfortunately, the inconsistencies between the regulations that still hampered the state-owned enterprises and the freedoms provided to the cooperatives encouraged the cooperatives to exploit those inconsistencies. The standard operating procedure was for the state-owned enterprise to sell raw materials to a cooperative that it controlled at the fixed price at which the state-owned enterprise acquired these materials from the state. (Although the cooperatives were supposed to purchase inputs at prices higher than those paid by the state-owned enterprises, these regulations were regularly ignored.) The cooperative could then either sell these materials at higher market prices or use the materials to make products that it could sell at market prices. The state-owned enterprise, as owner, enjoyed the profits.

It is well known that these initial economic reforms did not have the desired effect of increasing productivity and satisfying consumer demand. On the contrary, official economic output declined, as enterprises were released from some of their plan responsibilities and not all of the new nonplan economic activity was captured by the official statistics; net material product decreased by 4 percent during 1989 and reached a decrease of 21 percent in the fourth quarter

[11] T. G. Dolgopyatova, ed., *Malyy biznes v Rossii* (Moscow: Institute of Strategic Analysis and Development of Entrepreneurship [ISARP], n.d.), 30–31.

of 1991.[12] In addition, inflation increased as the previous very tight controls on cash were breached and as state-owned enterprises and the cooperatives were given more freedom to set prices and wages. These problems became painfully apparent to the general public as shortages became more and more acute; as of the spring of 1990, only five percent of 1,100 commodity groups were readily available.[13]

Furthermore, because these economic reforms were paralleled by political reforms encapsulated in such slogans as *glasnost* (transparency) and *democratizatsiya* (democratization), there was more flexibility than there had been since the 1917 revolution for other political figures and even the public at large to criticize the evolving economic conditions and propose other alternatives. Boris Yeltsin's election as chairman of the Presidium of the Supreme Soviet of the Russian Soviet Federative Socialist Republic in May 1990 intensified this contested political atmosphere, as he used his new platform to criticize Gorbachev and the Soviet authorities for their slowness in implementing reforms.

The public's views of economic reform were therefore evolving during an extraordinary period in which their new economic and political freedoms were accompanied by a worsening economic environment. Their correspondingly mixed views can be seen in an extensive 1990 survey that polled 101,000 residents in all fifteen Soviet republics regarding their views of cooperatives. Because the cooperatives were one of the most visible manifestations of the reforms, and were also increasingly used as a scapegoat for problems such as higher prices, the survey is particularly appropriate for this discussion. The results convey two clear messages. First, outright support for cooperatives was limited to 15 percent of the respondents. Second, there was a very high level of ambivalence; 56 percent of the respondents either were indifferent, ambivalent, or didn't know what to think.[14] Given the historic antipathy to private enterprise, as well as the worsening economic situation, it is not surprising that 29 percent of the respondents were explicitly opposed to cooperatives. The key criticism

---

[12] Anders Aslund, *How Russia Became a Market Economy* (Washington, D.C.: Brookings Institution, 1995), 36 and 41.

[13] Jones and Moskoff, *KO-OPS*, 122.

[14] Thirteen percent were indifferent, 27 percent were ambivalent, and 16 percent didn't know what to think.

of the cooperatives, cited by 86 percent of the respondents, was their excessively high prices.[15]

To convey the other half of the picture it is instructive to note the challenges faced by the cooperatives. According to a 1989 survey of cooperative members, the two organizations that created the most difficulties for them were local authorities and racketeers, in that order.[16] The theme of interference by local authorities was to become a perennial one.

Perhaps the most poignant example of the conflicting points of view during this tumultuous period is the decision of the Soviet Council of Ministers in August 1990 regarding small state-owned enterprises. Parallel to the development of the cooperatives, republic-level ministries had been authorized to experiment with creating smaller state-owned enterprises that would be more flexible and responsive to consumers. The results of these experiments had been perceived quite favorably, particularly in the case of Estonia. Because Estonia had managed to avoid the worst of the consumer goods deficits that plagued many of the Soviet republics, it was able to absorb the output of these small enterprises and avoid the consumer complaints over high prices that arose in Russia. In June 1989 a Soviet Council of Ministers committee had noted the positive results of Estonia's economic experimentation. The council was then due to follow up with a formal resolution regarding further development of small enterprises.

There was intense debate over whether this resolution would allow for the creation of small enterprises that were privately owned; the legal forms of private economic activity were still only individual labor activity, cooperatives, and joint ventures. Ultimately, the conservative viewpoint prevailed, and the August 1990 resolution, entitled "On the Means for Founding and Developing Small Enterprises," referred only to the creation of state-owned small enterprises (defined as those with up to one hundred employees). The Soviet authorities were still not ready to take the final step toward unrestrained private enterprise. With the complete disintegration of the Soviet Union only slightly more than one year in the future, this resolution has the retrospective air of holding one's fingers in a dike against an impending tidal wave.

---

[15] Survey cited in Jones and Moskoff, *KO-OPS*, 103–4.
[16] Jones and Moskoff, *KO-OPS*, 93.

President Yeltsin contributed to the creation of this tidal wave by using the conservatism of the Soviet authorities as a lever to increase his own popularity and authority. Russia had already declared sovereignty in June 1990, and, as Gorbachev backed away from the chaos of economic reform in the fall of 1990, Yeltsin seized on privatization as his battle cry. The privatization theme was useful both for demonstrating Yeltsin's progressiveness and for laying claim to assets on Russian territory—that is, territory that no longer belonged to the Soviet Union. As a result, just three months after the Soviet resolution of August, in November 1990 Russia adopted the Law on Land Reform, which was its first privatization law. Then in December 1990 Russia adopted two laws that removed essentially all restraints on private economic activity: the Law on Ownership and the Law on Enterprises and Entrepreneurial Activity. The Law on Ownership provided equal legal rights to all forms of property, private and state, while the Law on Enterprises and Entrepreneurial Activity removed remaining restrictions on private enterprise, including hiring labor, and allowed the full range of economic associations, including partnerships and joint stock companies. In five tumultuous years, private economic activity had gone from being a criminal act to one that was fully legalized by the Soviet Union's leading breakaway republic.[17]

Initial Consolidation, 1991 to August 1998

The initial consolidation period for the development of small entrepreneurs in Russia began in 1991 with a shift in the stage from the Soviet Union to Russia and ended with the 1998 financial crisis. The analysis shifts as well from the introduction of private enterprise, which was the key theme in the preceding period, to the development of small business. Although this period was quite dramatic in terms of political events, including the storming of the Russian White House (the building that housed the Congress of People's Deputies and the Supreme

[17] The debates of this final year of Soviet power are discussed in A. D. Yoffi, V. Shch. Kaganov, and A. I. Mishchin, eds., "Maloye predprinimatel'stvo v Rossii: Sostoyaniye, problemy, perspektivy," analytical materials prepared for the Second All-Russian Congress of Representatives of Small Enterprises, Institute of Entrepreneurship and Investment, Moscow, 1999.

Soviet of the Russian Soviet Federative Socialist Republic) in 1993 and the rise of the "oligarchs," Russia's new business elite, the key theme for small business was that it put down roots and grew. The initial acceptance of Russian small business as a fact of Russian economic life was reflected in the Law on State Support for Small Entrepreneurship of 1995 and the First All-Russian Congress of Representatives of Small Enterprises in 1996.

In 1991 the Soviet Union and Russia experienced an extraordinarily tumultuous year, concluding with the dissolution of the Soviet Union and with Gorbachev's resignation. As the conclusive struggle between Russian and Soviet power was waged during that year, authorities on both sides implemented economic measures in an attempt to assert their sovereignty, as well as to impress the population with their superior ability to implement economic reform. Of these measures, the most important for the further development of private enterprise was the July 1991 Russian Law on Privatization of State and Municipal Enterprises. The passage of this law (as well as a law on housing privatization) by the Russian government followed an unsuccessful attempt at the Soviet level to pass a privatization law in June. Although Gorbachev tried to make up for this failure with a decree on privatization issued on August 10, the putsch attempt of August 18 soon rendered lawmaking at the Soviet level irrelevant.

A noteworthy development for small business during this incredible year was a June decree by the Russian Council of Ministers entitled "On Means to Support and Develop Small Enterprises in the Russian Federation." This decree defined a small enterprise, recommended the development of programs specifically for small enterprises, and introduced tax incentives.[18] The decree marks the first entry of small privately owned business into the policy realm; the potential of small business had maintained the attention of policymakers despite their many distractions. However, except for an effort by the State Antimonopoly Committee of the Russian SFSR to sketch out a support program for small business in September, immediately following the failed putsch, the attention of policymakers was soon fully absorbed

---

[18] The decree defined small enterprises on the basis of the number of employees as follows: industry and construction—up to 200; science and research—up to 100; other manufacturing—up to 50; retail and services—up to 15.

by other economic challenges. Throughout the 1992–94 period the Antimonopoly Committee served as the leader and coordinator of the state's limited small business support efforts, which were primarily focused on providing tax incentives.

The introduction of "shock therapy" made 1992 a pivotal year for economic reform in Russia—and for small entrepreneurs. Expressed in its simplest form, shock therapy was based on the assumption that if market forces were allowed to take over in one "shocking" wave, Russia would quickly have a full-fledged market economy. Shock therapy included the liberalization of essentially all prices and assumed the rapid privatization of state-owned assets, following the privatization laws of the previous year.

Although shock therapy seems naive in retrospect, it is largely thanks to Russia's experience that we now understand that its missing ingredients include the wide range of institutional, legal, and regulatory infrastructure that underpin the functioning of a market economy. This infrastructure is typically taken for granted in market economies, because it developed over a period of decades and even centuries and therefore no one remembers what it was like when there was no infrastructure. However, because this infrastructure—from an independent court system to monetary policy to capital markets—did not exist in Russia, Russia's experience soon revealed the shortcomings of the shock therapy approach. New forces did indeed rush to fill the vacuum left by removing the economic role of the state, but they did not create the type of American or Western European economy that had been expected.

Shock therapy affected the development of small entrepreneurs in three major ways. When combined with the "shocks" that state-owned enterprises had endured beginning with perestroika, shock therapy spelled the final kiss of death for many of those that had managed to survive until this point. The collapse of these enterprises created a pool of unemployed workers, who fueled the growth of small enterprises; it also created a shortage of the goods that these enterprises had produced—and hence sales opportunities for new entrepreneurs.

In addition, the general economic disarray included a nonsensical tax regime that was enforced unpredictably and irregularly. As a result, small enterprises began to markedly favor businesses whose profits were more difficult to assess, such as trading consumer products from impermanent locations, instead of manufacturing and construction. (Difficulties in obtaining financing also contributed to this proclivity for less capital-intensive activities.)

Finally, the overall confusion of this period, including a rapidly changing and incoherent legal and regulatory environment, led to a marked breakdown of law and order. Almost all small businesses were therefore forced to rely on the protection groups, or what sociologist Vadim Volkov refers to as "violence-managing" or "force-wielding" organizations, that had begun to emerge during perestroika. Criminal groups first discovered this market protection "niche" in the outdoor markets that flourished during perestroika and exploited it by creating an environment in which sellers were not safe without a *krysha* (roof), a protection group. Volkov makes an important distinction between the criminal organizations whose intention was to practice extortion or take over businesses by illegal means and the more-or-less legitimate businesses that offered the basic protection of property and rights that would typically be provided by the state. Both types of groups competed with each other for *krysha* clients, and sometimes entrepreneurs turned to the genuine security businesses for protection from the criminal organizations.[19] Although we should not underestimate the horrible circumstances that forced entrepreneurs to rely on their *krysha*, entrepreneurs quickly adapted to them as a way of life; as I noted earlier, a 1989 survey revealed that local authorities created the most difficulties for cooperators, followed by the protection rackets.

The number of small enterprises grew rapidly from 1991 to 1993, reaching a total of 865,000 as of year-end 1993. The tendency for there to be more entrepreneurial activity in Russia's central region established itself quickly; it accounted for 36 percent of Russia's small enterprises, with Moscow alone accounting for 23 percent as of 1993.[20]

[19] Volkov defines a *krysha* as a "private enforcement partner, criminal or legal, and signifying a complex of services provided to clients to protect them physically and minimize their risks." The protection business became increasingly professionalized with the 1992 adoption of the Law on Private Protection and Detective Activity and the growing involvement of former security and police professionals. Vadim Volkov, *Violent Entrepreneurs: The Use of Force in the Making of Russian Capitalism* (Ithaca: Cornell University Press, 2002).

[20] Yoffi et al., "Maloye predprinimatel'stvo," 14.

Although there is no question the growth trend portrayed by this data is accurate, Russian small business data has shortcomings that have persisted up to today. Small businesses everywhere are tempted to maximize the use of cash in order to underreport taxable income, but this was a particularly powerful incentive in Russia in the early 1990s, with its inconsistent tax regulations, bribe-seeking government inspectors, and protection groups looking for clients. To reflect this underreporting, tax authorities revised their initial count of 480,000 small enterprises as of year-end 1993 and almost doubled it to 865,000.[21] Furthermore, Russian small business is defined differently than in the European Union and the United States, frequently leading to the incorrect conclusion that Russian small business lags substantially in its contribution to the economy.

The growth of small business had a further impetus from Russia's privatization program, which initiated the privatization of small state-owned enterprises in 1992. Small enterprises were defined for the purposes of the privatization program as having up to two hundred employees and a book value of under one million rubles. These enterprises were to be sold competitively—by auction or public tender—or the enterprises could be leased and the employees could obtain a right to buy it out. Because the privatization of small enterprises was relatively straightforward, local authorities were encouraged to implement the process quickly in order to demonstrate the momentum of privatization overall.

The results in terms of speed and the number of small enterprises privatized were impressive; between February 1992 and June 1994 87,189 small enterprises were privatized, representing over 70 percent of the total. Even by May 1993, about half of all Russian restaurants and bars, retail outlets, and consumer-service businesses were privately owned.[22]

These new small private businesses, whether privatized or genuinely new, had to hold their own in a nightmarishly unstable economic and political environment. Although political pressure brought a quick

[21] Tatiana Alimova, Russian SME research specialist, correspondence with author, July 2, 2005.
[22] Aslund, *How Russia Became a Market Economy*, 241–42 and 248–52.

end to shock therapy after only several months, the price liberalization added to a gathering wave of inflation that hit 2,562 percent by the end of 1992 and, while subsiding, was still a horrific 847 percent at the end of 1993.[23]

To add insult to injury, GDP continued to fall as well. Official figures registered a GDP decline of 12.9 percent in 1991, 18.5 percent in 1992, and 12 percent in 1993.[24] Even though GDP figures for the Soviet period could be criticized for reporting production of at least some products that no one wanted or used, these consistent declines in output were devastating.

These economic reversals also had political repercussions, with the Russian Congress—the Duma—going so far as attempting to impeach President Yeltsin in March 1993. Although Yeltsin kept the upper hand by dissolving the Duma and the Council of Federations in September, he and his remaining reformers were chastened by the parliamentary elections of December, in which the democrats and reformers were soundly routed. Victor Chernomyrdin, who had been named prime minister in December 1992, expressed his reading of these results when he commented in January 1994 that "market romanticism" was over.[25]

Compared to all of the preceding economic and political excitement, the period beginning in 1994 until the convening of the First All-Russian Congress of Representatives of Small Enterprises in 1996 was one of relative calm. Although small business growth slowed down substantially during this period, with a net increase of only twelve thousand new small businesses during 1994 and 1995, this decline can now be seen as heralding a new era in small business development. Not only was the worst shock of unemployment from the collapse of state-owned enterprises over but the economy was beginning to stabilize sufficiently so that the windfall profits available to traders were beginning to abate. The arbitrage schemes between state-owned enterprises and privately owned companies had

[23] Aslund, *How Russia Became a Market Economy*, table 4.2, 119.

[24] Alternate estimates, which attempted to pick up unofficial economic activity, showed declines of 7 percent in 1991, 12 percent in 1992, and 9 percent in 1993. Aslund, 278.

[25] Quoted in Aslund, *How Russia Became a Market Economy*, 201.

also run their course. Small business was no longer seen as the road to riches.[26]

In fact, arguably the most impressive development is that small business began to show signs of emerging from the shadows. Despite the lower number of new business starts, investment in small business in 1995 increased by four times and investment in the manufacturing sector of small business increased by 8.4 times.[27] Those small businesses that had survived were clearly planning on having a future.

The relative stability of this period also enabled the state to turn its attention back to small business, albeit with mixed results. The 1994–95 Federal Program of State Support for Small Entrepreneurship, approved in April 1994, aptly illustrates the nature of state support for entrepreneurs during this period. On the positive side, the program was created and implemented by decree, thereby illustrating a certain degree of administrative and political support for small business. On the negative side, however, of the 18.4 billion rubles targeted for the program, only 5.7 billion were allocated.[28]

The program was followed by the June 1995 adoption of the Law on State Support for Small Entrepreneurship. This law was also viewed by specialists as having the characteristics of a glass half full and half empty. The law had five key elements.

First, small business was defined using different employment levels than before. Although the changes varied from sector to sector, the overall impact on small business was negative in terms of its perceived contribution to the economy following the changes. Most notably, the previous definition of small business manufacturing had encompassed businesses with up to two hundred employees, while the new definition included only those with up to one hundred employees. Given the concern about the prevalence of small business trading operations, this new definition inadvertently reduced the incentives to create new manufacturing businesses.

---

[26] This interpretation is made persuasively by Yoffi et al., "Maloye predprinimatel'-stvo." Note also that the new civil code arguably had some effect on the data, because it forced small enterprises that had been created as partnerships to reregister, but this does not appear to have been the dominant factor.

[27] Goskomstat Rossiyskoy Federatsii, "Maloye predprinimatel'stvo v 1995 godu," Moscow, 1996.

[28] Yasin et al., "Maloye predprinimaltel'stvo," table 53, 162.

More positively, the number of employees in a small construction business was increased from fifty to one hundred, and the number of employees in a small retail business was increased from fifteen to thirty. In another important innovation, the definition of small business was expanded to include farmers and nonincorporated individual entrepreneurs. The new definitions were as follows:

Manufacturing and construction—up to one hundred employees
Agriculture—up to sixty employees
Science and technology—up to sixty employees
Wholesale trade and other activities—up to fifty employees
Retail trade and domestic services—up to thirty employees

Second, the definition specified that small businesses were those in which ownership by the state or non–small businesses was under 25 percent. This criterion reversed the perestroika-era practice in which state agencies had created small private enterprises.

A third important element of the law was the creation of permanent mechanisms for state support for small business. One was the annual Federal Program of State Support for Small Entrepreneurship, whose program and budget, which included support for regional and local programs, would be approved annually by the legislature. Another was the creation of the Federal Fund for the Support of Small Entrepreneurship, which was intended to provide various forms of financial support for small business, such as guarantees, as well as helping support a network of state and municipal small business support funds.[29]

Fourth, the law attempted to address registration and taxation issues. In an implicit reference to the problems that small businesses faced with overlapping registration requirements at different levels of government, the law stated that only registration at the federal level was required. The law also referred to efforts to simplify taxation for small enterprises, including providing a four-year grandfather clause.

---

[29] This fund was the successor to the Fund for the Support of Business and Competition, which had been established by the State Antimonopoly Committee to manage the limited funds available for small business support in the early 1990s.

Finally, the law allowed for the creation of credit cooperatives that would lend to their members.

While the law was extensive in scope, it suffered the shortcomings of much Russian legislation—lack of funding and lack of follow-up. The lack of follow-up, including the elaboration of implementation instructions, was both an implicit and explicit theme in the proceedings of the First All-Russian Congress of Representatives of Small Enterprises, held in Moscow in February 1996. As in the case of the law, the congress was a good news–bad news event. The good news was the simple fact that the congress took place and was very well attended with over three thousand delegates, including Russian officials, international donors, and thousands of entrepreneurs.[30]

The fact that President Yeltsin made the opening speech indicated the importance of this event. Furthermore, he frankly identified the challenges facing small business; the Antimonopoly Committee and small business lobbies had done an impressive job of cataloguing these challenges, and Yeltsin had no compunction about enumerating them. Yeltsin's speech even sounded a theme about the importance of small business that could easily have been lifted from a speech given by any U.S. politician. For example, Yeltsin stated that "the further we move along the path of market reform, the clearer it becomes that small business is—one of the anchors of the economy, the well-being of its citizens, the social-political stability of society and in many ways its moral recovery." At another point Yeltsin noted that small business represents "the formation of a powerful middle class, without which there cannot be stability in modern society." In five short years since the legalization of private activity in Russia, the concept of the importance of small business had become entrenched in the political lexicon.

Still in the category of good news, the output of the congress was impressive, including a detailed plan for the development of small business until the year 2000. The program anticipated that by 2000 small business would account for 20–25 percent of GDP and would

---

[30] The following discussion of the congress is based on "I Vserossiyskiy s"ezd predstaviteley malykh predpriyatiy," documents and materials from the congress, http://www.rcsme.ru/libList (accessed July 12, 2005).

employ 27–30 million people, of which 12–15 million would be employed on a full-time basis.[31]

The bad news about the congress was quite simple: there was limited follow-up. No political force was strong enough to ensure that small business remained an official priority. Not only did small business provide only a small portion of tax revenue to the federal government but this revenue came from thousands of small companies that had not consolidated themselves into a political force.

It is relevant to add for context that the presidential elections held in June 1996 demonstrated the significant role that Russia's new and most prominent multimillionaires—often referred to as "the oligarchs"—played in Russia's political affairs. One oligarch, Boris Berezovsky, went so far as to claim in an interview in London's *Financial Times* that a group of seven oligarchs "invested huge sums of money to ensure Yeltsin's election. Now we have the right to occupy government posts and enjoy the fruits of our victory."[32] Small business simply paled by comparison with the power and resources wielded by these wealthy individuals.

The dynamics of the development of Russian small business from the end of 1994 to the beginning of 1998 are outlined in table 2.1 (data do not include individual entrepreneurs).[33] Two points in the table should be highlighted. First, trade remained the dominant activity throughout this period. As I noted, trading provides more opportunities for those wishing to avoid the attention of tax authorities and other officials; it also requires a lower initial investment than construction or manufacturing. Second, the number of small businesses declined for three years in a row, from the end of 1994 through 1996, with a recovery beginning during 1997. The number of employees also dropped substantially. The main reason for these declines was the more limited definition of small businesses in the 1995 law, as well as an unfavorable change in the tax treatment of salaries. It is ironic that the changes introduced by a law designed to support small business indirectly served to reduce the incentives

[31] At the time of the congress, small businesses were estimated to account for about 10 percent of GDP and to employ about 8.9 million people on a full-time basis.

[32] *Financial Times* quote cited in Andrei Piontkovsky, "Berezovsky Still Powerful Despite Being Dismissed," *St. Petersburg Times*, November 17–23, 1997.

[33] There were an estimated 3.5 million individual entrepreneurs as of July 1997.

TABLE 2.1.
Russian Small Business Growth Trends

	Dec. 1994	Dec. 1995	Dec. 1996	Dec. 1997
Number of small businesses	896,900	877,300	828,000	862,685
Percent in trade	46.8	42.7	42.6	43.2
Percent in manufacturing	14.2	14.6	15.6	15.6
Percent in construction	13.8	16.6	16.5	16.5
Full- and part-time employees, in millions	15.5	13.9	8.5	8.6
Full-time employees, in millions	8.5	8.9	6.3	6.5
Percent of total full-time employment	22.7	20.7	12.9	13.2

Source: Goskomstat Rossii, various publications.

for support by reducing the perceived contribution of small business to the economy. It is even more ironic that the 1998 crisis helped to turn this situation around.

The Financial Crisis, August 1998 to 1999

Financial crisis and 1998 are synonyms in Russia, with 1998 shattered by a financial meltdown that made a mockery of the relative economic and political stability of the preceding few years. Although 1997 had witnessed Russia's first year of positive economic growth since the dissolution of the Soviet Union, the crisis made clear that this and other apparent signs of improvement had been facilitated by a government borrowing program that had grown out of control. On August 17, 1998, having reached a financial point of no return, Russia defaulted on its domestic treasury bills; declared a 90 day moratorium on foreign debt obligations; and devalued the ruble, which fell to 20.7/$1.00 by year end 1998, compared to 5.96/$1.00 one year earlier.[34]

The crisis had a devastating effect on Russia's economy—which fell by 4.9 percent in 1998—as well as morale. GDP per capita fell in

[34] Data cited are from European Bank for Reconstruction and Development, "Transition Report 2001: Energy in Transition," 189.

dollar terms from $2,960 in 1997 to $1,254 in 1999.[35] According to one survey, 32.4 percent of the respondents considered their losses from the crisis to be "catastrophic," while another 48.7 percent rated their losses as "extremely significant."[36]

Prior to the crisis most Russians had begun to believe that the trauma that had become a daily part of life was actually over; the fact that private consumption had risen by over 5 percent in 1997 provides evidence of that belief. The resulting tangible and psychological impact of the crisis was further worsened by the government's paralysis. Not only did the state fail to demonstrate any leadership but its inactivity provided opportunities for the owners of banks that had become essentially bankrupt to seize their assets before their creditors did. The depressed sense of a return to the morality free-for-all of the early 1990s was palpable.

Although the crisis seemed to deny Russia all hope for the future, it is clear in retrospect that it played an invaluable role in laying the groundwork for a more measured approach to economic development. This new approach did not offer quick fixes or large international rescue packages but was based on the long, hard slog of putting an appropriate legal and institutional framework into place and providing conditions for businesses—large and small—to address the normal challenges of doing business.

Russia's entrepreneurs stand out for the speed with which they accepted and responded to the new reality imposed by the crisis, compared to Russia's larger businesses. As I noted, by the mid-1990s the easy profits that used to be associated with small business, either because of untapped consumer demand or the ability to take advantage of connections with state-owned enterprises or official connections, had largely subsided. Therefore a significant proportion of the entrepreneurs operating in 1998 were accustomed to the day-to-day challenge of making a living.[37]

---

[35] International Monetary Fund, "Russian Federation: Staff Report for the 2000 Article IV Consultation and Public Information Notice Following Consultation," IMF Staff Country Report No. 00/145, November 2000, table 16, p. 51.

[36] "Osenniy krizis 1998 goda: rossiyskoye obshchestvo do i posle," Russian Independent Institute of Social and National Problems (RNIS and NP), Moscow, 1998.

[37] Furthermore, those who had not yet made the transition to functioning independently of the government were forced to do so after the crisis; one survey concluded that of nineteen potential challenges to small business, the relative position of independent small businesses had improved relative to "dependent" small businesses in fourteen areas following the crisis: "Osenniy krizis."

By contrast, the larger enterprises that had survived to this point were still accustomed to the privileges that come with being larger, especially in cases where they were the primary—or sole—local employer and therefore could not readily be closed down even if they were losing money.[38] According to statistics cited by Tacis (Technical Aid to the Commonwealth of Independent States—an EU program created in the early 1990s), during the first nine months of 1997, between 41 and 59 percent (depending on the sector) of large Russian enterprises realized losses, compared to about 20 percent of small enterprises.[39] The fact that there was no longer any support available for these large loss-making enterprises following the crisis came as a shock.

A second factor contributing to the flexible response of small businesses is that they tended to be diversified. According to research by the Russian think tank Liberal Mission, Russian small businesses had begun to diversify as early as the mid-1990s, so that by the time of the crisis over half of the small businesses whose primary activity was in a nontrading business also had some trading activities.[40] Not only does diversification reduce risk, but, in the Russian context, diversification could also help to keep businesses below the official "radar screen"; by developing a number of small businesses instead of one larger one, entrepreneurs could avoid attracting unwanted attention from tax inspectors and other officials.

A third factor that helped entrepreneurs was their relatively limited interaction with the banking sector. Small businesses were often cash businesses, since cash minimized the need for interactions with the formal economy, including banks. Also, as I discuss in chapter 3, few banks were actively trying to attract small business clients during this period. As a result, small businesses were less likely to have lost money in bank accounts due to the crisis. Furthermore, since dollars were

---

[38] The term "virtual economy" was coined to describe the situation in Russia at this time, with manufacturers consuming more in wages and raw materials than the value of their final product. As a result, there was a significant accumulation of pension and wage arrears, as well as government debt. Clifford G. Gaddy and Barry W. Ickes, "Russia's Virtual Economy," *Foreign Affairs* 78, no. 5 (September–October 1998).

[39] Yoffi et al., "Maloye predprinimatel'stvo," table 7, p. 28.

[40] Yasin et al., "Maloye predprinimaltel'stvo," 24.

TABLE 2.2.
Small Business before and after the Crisis

Indicator	Year	Total	Manufacturing	Construction	Trade and social services
Number of small businesses	1997	862,685	134,810	142,087	372,836
	1998	868,000	136,100	137,500	386,100
Percent change in number of small businesses	1997–98	0.6	1.0	–3.2	3.6
Total employment	1997	8,638,700	1,911,100	2,188,000	2,448,300
	1998	7,401,400	1,580,800	1,600,900	2,525,500
Percent change in employment	1997–98	–14.3	–17.3	–26.8	3.2
Total output (billions of rubles)	1997	303,056.3	67,895.4	67,579.3	102,487.4
	1998	261,908.0	63,084.8	67,275.0	71,113.5
Percent change in output	1997–98	–13.6	–7.1	–0.5	–30.6
Profit or loss (billions of rubles)	1997	37,900	6,650	9,103	13,115
	1998	–28,550	–4,725	2,516	–5,971

Source: Research Center for Small Entrepreneurship, "Malye predpriyatiya: Posledstviya krizisa," Tacis Project SMERUS9803, 2000, table 1, pp. 1–2.

typically preferred to rubles, those holding dollars benefited from the devaluation.[41]

We can get an overview of the magnitude of the crisis by comparing the condition of Russian small business before and after August 1998 (see table 2.2). Profits disappeared entirely, falling from 37.9 trillion rubles in 1997 to a loss of 28.55 trillion rubles in 1998. Even these figures understate the trauma of the crisis, however, because most losses occurred in the last four months of the year.[42] Therefore many

[41] Ironically, many borrowers were hurt by the crisis as well, because the underdeveloped ruble market had led to the widespread practice of making loans denominated in dollars. For those borrowers that had dollar-denominated loans but a ruble-based business, the ruble devaluation substantially increased the difficulty of repaying their loans. However, as I discuss in chapter 3, small businesses were not sought-after banking clients prior to the crisis, and therefore their borrowing was limited.

[42] Note, however, that small business profitability had been declining in the first seven months of 1998 compared to 1996 and 1997: "Osenniy krizis."

small businesses that had been realizing profits until the August crisis suffered enormous reversals afterward that eliminated those profits and created additional losses as well.

The other striking data concern employment, which fell by 14 percent overall and by a particularly painful 27 percent in construction.[43] In contrast, the official figures for the economy overall show a decline in employment of only 2 percent, despite the 4.9 percent decline in GDP. Even allowing for inaccuracies in the official data, there is a marked contrast between the rapid response of small business in laying off employees and the considerably more measured response of the rest of the economy, where businesses were still accustomed to the state's helping hand.

A different dimension of the impact of the crisis can be seen in the five major challenges cited by entrepreneurs before and after the crisis. Whereas interference by officials had been the biggest problem before the crisis, having been cited by 49.3 percent of respondents, this problem was completely pushed off the list after the crisis. It was replaced by purely business concerns, headed by sales; this issue was cited by 64.3 percent of all respondents, compared to only 36.5 percent before the crisis. Other business issues such as bad debts, unreliable business partners, and access to raw materials all became more acute after the crisis (see table 2.3).

Although these figures paint a clear picture of the devastating impact of the crisis, another series of surveys illustrates the remarkable response of entrepreneurs, in particular their intention to put their problems behind them and focus on the future. This attitude can be seen in the results of a survey conducted in October 1998, during the shell-shocked period immediately after the onset of the crisis. Although 19 percent of those questioned planned to reduce investment and 14 percent planned to reduce output, 26 percent planned to increase investment, and 34 percent planned to increase output.[44]

---

[43] Turnover in construction was almost unchanged, and the sector realized a profit in 1998; this presumably shows the impact of the timing of the crisis, with the high revenue level representing work done before the crisis, while the employment figures capture the layoffs in effect at the end of the year. The fact that trade and retail services increased employment, despite the decline in turnover, undoubtedly contributed to that sector's losses.

[44] "Osenniy krizis."

TABLE 2.3.
Five Major Challenges Cited by Entrepreneurs before and after the Crisis (in percent)

Precrisis	Percent of respondents	Postcrisis	Percent of respondents
Interference by officials	49.3	Sales	64.3
Nonpayment, unreliable partners	48.5	Nonpayment, unreliable partners	59.0
Obtaining working capital	40.2	Obtaining working capital	58.7
Lack of legal protection	37.6	Obtaining raw materials	52.4
Sales	36.5	Paying taxes	47.3

Source: A. D. Yoffi et al., "Maloye predprinimatel'stvo v Rossii," tables 4 and 5, pp. 32–33.

This positive response was due to the silver lining in the crisis upheaval: foreign goods were no longer affordable. Not only did foreign consumer goods fall from 49 percent of all consumer goods sales in Russia at the beginning of 1998 to 30 percent during 1999 but these figures understate the drop in volume of foreign consumer goods sold, because a ruble in 1999 bought so much less than in 1998.

The opportunity provided for those in the manufacturing sector in particular can be seen clearly in table 2.4. At the Second All-Russian Congress of Representatives of Small Enterprises in November 1999, just slightly over one year after the onset of the crisis, 60 percent of the small manufacturing businesses surveyed said the crisis had had positive effects.

I should stress that the delegates to the congress were not a representative sample of all Russian entrepreneurs, because they came from businesses that had survived the crisis and had the initiative and resources to participate in the congress. Nevertheless, the attitude of this group is quite important; as survivors, they were leading the way into the future of Russia's small business.

This survivor attitude can also be seen by the response of those in the trading sector; these businesses were hurt much more seriously by their reduced ability to import goods and by reduced consumer purchasing power. Even this group had a marginally positive assessment of the crisis; 46 percent of the respondents rated the impact of the crisis as positive, while 43 percent rated it as negative.

TABLE 2.4.
Assessments of the Impact of the Crisis

Impact	All small businesses (%)	Small businesses in trade (%)	Small businesses in manufacturing (%)
Overall impact			
Positive	52	46	60
Neutral	15	11	14
Negative	33	43	26
Impact on financing			
Positive	23	17	32
Neutral	24	14	21
Negative	53	69	47
Impact on demand			
Positive	40	33	59
Neutral	11	7	10
Negative	49	60	31
Impact on competitiveness			
Positive	45	44	60
Neutral	21	19	19
Negative	34	37	21

Source: Research Center for Small Entrepreneurship, "Malye predpriyatiya: Posledstviya krizisa," Tacis Project SMERUS9803, 2000, diagrams 1, 2, 4, and 5, pp. 7–8.

Perhaps the most telling results are provided by the delegates' comparison of the state of affairs in 1999 and the prognosis for 2000. On all counts, the entrepreneurs expected a more positive future (see table 2.5). As one example, whereas 40 percent of small businesses assessed their status in 1999 as "good," a full 61 percent expected to achieve "good" status by 2000. Although the effect of this positive attitude is impossible to quantify, it undoubtedly played a role in positioning these small businesses to take advantage of the opportunities provided by the crisis, rather than bemoaning their bad luck.

In fact, summary data for 1999 largely bears out the expectations of the survey: during that year the number of small enterprises grew by 2.6 percent, the number of employees increased by 4.5 percent (full-time employees increased by 1.9 percent), and turnover increased by 61.8 percent.[45] Small business was already on the way to recovery.

[45] Goskomstat Rossiyskoy, Maloye predprinimatel'stvo.

TABLE 2.5.
Assessment by Small Businesses of Their Current and Future Status

Assessment	By all small businesses (%)	By small businesses in trading (%)	By small businesses in manufacturing (%)
Current status, 1999			
Good	40	44	45
Acceptable	48	39	48
Bad	12	17	7
Anticipated status, 2000			
Good	61	61	71
Acceptable	31	29	21
Bad	8	10	8

Source: Research Center for Small Entrepreneurship, "Malye predpriyatiya: Posledstviya krizisa," Tacis Project SMERUS9803, 2000, diagram 6, p. 9.

"For us the crisis was exclusively positive."

Oleg Gamazin is a stocky young man who exudes openness and goodwill. The son and grandson of military officers, he decided in the early 1990s, when he was also serving as an officer, that his goal in life was to be independent. Over the considerable opposition of his entire family, Gamazin moved to Moscow in 1995, where, as he put it: "I couldn't even have a beer with anyone; I didn't know a single person." Ten years later, as he recounted the development of his business, Gamazin expressed his gratitude to Moscow, "the only city in Russia where you can start from nothing."

Gamazin found work in an advertising agency and within a year had concluded that a specialized advertising agency could do well in the market. Because he knew the automotive business well and by this time had made some friends, four of them joined as partners to open the Cabrio advertising agency in 1996. The start was far from glamorous; they had to borrow half of the $600 registration fee, and for the first month they all worked from a desk with one phone in the office of a friend. Even after the business got started, it took Cabrio four months to buy its first computer, and Oleg took home only $50–100 per month.

The 1998 crisis was devastating for Cabrio. Not only did all businesses stop advertising but the company lost money that clients had paid to them and that was to be used to pay for newspaper and other advertising space.

This money was in an account at a bank that had been one of Russia's largest and most prestigious but which lost its license relatively early during the crisis. It took Cabrio two years to be able to reimburse its clients.

Nevertheless, Gamazin insists that "for us the crisis was exclusively positive." The crisis brought him and his partners to the conclusion that they "didn't know anything about business" and that therefore they should all study business formally. They kept Cabrio open by explaining the situation to their sixteen employees and agreeing that 40 percent of the company's profits would be allocated to salaries. All of the staff decided to stay.

The positive outcome of communicating openly with the company's staff, combined with their subsequent business training, convinced Gamazin and his partners that the best way to achieve good results is to be very clear about an employee's responsibilities and how these are related to potential benefits. The company has introduced a share ownership plan for particularly promising staff members.

By the end of 2005 the original advertising business had expanded into three businesses—advertising, creative services, and business training—joined together in a holding company, Synergo.[46] Annual turnover had reached the range of $15 million, and the three companies had approximately eighty employees. Nevertheless, financial issues have continued to pose a challenge for the group. Although they have been able to obtain short-term financing from several banks, including KMB Bank, it is an ongoing challenge to find banks able to work with medium-sized and growing companies.

Gamazin observed that one of the biggest shortcomings of Russian economic development programs, whether instigated by domestic or foreign agencies, is that they don't take growth into account. Since the company's borrowing needs no longer fit into the category of small business loan programs, it falls into a financing void of companies needing to borrow over several hundred thousand dollars but less than several million.

An even more serious issue for Synergo is that without additional equity investment the company will not be able to build on its existing successes and continue to grow. Furthermore, maintaining the status quo is not an attractive option; the market is still growing quickly enough that companies that can't grow will fall behind.

---

[46] The company's website is http://www.synergo.ru.

How does Gamazin explain his success to date? First, his partners and employees; second, a clear strategy; and third, an overwhelming desire to succeed. He has had many sleepless nights, especially during the crisis and now as he ponders how Synergo can continue to grow. But he wouldn't have it any other way.

Mainstream, 2000–2006

The mainstream stage for Russian entrepreneurs spans the period from the beginning of 2000, following the convening of the Second All-Russian Congress of Representatives of Small Enterprises in October 1999, through 2006. This stage is characterized by the new attitude of Russian entrepreneurs toward their role in the economy. They no longer saw their role as unique or unusual, as it had seemed in the early days of market reform, but one that was central to economic development overall. As important, they were able to convince the state to share this view.

In addition, despite a burst of state support at the beginning of this stage, the attitude of small business toward its relations with the state underwent a significant shift. As former prime minister Yevgeniy Primakov, then president of the Russian Chamber of Trade and Industry, said at the Fourth All-Russian Conference of Representatives of Small Enterprises held in April 2003, the challenge was becoming how to protect small business *from* the incursions of the state, instead of the previous approach of seeking protection *by* the state.[47]

Perhaps the best summary of the period is again provided by Primakov, this time in his comments at the Fifth All-Russian Conference of Representatives of Small Enterprises in March 2004. He observed that the three major economic challenges facing the state were the goal of doubling GDP by 2010, diversifying the economy, and eliminating poverty. And, in keeping with the theme with which small

---

[47] "Itogovye materiali, IV Vserossiyskoy konferentsii predstaviteley malykh predpriyatiy "Vzaimodeystvie malogo i krupnogo biznesa," 22. www.rcsme.ru/libList (accessed July 12, 2005).

business kicked off its new stage at the 1999 congress, Primakov noted that small business was an inherent part of the solution to all of these challenges.[48] Put differently, small business had become part of the mainstream.

It was far from predictable that the postcrisis period would start so promisingly for Russian small business. In fact, the Russian Chamber of Commerce and Industry debated whether to even hold a second congress, given the disappointing results of the first one. Despite the initial enthusiasm created by that congress, the lack of results was well illustrated by the lack of any federal funding to support small business in 1998 and 1999, accompanied by the disbanding in 1998 of the State Committee for Support and Development of Small Entrepreneurs. However, the debate about whether to hold the congress led to identifying the theme that moved small business squarely onto the state's agenda: small business was a key partner in building a market-based economy and a democratic society; its development was not an isolated, optional policy objective.[49]

The success of the congress in making this point was reflected in acting president Putin's interest in small business, which was reminiscent of former president Yeltsin's support for small business right before the 1996 elections. (Putin was elected president in May 2000.) Putin's support galvanized an unprecedented flurry of activity by government officials. By the time of the follow-up conference held just five months later in March 2000, minister of Antimonopoly Policy and Support for Entrepreneurship Ilya A. Yuzhanov informed the participants that 80 percent of the resolutions of the October congress had been implemented. Although this level of responsiveness was not sustainable, it provided an important impetus to small business development at the beginning of this period.

---

[48] "Sbornik informatsionno-analiticheskikh materialov: V Vserossiyskaya konferentsiya predstaviteley malykh predpriyatiy 'Uskorennoye razvitie malogo predprinimaltel'stva kak faktor ustoychogo rosta ekonomiki,'" www.rcsme.ru/libList (accessed July 12, 2005).

[49] The discussion of the Second Congress is based on V. P. Yermakov and V. Sh. Kaganov, "Razvitie malogo predprinimatel'stva v Rossii: Glavnye napravleniya (po materialiam II Vserossiyskogo s"ezda malykh predpriyatiy)," analytical materials, 2000. The preparation for the congress included seventy-two regional congresses at which this approach was refined. Not only was the congress well focused, but the views stated can also be considered an accurate reflection of the views of grassroots small business.

In his address to the Second Congress, Yuzhanov outlined the following groups of issues facing small business: strengthening relations between small business and the state; reducing administrative barriers (such as registration, licensing, certification)[50]; improving the availability of finance.

Because these issues are key themes throughout the period under discussion, this section focuses on the first two issues, while the third, finance, is the topic of chapter 3. This section concludes with a discussion of regional development and how data issues affect Russian small business development.

The Second Congress was notable for its articulated frustration over the state's inadequate response to the needs of small business, including, as a resolution noted, its "ignoring" the resolutions of the First Congress. This frustration was evident in a survey conducted at the Second Congress regarding the performance of six official bodies in supporting small business. The worst rating in the survey, a negative assessment of 79 percent for the Russian Duma, was only marginally worse than the best rating, a negative assessment of 64 percent for implementing bodies below the federal level.[51]

In the analytical materials summarizing the congress, two explanations for this negative assessment were highlighted. Because there was no comprehensive strategy for the development of small business, various uncoordinated efforts were taken at different levels of government. These efforts tended to have little actual impact, but they did create confusion. As the congress noted, "The state's policy toward small business is declaratory; it consists of 'cosmetic' and inconsistent measures that do not and will not create a positive breakthrough in the development of this economic sector."

In addition, small business was not effective in making its views known to the state. Although dozens of small groups representing different geographic and business interests had emerged, none of them had sufficient membership coverage, resources, or access to the state

---

[50] Yuzhanov also noted a fourth group of issues, which was improving the legal and regulatory environment. This topic is included in the discussion of administrative barriers, which are largely the result of legal and regulatory shortcomings.

[51] The other ratings were: Federation Council—71 percent; Russian federal government—70 percent; legislative bodies below the federal level—68 percent; Ministry for Antimonopoly Policy and Support of Entrepreneurship—66 percent.

to be effective. A small sample of these organizations included the Yekaterinburg Association of Producers, the Moscow Association for Small Business, the Russian Union of Young Entrepreneurs, the Association of Women Entrepreneurs, and the Association of Farm and Rural Cooperatives.

Ineffective representation at the national level had already been a concern to small business leaders and had been discussed at a conference in September of that year on "The Role of Associations of Entrepreneurs in the Development of Small Business."[52] Participants at the congress were therefore poised to address this shortcoming, leading to the creation of the Association of Organizations of Small and Medium-Sized Enterprises (OPORA) in September 2001.[53] OPORA's declared mission was "to consolidate the efforts of associations of small and medium-sized businesses, to create positive conditions for the development of entrepreneurship in Russia, to represent and defend the interests of entrepreneurs in dialogue with all levels of government, and to participate in the creation of a national 'middle class' on the basis of the best traditions of national entrepreneurship and Russian business culture."[54] President Putin provided OPORA with an invaluable stamp of credibility by supporting its work. OPORA's ongoing ability to gain access to decision makers was further ensured by the membership of its board of trustees, which includes major government and legislative figures.

A caveat about OPORA, however, is precisely these close state ties, which led some to believe that OPORA was created to consolidate political support for Putin among small business owners. Although this could have been a motive for the state's support, and while the structure of the board of trustees certainly reduces OPORA's potential autonomy, the key objective at this point in the development of Russian entrepreneurship was to create representation at the national level. Furthermore, at least at this early stage of its existence, OPORA did

[52] The conference was organized by the Institute on Entrepreneurship and Investment and the Chamber of Trade and Industry, with support from the Eurasia Foundation.

[53] OPORA's Russian name is Obshcherossiyskaya Obshchestvennaya Organizatsiya Malogo i Srednogo Predprinimaltel'stva. The word *opora* in Russian means *support*. OPORA is an association of associations; it has a parallel organization, OPORA Russia, which consists of individual entrepreneurs and small businesses as members.

[54] http://www.opora.ru (accessed February 28, 2005).

not have an agenda that required autonomy for it to be realized. The goal—which was realized—was to ensure an ongoing voice in the state's decision-making process.

One important aspect of OPORA's mission was public relations, as seen in its reference to the "best traditions of national entrepreneurship and Russian business culture." Ensuring small business's position as part of the Russian economic mainstream required ridding itself of the negative stigma that persisted from Soviet culture. This stigma had attenuated to some degree with the passage of time. In addition, the display of greed by some of Russia's oligarchs during the crisis had cast the day-to-day struggles of small entrepreneurs in a more favorable light.

The congress's materials emphasized this point in noting that "small business, like the entire Russian population, became the scapegoat for the fact that previous governments, together with the oligarchs, had brought Russia to the brink of complete financial default." It was also noted that small business development objectives could only be achieved by "creating positive attitudes by various levels and groups of the population toward entrepreneurial activity, not only as a source for satisfying material needs but also as a worthy way of life." It is therefore quite apt that OPORA's website includes the catchy phrase, "What is good for entrepreneurs is good for Russia."

The second theme that had been highlighted by Yuzhanov and that emerged very clearly from the congress was the burden on small business of the administrative barriers imposed by various levels of government. During the 2001–02 period, for example, firms with eleven to twenty employees required an average of twenty-six person-days to register a new business; an average of sixteen person-days to acquire only one of the multiple certifications that were required; and an average of seventeen person-days to acquire a single license. In addition, management of small businesses spent 11 percent of its time on inspection-related issues.[55]

---

[55] The process was slightly shorter for firms with fewer employees and longer for those with more employees. Center for Economic and Financial Research (CEFIR) and the World Bank, "Monitoring of Administrative Barriers to Small Business Development in Russia: The First Round," Moscow, Summer 2002, http://www.cefir.ru (accessed February 28, 2005).

"We're growing despite the government's efforts to help us."
Vadim Samsonov is the self-assured founder of DeloShop (The Business Shop), a business brokerage firm that he created in 2000.[56] As a member since 1991 of one of Russia's first private law firms, Samsonov had almost a decade of experience helping clients buy and sell businesses. The aftermath of the crisis substantially deepened this market; not only were there more sellers of businesses but there were also buyers, as Russian manufacturing became viable in the face of suddenly unaffordable foreign products.

Samsonov's selling clients are typically people who are retiring, who have inherited a business or have simply gotten tired of running a business, or who have to move for family reasons. Buyers are those who want to own and possibly run a business but don't want to go through the effort of starting from scratch. Possible acquisitions are listed on the company's website in two categories: prices below and prices above $50,000. As of early 2006, the company's most recent sales were a beauty salon in St. Petersburg, a video store in Nizhny Novgorod, a café in Nizhny Novgorod, a dentist's business in Moscow, and a preserves factory in Ukraine. To date buyers have been providing their own financing, although Samsonov is thinking about whether he can assist them in the future. He's quite certain that there will always be a market for his brokerage services. As he says, "Businesses will always exist, but people change."

As of the end of 2005, Samsonov hasn't looked back; he's built the business up to thirty employees and will close between thirty and forty business sales for the year. Although DeloShop qualifies as a "small business" according to Russian law, because it is a service company with up to thirty employees, these considerations are irrelevant for Samsonov. As he put it, "We're growing despite the state's efforts to help us."

The single most impressive result of the congress was ensuring President Putin's support for reducing these burdens on small business. The key initiatives, collectively known as the "administrative reform package," were in the areas of inspection, licensing,

---

[56] The company's website is http://www.deloshop.ru.

TABLE 2.6.
The Administrative Reform Package

Name of law	Effective date	Key changes introduced
Law on Inspections	August 2001	Each agency to have planned inspections no more than once every two years
Law on Licensing	February 2002	Reduced number of activities requiring a license, reduced the cost of a license by over 50 percent and extended the term of a license to five years (previously three)
Law on Registration	July 2002	"One stop" for registering new business, a maximum five-day registration period, cap on registration cost
Law on Standardization and Certification	January 2003	Reduced certification requirements
Law on Simplified Tax System	January 2003	For firms with revenue below 11 million rubles and fewer than 100 employees, can pay one unified tax of 15 percent of profit or 6 percent of revenue.*

Source: Table based on CEFIR and the World Bank, "Monitoring the Administrative Barriers to Small Business Development in Russia: The Second Round," executive summary, http://www.cefir.ru (accessed February 28, 2005).
  * According to the 1995 law, firms with revenue below 7.5 million rubles and fewer than 20 people can pay 10 percent of their profit to the federal budget and under 20 percent of their profit to the regional budget (depending on the region) or 3.3 percent of their revenue to the federal budget and under 6.7 percent of revenue to the regional budget.

registration, certification, and taxation. The legislation that was adopted and the key changes introduced can be seen in table 2.6.

Although Russian laws are notorious for becoming ineffective at the implementation stage, this administrative reform package actually did achieve noteworthy results. As an example, the average number of inspections per company in a six-month period fell from 3.32 to 2.39 between 2001 and 2003. Also, whereas only 17 percent of new companies were able to register within one week in 2001, this percentage had increased to 47 percent as of 2003.

Even more important for the long-term development of Russia's economy, the proportion of surveyed firms using the new simplified tax-reporting system increased from 40 percent immediately after the changes were introduced in January 2003 to 59 percent as of the spring of 2004.[57] Federal revenue from the simplified tax system increased by 48.9 percent in 2004 and another 21.3 percent in 2005.[58]

Finally, the number of registered small businesses increased, by a particularly encouraging 6.5 percent growth rate during 2004, another 3.0 percent in 2005, and a further 5.0 percent during the first half of 2006.[59] Even more noteworthy, investment in fixed assets increased by 47.4 percent during 2004 and another 21.4 percent during 2005. Despite the shortcomings with small business data that I discuss later in this chapter, the trend is clearly positive.[60]

Part of the credit for the relative success of the reform package was the high degree of public scrutiny accompanying the reforms, fostered by a rigorous series of implementation surveys undertaken by the Moscow-based Center for Economic and Financial Research (CEFIR) and the World Bank.[61] Data from the fifth survey, completed in the fall of 2004, shows how Russian entrepreneurs ranked the major challenges to their businesses before and after the administrative reforms (see table 2.7).

Although this table is rich in information, three points merit particular attention. First, with the exception of competition and anticompetitive barriers, the severity of the other seven challenges all decreased between 2001 and 2004. Furthermore, some of the problems typically assumed to be overwhelming challenges for Russian entrepreneurs, such as financing and corruption, were rated lower than might have been expected. Finally, none of the top three constraints in 2004— macro instability, competition and the taxation level—is unique to Russia; arguably, entrepreneurs anywhere in the world would cite similar

---

[57] CEFIR and World Bank, "Monitoring the Administrative Barriers to Small Business Development in Russia: The Fifth Round," Moscow, November 2005, http://www.cefir.ru (accessed August 16, 2006).

[58] A. M. Shestoperov, "Dinamika razvitiya malogo predprinimatel'stva v regionakh Rossii," report for 2004, dated May 2005; report for 2005, dated May 2006; National'nyy Institut Sistemnykh Problem Prednimatel'stva, http://www.nisse.ru (accessed August 15, 2006).

[59] "Malyy i sredniy biznes pokazali rekordnye tempy razvitiya," *Rosbalt*, September 21, 2006, http://www.rcsme.ru/news.asp (accessed September 21, 2006). The 2006 figure is from http://www.opora.ru (accessed December 20, 2006).

[60] Rosstat (Federal Service of State Statistics), "Maloe predprinimatel'stvo v Rossii, 2005," Moscow, 2005; and "Pokazateli deyatel'nosti malykh predpriyatiy za 2005 g.," Moscow, 2006.

[61] The surveys were financed by the World Bank and USAID.

TABLE 2.7.
Business Climate for Entrepreneurs

2001	Rating*	2004	Rating	Change
1. Tax level	3.52	1. Macro instability	2.89	0.39
2. Macro instability	3.28	2. Competition	2.86	−0.23
3. Tax administration	3.11	3. Tax level	2.78	0.74
4. Regulation	2.91	4. Tax administration	2.59	0.52
5. Access to capital	2.65	5. Regulation	2.45	0.46
6. Competition	2.63	6. Access to capital	2.42	0.23
7. Anticompetitive barriers	2.27	7. Anticompetitive barriers	2.30	−0.03
8. Corruption	2.10	8. Corruption	2.03	0.07
9. Rackets	1.34	9. Rackets	1.21	0.13

Source: CEFIR and World Bank, "Monitoring the Administrative Barriers to Small Business Development in Russia: The Fifth Round," Moscow, Summer 2002, http://www.cefir.ru.
* The rating scale is as follows: 5—threatens the existence of the firm, 4—a very serious problem, 3—a serious problem, 2—a slight problem, 1—not a problem. The survey is based on a sample size of 2,000 firms in 20 regions, with a median employee number of 11.

constraints. Although entrepreneurs in some countries might rank the severity of these constraints lower than in Russia, these results nevertheless reveal another dimension on which Russian entrepreneurs have joined the mainstream—in this case an international one.

Encouraging as these results are, it is also important to note the shortcomings of the reform package. Some of its provisions simply were not implemented, such as the "one-stop" registration process. Others, such as simplified licensing, were only partly implemented, with 38 percent of the surveyed firms during the fifth round of the study still having to obtain licenses that were not required by law. Furthermore, it is not clear how long some of the improvements can be sustained. Between the fourth and fifth round of surveys, for example, the proportion of firms that had to pay bribes to licensing organizations increased from 35 percent to 56 percent. Concern on this point is underscored by the conclusion of a World Bank study that the accountability of Russian bureaucrats worsened from a rating of 36.4 in 2002 to 25.7 in 2004.[62]

[62] Daniel Kaufmann, Aart Kraay, Massimo Mastruzzi, "Governance Matters IV: Governance Indicators for 1996–2004," Policy Research Working Paper, Report no. WPS3630, World Bank, June 1, 2005.

This type of backsliding underscores the strength of the traditions and incentives that encourage extralegal activities by Russian officials, and the corresponding challenge faced by policy and lawmakers to address these problems in practical ways.

Although seeking the political support of entrepreneurs makes political sense for Putin, supporting entrepreneurs makes economic sense as well. Russian small business has consistently been more profitable than larger businesses, with government statistics showing that 66.6 percent of small businesses reported profitability in 1997 compared to 49.9 percent of large and medium-sized businesses. Although the difference between them has diminished over the years, small business has continued to show superior performance; 68.6 percent of small businesses reported profitability in 2004 compared to 61.9 percent of large and medium-sized businesses.[63]

Because the Second Congress successfully set the tone and laid out the agenda for small business issues throughout the maturity period, it is not necessary for the purposes of this chapter to discuss the proceedings of each of the following five events, which were called *conferences*—the most recent of which was held in May 2006—in detail. The key theme that emerges from these successive conferences is the increasing sophistication of the issues that they addressed. The Fourth Conference (2003), for example, focused on the relationship between small business and big businesses, while the Fifth Conference (2004) focused part of its proceedings on globalization issues. Small business not only succeeded in making itself part of the economic mainstream but it was increasingly sensitive to the larger context within which it operated.

The Sixth Conference (2005) focused on an increasingly important aspect of small business development: regional and local policies.[64] Background information about the geographic distribution of small businesses in Russia's seven administrative regions as of January 2006 can be seen in table 2.8. (The data do not include the self-employed.) As the table shows, the northwestern region, which includes St. Petersburg, and the central region, which includes Moscow, dwarf the other

---

[63] "Maloye predprinimatel'stvo v Rossii 2002 and 2005," Statistical handbook, Goskomstat (2002), Rosstat (2005), Moscow.

[64] http://www.siora.ru (accessed December 20, 2005).

TABLE 2.8.
Geographic Distribution of Small Businesses

Administrative region	Number of small enterprises per 100,000 inhabitants	Increase, 2005–2006
Russian Federation	682.6	18.3 percent
Northwest	1189.3	68.5 percent
Central	898.6	19.7 percent
Far East	582.4	–9.1[a]
Urals	539.9	46.4 percent
Siberia	524.9	–6.1 percent[b]
Privolga	523.0	9.4 percent
Southern	479.4	11.0 percent

Source: A. M. Shesteperov, "Dinamika rasvitiya malogo predprinimatel'stva v regionakh Rossii v 2005 godu," table 1.1, p. 5, National Institute for Systemic Study of the Problems of Entrepreneurship and the Working Center on Economic Reforms of the Russian Government, May 2006, www.nisse.ru (accessed August 18, 2006).
[a] Note that growth in the Far East the previous year was 86.7 percent.
[b] Growth in Siberia the previous year was 30.9 percent.

regions, with the northwestern region in particular having more than twice the number of small businesses per 100,000 inhabitants than five of the other six regions. Furthermore, the 68.5 percent growth in the number of these businesses outpaces that of all the regions.

Moscow has consistently been the preeminent location for small business since the beginning of perestroika, reflecting the synergies of so many goods and services being produced and consumed in a concentrated area, the higher spending power of its residents, and its considerable volume of domestic and international visitors. However, an illuminating survey of regional conditions for small entrepreneurs led by OPORA concluded that the cities and regions with a high level of socioeconomic development have become the most challenging for further small business growth.[65] (The survey covered Russia's seventy-eight regions and the two cities of St. Petersburg and Moscow.) These markets are also attractive to large companies, therefore creat-

[65] OPORA Russia and All-Russia Public Opinion Research Center, with the support of INTERROS Holding Company and the U.S. Russia Center for Entrepreneurship, "Conditions and Factors Affecting the Development of Small Entrepreneurship in the Regions of the Russian Federation," Moscow 2005, http://www.opora.ru (accessed August 16, 2006).

ing a more demanding competitive environment; the good health of the local economy makes the administration less concerned about the conditions for small business; and the standard small business niches, such as services and small trading operations, are already well occupied. Partly as a result of these considerations, the entrepreneurs in the survey ranked Moscow's entrepreneurial climate seventy-eighth out of eighty locations, while St. Petersburg was ranked sixty-ninth. (Yamalia, an *okrug,* or autonomous district, in northwest Siberia, was ranked first.)

The summary results of the survey are shown in table 2.9. (A ranking of over 100 indicates a "rather favorable" response.) The financial situation assessment, which received the highest positive ranking, is discussed in chapter 3. The transaction costs assessment, which is also relatively positive, corresponds with that of other surveys; although corruption is widely acknowledged, entrepreneurs appear to have adapted to it.

The survey also provides revealing information about the competitive environment, with only three out of the eighty locations providing positive results. A total of 50.5 percent of the survey respondents noted that there were branches of the economy to which access had been artificially restricted, while 65 percent stated that members of the regional administration supported individual firms "frequently" or "occasionally." The highest level of official interference was in construction and installation work, with 43.4 percent of the respondents in that sector stating that the regional administration had its own commercial interests in the sector and therefore restricted competition. The least restrictions were in retail trade and public catering (noted by 33.6 percent) and consumer services (24.6 percent). These results provide an important perspective on the often-voiced complaint by policymakers that Russian small businesses do not contribute to the economy because all they do is trade—they don't produce or build anything.

Although the picture painted by the summary is mixed, the most important point is that this type of research is being done. At a minimum, the results might provide some "name and shame" incentive for regions that receive low rankings for factors that are under their control. More broadly, this type of information has enormous potential for designing and assessing reforms to assist small entrepreneurs.

TABLE 2.9.
Evaluation of the Environment for Entrepreneurs

Aspect of entrepreneurial climate	Brief description	Average value of index for all regions	Number of regions with index over 100
Financial situation	Self-assessment of the financial situation of their business	124.5	71
Transaction costs	Assessment of expenditures of resources on interaction with the authorities, including corruption-related expenses	114.3	68
Support for small entrepreneurs by authorities	Assessment of the treatment of small entrepreneurs by regional and local authorities	113.2	57
Business motivation	Assessment of the situation in the region regarding conditions for small entrepreneurship and the outlook	93.5	27
Level of security	Assessment of the risk level of interaction with the administration, law enforcement organizations, and criminal milieu	68.7	7
State of competitive environment	Presence/absence of restrictions on market entry	75.8	3
Property resources	Assessment of the accessibility of production space	55.3	3
Legal conditions	Adequacy of availability of legal (judicial) protection	47.6	0

Source: OPORA Russia and All-Russia Public Opinion Research Center, with the support of INTERROS Holding Company and the U.S. Russia Center for Entrepreneurship, "Conditions and Factors Affecting the Development of Small Entrepreneurship in the Regions of the Russian Federation," table "Evaluation of the Entrepreneurial Climate," p. 9, Moscow, 2005, http://www.opora.ru (accessed August 16, 2006).

The Russian government's 2005–08 SME development program takes regional issues and a number of the other issues raised in this chapter into account. Starting with the premise that much of the federal-level legal and regulatory reforms to facilitate entrepreneurship have already been implemented or are being finalized, the program emphasizes the responsibility of regional and local governments to comply with this federal framework. The program also includes the principle that requests from regional and local governments for federal SME support will be evaluated based on data from analyses such as OPORA's survey. One final positive element of the program is that it has been expanded to include medium-sized enterprises; one of the "accents" of the program is to help SMEs grow.[66]

This recognition of the importance of medium-sized enterprises takes us to a final important development during the 1999–2006 maturity period: increased appreciation of the weakness of entrepreneurship data and the resulting policy implications. The weaknesses of these data have made it difficult to measure the impact of policy measures on such variables as the number of small businesses, turnover, profit, and employment. Furthermore, incomplete data have deprived entrepreneurs of their potential political clout. Even though entrepreneurs have been successful in incorporating themselves into the state's thinking on economic development, the intensity of that thinking would clearly vary depending on the overall contribution of entrepreneurs to GDP.

The relevance of data issues was emphasized by two successive studies that estimated that entrepreneurs played a much more significant role in Russia's economy than was typically believed. It has been consistently estimated that small business accounted for 10–12 percent of GDP, a figure that was considered woefully low. However, a Tacis study in 2001 redefined the measurement categories in order to compare Russian entrepreneurship overall with entrepreneurship in the European Union. Whereas the European Union uses SME data to measure entrepreneurial activity and defines SMEs as businesses with up to 250 employees, Russian statistics on entrepreneurs are limited to small businesses as they are defined by the 1995 Law on State Support for Small Entrepreneurship. The number of employees varies by the business, but in no case exceeds one hundred.[67] In addition, Russian small business statistics do not include the self-employed, who constitute most of the small businesses in Russia—as they do throughout the world.[68] Furthermore, there are no official Russian statistics for

[66] http://www.smb.economy.gov.ru (accessed September 2, 2006).

[67] The EU definition for SMEs that was introduced after this study also established financial limits for balance sheet size and turnover, one of which can be exceeded, in addition to the number of employees and the degree of private ownership. The 2001 survey used only the employee criterion.

[68] To make matters even more complicated, the self-employed in Russia are entitled to hire other employees, therefore making the lack of data capture even more significant.

medium-sized enterprises, which are not defined by law. It is hardly surprising that the available Russian entrepreneurship figures are so much lower than the comparable EU figures.

When the Tacis study adjusted the Russian data to make them more comparable with the EU data, it concluded that Russian SMEs accounted for approximately 40 percent of the national output of goods and services and at least 45 percent of Russian employment.[69] Although these figures were still lower than the comparable EU figures (57 percent share of sales and 66 percent share of employment), they painted a startlingly different picture of Russian entrepreneurs than the commonly accepted one. As the Tacis report noted, "The basic level of development of the Russian SME sector does not lag as far behind the European Union as has been commonly believed. . . . Russia is now very much a country with a market economy populated mainly by SMEs."[70]

Although a single study might well have been dismissed as an aberration, or the estimates and adjustments might have been erroneous, comparable results were achieved in 2003 by the Russian SME Resource Centre and USAID. Using the same definition of an SME as a company with up to 250 employees, the study concluded that Russian SMEs account for 39 percent of Russian national output and 45 percent of employment.[71]

Although at first glance these different definitions appear to be easily resolvable, the process is quite complex. A new definition of Russian SMEs would require amending the Law on State Support for Small Entrepreneurship. Laws are rarely easy to amend in any country, and in Russia entrepreneurs have never been important for long enough to make these amendments a priority. Once the definitional changes are made, the regulatory and statistical procedures for obtaining the new data will have to be designed and implemented. In addition, political and financial considerations play a role in defining various business groupings, because these definitions are also used to

[69] Tacis, Resource Center for Small Entrepreneurs, "Russian SME Observatory Report 2001," Moscow, June 2002.

[70] Tacis, "Russian SME Observatory Report 2001," Executive Summary, Moscow, June 2002, p. 2.

[71] USAID and Russian SME Resource Centre, "Analysis of the Role and Place of Small and Medium-Sized Enterprises in Russia," Moscow, 2003.

determine government support. Therefore, appropriate adjustments have to be made to differentiate between definitions to be used for statistical purposes and definitions to be used for determining financial and other forms of government support.[72]

There are also other complex measurement issues. The data collected on Russian small businesses, for example, have been based on output and do not include the information needed to calculate their contribution to GDP.[73] Another example is the misleading impact of "shell" SMEs, the result of larger enterprises trying to reduce their taxes by creating smaller trading companies to which they sell their products at below-market prices.[74]

Despite these complications, progress is being made in introducing amendments that will revise the definition of a small business (up to 100 employees) and introduce new definitions of medium-sized businesses (from 101 to 250 employees) as well as microbusinesses (from one to 15 employees). If the data collected based on these new definitions encourage Russian policymakers to make better informed decisions about how to encourage entrepreneurship, the effort will be a success.

In this chapter I have outlined the key challenges facing Russian entrepreneurs and have attempted to present them in a context that demonstrates their positive evolution. This perspective should not be interpreted to mean, however, that the life of a Russian entrepreneur is easy. Merely because entrepreneurs have become accustomed to paying a certain proportion of their income in various bribes, for example, and therefore rank bribes relatively low on their list of concerns, does not mean that bribes are no longer a serious problem.[75] Furthermore, even as existing issues are addressed, new issues will emerge to replace them. Nevertheless, when compared to the agenda of unresolved issues that

[72] Anatoly Aksakov, Duma deputy, interview with author, Moscow, April 19, 2005.

[73] Because the Russian acronym for gross domestic product and output is the same—VVP—this point is often misunderstood. It was pointed out to me by Tatiana Alimova.

[74] A World Bank study that recalculated the size of Russia's trade sector to adjust for the creation of trading companies estimated that its actual share of GDP was more likely in the range of 9–11 percent, compared to the 31 percent derived from official Russian statistics. World Bank, "Russian Economic Report #7," World Bank Russian Country Department, Economics Unit, February 2004.

[75] A World Bank study on corruption observed that the number of respondents (not only small businesses) who considered corruption a problem for their business

has confronted entrepreneurs and policymakers since the mid-1980s, the progress in working through that agenda is clear.

The experience of the past two decades has reaped four major achievements. First, Russian entrepreneurs have largely achieved political and social acceptability. While a number of entrepreneurs in the late 1980s and early 1990s were able to make profits due to their connections and their ability to exploit market imperfections, increasingly over the past decade entrepreneurs have been forced to make money the old-fashioned way—by hard work. Neighbors and customers inevitably take note and are less grudging—and sometimes admiring—of an entrepreneur's perseverance and success.[76]

Second, Russian entrepreneurs have achieved recognition of the economic value of their work. Although the official policy response to this recognition continues to be better than its implementation, the development of entrepreneurship has become part of the standard agenda of Russia law and policymakers.

Third, through OPORA, Russian entrepreneurs have created their own permanent voice in policymaking. This platform may well become more important in the future, as issues such as the competitive environment become increasingly relevant to ensuring the further growth of entrepreneurs. OPORA's work in monitoring regional disparities in entrepreneurship policies and development is an encouraging example of the kind of contributions it can make to improving the environment for entrepreneurs.

Finally, and most impressively, Russian entrepreneurs have continued to adapt and to grow, with two studies estimating that Russian SMEs account for as much as 45 percent of employment and approximately 40 percent of national output. The 5 percent increase in the number of registered small businesses in the first six months of 2006 is another positive development.

---

had increased from 30 percent in 2002 to 40 percent in 2005, even though the relative level of bribes has decreased. James H. Anderson and Cheryl W. Gray, "Anticorruption in Transition 3: Who Is Succeeding . . . and Why?" World Bank, 2006. These results seem to indicate an increasing lack of patience for such bribes.

[76] When asked about their attitudes toward the owners of SMEs in a 2005 survey, 80 percent of those questioned answered "good" or "rather good." Nikolai Popov, "A Fateful Triangle: Business, Government, and the People," *Novoe Vremya* 19 (May 18, 2005), reprinted in Johnson's Russia List, http://www.cdi.org/russia/johnson.

To conclude on a point that I highlighted at the beginning of this chapter, Russian entrepreneurs are in an ongoing process of development; they have not maximized their growth potential. It would be a serious mistake to design financing or other programs that assume that entrepreneurs need some type of unusual assistance. What is unusual about Russian entrepreneurs is that they have survived and grown since the early days of perestroika, despite impediments that are almost unimaginable.

Chapter 3

RUSSIA'S FINANCIAL SECTOR

The perceived low level of Russian MSE development is often blamed on Russian banks. Indeed, with MSE lending accounting for approximately 3 percent of total bank lending in Russia, this conclusion is easily understood.[1] Furthermore, while I argued in the preceding chapter that the level of MSE development in Russia is not as low as we typically assume, I can't argue that MSE lending is higher than it appears. However, the situation is considerably more complex than simple percentages can convey and can best be understood in the larger context of how Russia's banking sector has developed.

This bigger-picture perspective shows that until the 1998 crisis the majority of Russian banks were distracted by a number of activities that were substantially more profitable than lending. Russian banks were not discriminating against small borrowers; for many of them lending at all was not a priority. Instead, a key characteristic of the

[1] Although the comparison is not exact, SME lending in EU countries represents approximately 15 percent of total lending. Hubert Kulikowski, "Basel II Impact on Availability and Cost of Financing for SMEs," May 11, 2004, http://www.pwcglobal.com (accessed January 16, 2006). Estimated lending to small businesses by Russian banks at year-end 2005 was $5 billion, with a further $500 million in bank lending to microbusinesses. Total banking-sector lending at year-end 2005 was $195 billion. Russian data is from the Russian Microfinance Center, "Mikrofinansirovaniye v Rossii," presentation made to the Advisory Council of the National Association of Microfinance Providers and the Council on Federations of the Russian Federation, June 29, 2006, http://www .rmc.ru (accessed September 21, 2006).

chaotic environment of perestroika and its aftermath was the strong ties of mutual dependence that developed between the banks, the central bank, and the government.[2] These relationships led these parties to focus more on the benefits they could gain from one another than on creating a legal and regulatory environment that would be a foundation for economic growth.

Partly because of the relatively low level of MSE lending, which persists until today, the fact that Russia has been building an inclusive financial sector from the outset is typically overlooked. Microfinance in Russia has always been seen as a standard banking product, having been introduced as a tool for financing new entrepreneurs and contributing to economic growth. Because this view of microfinance is critical for ensuring the commercial bank involvement necessary to close the global microfinance lending gap, Russia is a particularly useful case study. It also provides an important cautionary note: well-intended government efforts to further accelerate MSE lending could derail the momentum that the inclusive financial sector approach has helped to create.

I begin the chapter with a description of the Soviet banking system before perestroika, in order to lay the groundwork for understanding the effect of the perestroika reforms. I then chronicle the development of Russia's financial sector according to four stages. The first stage, "perestroika," began with a restructuring of the Soviet banking system that inadvertently created a chaotic environment that mirrored the overall economic disarray discussed in chapter 2. This chaos led a number of organizations to create their own banks to protect themselves from the growing unpredictability of the banking sector. The chaos also created opportunities for newly created banks to reap large profits. The strong bonds of mutual dependence between the banks and the central bank took root during this period, as each relied on the other for support in at least protecting themselves, if not actually benefiting politically or financially, in the unpredictable environment. The perestroika stage ended in July 1990 when the Russian Supreme Soviet, headed by Boris Yeltsin, announced that

---

[2] I use the word *government* to refer to the legislative and executive branches of the state and to distinguish them from the central bank, which is also an organization of the state.

all state-owned (i.e., Soviet) banks on the territory of Russia would become the property of the Russian Federation.

During the subsequent "oligarchs" stage, which extended until the 1998 crisis, the level of mutual dependence reached its peak. The Russian central bank (CBR) and government provided benefits such as a lax regulatory environment and inexpensive funding to the banks. The banks in turn used their growing wealth to support the government, from financing favored projects to ensuring President Yeltsin's reelection in 1996. The relative irrelevance of lending—to MSEs or any other borrowers—also reached a peak during this period, in which there were many other more profitable ways to make money.

The "crisis" stage, from August 1998 until early 2000, put an end to these profit-making opportunities. Furthermore, although the government and CBR exercised a light regulatory hand that protected banks as they hid their assets from creditors, the crisis ultimately weakened the fabric of mutual dependence. The government and CBR had little more to offer the banks, and the bank-owning oligarchs that survived the crisis largely turned their attention to other businesses.

The fourth and final stage, "a new start," began in 2000 and is still unfolding as I write at the end of 2006. The most noteworthy characteristic of the fourth phase is the changed incentive structure; because the precrisis methods for making money had evaporated, banks that wished to survive were forced to turn to lending. And, as competition has grown, including increased foreign investment in Russia's banking sector, bank lending has been expanding to include relatively untapped markets such as consumers and MSEs.

Starting Conditions

Understanding the effects of the perestroika reforms on the Soviet banking system requires understanding the basic features of the Soviet banking system as it had functioned previously.[3] This earlier system consisted of Gosbank, literally the state bank (*gos* is an abbreviation

---

[3] Unless otherwise noted, this discussion of the Soviet financial system is based on George Garvy, *Money, Financial Flows, and Credit in the Soviet Union* (Cambridge, Mass.: Ballinger Publishing for the National Bureau of Economic Research, 1977).

for *gosudarstvenniy,* which means *state*), and two smaller specialized banks and one banking network that were supervised by Gosbank.[4] Gosbank's chairman reported directly to the Council of Ministers, which was the highest level of the state bureaucracy and which in turn reported to the Communist Party of the Soviet Union, the country's highest level of power. Gosbank performed all financial transactions for the state by administering the flow of funds associated with the annual economic plan that controlled essentially all economic activity. Three characteristics of the Soviet banking system are important to stress.

First, the banking system was a passive implementer of the economic plan that was approved each year by the Communist Party. The plan itself was measured in terms of physical output, and money was a convenient accounting unit of secondary importance. The banking system was responsible for funneling the allocated funds to the pre-determined recipients and for monitoring the financial measures of plan fulfillment, such as ensuring that funds were utilized on schedule, that funds transfer between enterprises took place as expected, and that "profits" were remitted back to the state. In a system in which money and finance were distasteful tools of capitalism, it is not surprising that the banking system was assigned such a subsidiary role. Viktor Gerashchenko, who was a governor of the Soviet central bank and later the Russian central bank, memorably referred to the Soviet banking system as "little more than a settlement house."[5]

Second, although Gosbank was empowered to make temporary short-term loans, primarily to cover gaps between an enterprise's acquiring raw materials and being paid for its finished goods, these amounted to grants. They were issued almost automatically and there were no standard sanctions for failure to repay the loans. Nonpayment in the agricultural sector in particular was so egregious that in several cases large loan obligations were simply forgiven and cancelled.

A final function of the Soviet banking system at first seems obscure but is actually vitally important: its role in maintaining a separation

[4] The two specialized banks were Stroibank (the construction bank), which financed long-term investment projects, and Vneshtorgbank (the foreign trade bank), which was responsible for foreign currency transactions. The Sberkassa system, which was part of Gosbank, served the limited financial needs of the population.

[5] Martin Wolf, "Soviet Banker with Revolutionary Ideas," interview with Gosbank chairman V. Gerashchenko, *Financial Times*, March 22, 1990, sec. 1, 23.

between cash and noncash transactions. Ownership of physical cash gives individuals and enterprises the ability to make independent economic decisions and therefore conflicts with the control imperative of the planned economy. If you're walking down the street with money in your pocket and see an expensive item that you want to buy, it's easy to do so. But, if you are living in the Soviet planned economy and only a certain number of those items are produced every year, your purchase—and that of thousands of others like you—will throw off the plan's balance, unless the planners miraculously had anticipated how many of you would want to buy the item. And, since the priority of the Soviet economic plan was to maximize industrial output, not to satisfy consumer demand, the chances of a popular consumer item being made in sufficient quantity to satisfy demand were nil. It was much simpler for planners to keep a lid on demand by limiting the supply of cash.

As a result, the circulation of physical cash in the economy was kept to the minimum necessary. Enterprises operated largely on the basis of "noncash" rubles; these were essentially bookkeeping entries that were transferred between enterprises to reflect the fact that physical goods had changed hands and that gave enterprises the rights to acquire raw materials. However, and this is key: these rubles could only be converted to physical cash according to strictly defined criteria, such as for salary payments. The banks were responsible for enforcing these criteria and only disbursed cash against carefully verified documentation. Large enterprises typically had a bank branch on their premises to ensure the segregation of cash and noncash and to supervise the enterprises' other financial activities.

These three characteristics of the Soviet banking system—its passive role as implementer of government instructions, its lack of differentiation between loans and grants, and its role in segregating cash and noncash—all took on lives of their own as a result of the perestroika reforms.

Perestroika, 1985–1990

In chapter 2 I described the reforms introduced during the perestroika period to provide Soviet enterprises with more autonomy and accountability, including ensuring their own financial viability. Corresponding changes were also required in the banking sector, so that it could respond to the enterprise sector's new demands.[6] The result was the 1987 Decree on the Improvement of the Banking System and Strengthening Its Influence on the Promotion of Economic Efficiency. This decree created a two-tier banking system by transforming the state bank, Gosbank, into a central bank and creating five banks out of the former system to serve specified branches of the economy.[7]

The five new specialized banks were required to serve the financial requirements of the state-owned enterprises in the sector assigned to them, according to detailed credit and cash allocation plans created annually by the Ministry of Finance. They were also given the right to finance activities not covered by the plan, such as the needs of the cooperatives and the nonplan activities undertaken by the state-owned enterprises. By providing this financing on their own initiative and at their own risk, the banks were expected to replace the financial discipline that had previously penetrated the economy on the basis of the annual economic plan.

The pivotal effect of this reform was on Gosbank, which was newly constituted as the central bank. Although Gosbank was given ostensible supervisory authority over the other banks, it had no legal or regulatory tools with which to exercise its supervisory responsibilities, nor any experience in how to do so. Furthermore, the new specialized banks were not only elevated to the same hierarchical level as Gosbank but were expected to fulfill the requirements of the ministries covering their respective industries. This new organizational structure rendered unanswerable the question of who had ultimate authority over the banks—the central bank or the relevant industrial ministry. Finally, the people and the physical and financial assets used to create these new banks were almost all taken directly from Gosbank

[6] The discussion of Gosbank's response to the perestroika reforms, as well as the development of the specialized banks and the new privately owned banks, is based on Joel Scott Hellman, "Breaking the Bank: Bureaucrats and the Creation of Markets in a Transition Economy" (PhD diss., Columbia University, 1993), chapters 3 and 4.

[7] These banks were Sberbank, the savings bank; Vnesheconombank, the foreign trade bank; Promstroibank, the bank for industry and construction; Zhilsotsbank, the bank for housing and social needs; and Agroprombank, the agricultural bank.

or the banks it had previously supervised. Therefore, Gosbank was not only assigned new responsibilities for which it had no experience, no implementing instruments, or even a clear mandate, it was demoted by its loss of assets, staff, and hierarchical prestige.

Gosbank and the new specialized banks wasted no time in identifying one another as the source of the many problems that arose in fulfilling their new responsibilities. The specialized banks complained that Gosbank's regulatory efforts made it impossible for them to do their business; according to one banker, Gosbank had sent him at least one thousand instruction documents in one year. Gosbank in turn accused the specialized banks of ignoring its authority. The situation was worsened by an almost 10 percent decline in short-term lending in 1988, due to a deliberate reduction in official lending intended to encourage enterprises to seek more independent financing.

It quickly became clear that the banking reform would not achieve its objective of providing enterprises with more responsive, yet also responsible, banking services. The reformed banking system simply did not have the appropriate regulatory framework, flexibility, or incentives to replace the planned lending with voluntary lending. The government's response to this dilemma was similar to the snowballing reform efforts in the economy at large, where failed attempts at partial liberalization were followed by ever-bolder liberalization measures. Within one short year the banking reforms progressed from liberalizing the operations of the state-owned banks to allowing the creation of fully private cooperative banks, as authorized by the May 1988 Law on Cooperatives.

Gosbank played an active role in the development of this legislation, and, as Joel Hellman convincingly has argued in his insightful dissertation research, it had a strong institutional incentive to do so. These new banks could be more readily controlled than the specialized banks, therefore enabling Gosbank to assert its authority. The new banks also posed a commercial challenge to the specialized banks that would presumably reduce the specialized banks' relative importance over time, thus also helping to fortify Gosbank's position. The relationship of mutual dependence between the banking sector and the regulatory authorities dates from this period, when Gosbank perceived its interests as being aligned with the rapid development of the new private banks. Hellman quotes the head of Gosbank's research institute, Aleksandr Khandruyev, who stated in an interview that "Garetovskii [the chairman of Gosbank] needed a 'third force' in his struggle against the spetsbanks. He needed to undermine their monopoly position in the banking system."[8]

The incomplete legal and regulatory environment played a critical role in the development of this relationship, because it gave Gosbank enormous latitude to help the new private banks get started. As one example, Gosbank neglected to enact specific regulations on the licensing and regulation of the new private banks until January 1989, a full seven months after the Law on Cooperatives had been adopted, and after it had already licensed forty-one banks. Furthermore, these regulations were structured so broadly that Gosbank retained the ability to make highly subjective licensing decisions.[9] Gosbank also took the enormous liberty of expanding upon the Law on Cooperatives by declaring that any legal Soviet entity had the right to form a commercial bank; the law had actually provided this right only to cooperatives.

Not only did Gosbank have the opportunity to confer banking licenses, it also took the initiative to provide the privately owned banks with unique advantages. The specialized banks were located awkwardly between the command economy and the perestroika economy, with responsibilities to fulfill the evolving demands of the perestroika economy as well as the control functions of the planned economy. Not only were they subject to annual plans created by the Ministry of Finance that specified their lending activities, these plans also detailed the loan terms and interest rates. The new privately owned banks, by contrast, were unfettered by any obligations to state-owned enterprises, as well as being free to set their own interest rates and other conditions for loans and deposits. Gosbank took that advantageous starting point one enormous step further by freeing the private banks from one of the strictest controls of the planned economy: the requirement to segregate cash and noncash.

[8] Hellman, "Breaking the Bank," 138.

[9] There were three general reasons for denying a license: the charter did not comply with existing legislation and banking regulations; the bank's objectives did not correspond with "the interests of the economy"; the bank had weak development prospects. In addition, the minimum capital requirement of five million rubles did not have to be fully paid-in by the time the bank began operations, while a requirement that the bank's chief executive have at least five years of banking experience was dropped due to lobbying pressure.

The lifting of this restriction converted a banking license into an outright license to create money. The private banks bought the noncash balances of the state enterprises at large discounts; the enterprises were pleased to get any cash at all, and the banks profited from keeping the rest. Furthermore, any accounts opened at the private banks were free from the cash/noncash differentiation from the outset. Although the perestroika period witnessed many reforms that chipped away—deliberately or accidentally—at the controls of the planned economy, the failure to maintain the cash/noncash segregation had one of the most far-reaching results. The sudden availability of cash gave individuals and enterprises vastly more options than they had ever had previously. It also contributed to the hyperinflation that erupted in the early 1990s.

These long-term considerations were of course irrelevant to any organization struggling to survive or even take advantage of the evolving circumstances, whether it was a cooperative, a state-owned enterprise, a regional or local government, or even a ministry. Furthermore, many of these organizations soon realized that private banks could not only offer more flexibility than the specialized banks but owning their own bank would provide even more advantages. Ultimately, even the specialized banks began opening private banks. In a reflection of how organizations other than the cooperative banks seized the opportunities provided by the new banking regulations, there were 433 private banks by August 1990, of which cooperative banks accounted for less than 3 percent of the total share capital.

At one end of the spectrum, owning one's own bank was a form of protection against the growing unpredictability of the banking system: the payment system was disintegrating, account balances at the specialized banks paid very low rates of interest, and the outcome of loan requests was unpredictable. State-owned enterprises still had annual plan obligations in this difficult environment; they were only free to undertake other activities in addition to fulfilling these obligations. Therefore, the confusion in the state-owned banking sector created particular problems for these enterprises, each of which had been assigned to a specialized bank at the time of the 1987 reform.[10]

---

[10] In March 1989 the enterprises were given the right to choose their own specialized bank partner.

Creating their own banks gave these enterprises a fully owned ally and more flexibility in their attempts to survive, or even prosper. Among the survival techniques the banks could implement were converting enterprise noncash accounts to cash, borrowing funds from the CBR to lend to their shareholders, and implementing transfer pricing programs that enabled their shareholders to conceal part of their earnings.

At the other end of the spectrum from simply surviving, owning one's own bank was a potential route to riches, from transactions that included using cash surpluses to buy and sell hard-to-obtain consumer goods, such as computers; creating offshore accounts for protecting hard currency profits; converting noncash to cash; and simply "privatizing" money by moving it out of government accounts.[11] Regarding the last activity, Duma hearings in 1992 revealed that over one billion rubles of Communist Party funds had been transferred to private banks.[12]

Under the circumstances, it is not surprising that a relationship of mutual dependence developed as it did. Gosbank was operating in a freewheeling environment in which it had the ability to confer upon applicants the right to make money, or at least protect their current operations. With so much at stake from Gosbank's decision, it is not difficult to imagine prospective bank owners being willing to make or entertain proposals for informal ways to facilitate the process, such as paying bribes or being receptive to subsequent loan requests from Gosbank officials.

Furthermore, as I discussed, Gosbank saw the creation of private banks as being in its interests; its objective was not to limit the number of licenses so that it could adequately supervise the banking sector but to issue enough licenses to reduce the influence of the specialized banks. Therefore, the scope for individualized relationship building between banks and regulators was immense. The fact that the local Gosbank branch and the local government also had to agree to a bank license request served to create an even broader net of relations and obligations, implicit or explicit.

---

[11] Creating offshore banking accounts was not allowed but was almost impossible to prevent in the rapidly changing regulatory environment.

[12] Juliet Johnson, *A Fistful of Rubles: The Rise and Fall of the Russian Banking System* (Ithaca: Cornell University Press, 2000), 41.

Although it's easy for those of us who grew up in relatively stable, developed market economies to turn up our noses at this type of behavior, it is more useful to put ourselves in the shoes of a prospective banker or regulator at that time. Russia did not have a culture of strict delineation between the public and the private sector and the related concept of the civil servant whose responsibility was to help enforce that delineation. There was certainly no such separation during the Soviet period: not only was there essentially no private property or private sector but even the realm of personal privacy was regularly invaded by the state.

This deep-rooted lack of differentiation between the public and private sector suddenly overlapped with the perestroika environment, in which all of the controls and certainties of the previous decades were rapidly disintegrating. Furthermore, as I noted in chapter 2, the use of bribes and tips had long been an entrenched part of Soviet culture. It's therefore not difficult to understand that regulators and potential bankers were willing to make whatever private arrangements they made to be able to survive, and possibly prosper, amid the uncertainty.

Bank lending, and in particular lending to small newly created companies, was not a priority in this environment. The specialized banks were expected to fulfill lending plans for the state-owned enterprises, but these were based on instructions and funding provided by the Ministry of Finance. Although the specialized banks had the authority to lend to cooperatives, the bureaucratic burden under which they operated prevented this from becoming a major new activity.

For the newly created private banks, lending was only one of a wide range of activities. Particularly for those banks that were created defensively, in order to help their founders survive, lending to their shareholders, their suppliers, and clients made sense—it was the reason for founding the bank.[13] And, as part of the survival objective, the banks often charged such low interest rates on these loans that they were actually loss making; the banks typically made sufficient profits from their other activities to subsidize this lending.

---

[13] Hellman notes cases in which bank employees expressed dissatisfaction with being forced to lend to their shareholders, but the shareholders certainly considered this an important function of "their" bank.

Although lending to shareholders and related parties may have made sense, lending on an arms-length basis to third parties did not. Such lending was unusually risky in an environment in which no one had any credit history and there was no effective legal framework for enforcing creditors' rights. Furthermore, as I discussed in chapter 2, the considerable suspicion that dogged private entrepreneurs did not usually make them desirable potential borrowers. It took much less effort and was less risky and more profitable for banks to keep cash turning over quickly by trading popular consumer items or trading foreign currency at black market rates.

As a result of these considerations, lending to the cooperatives—which were still the only legal form of private enterprise, other than individual entrepreneurship and foreign joint ventures—was relatively low. Using the data available about lending to cooperatives by the private banks, and assuming a similar situation at the specialized banks, loans to cooperatives as of mid-1990 accounted for under 2 percent of total lending.[14] Lending therefore did not correspond to the proportion of the cooperatives' contribution to GDP, officially estimated at 4.3 percent at year-end 1989 and assumed to be higher.

Although the emphasis in this chapter is on lending by banks, it is important to bear in mind that Russian entrepreneurs, like entrepreneurs throughout the world, also turned to informal sources of finance, including friends and neighbors. Particularly in countries with large informal economies and weak banking sectors, individuals with extra cash often prefer to lend it directly to someone they know instead of putting the money in a bank that might fail or might ask questions about where the money came from. Almost 16 percent of Russian small businesses and individual entrepreneurs surveyed as recently as 2005 financed the creation of their businesses with funding from relatives and acquaintances.[15]

---

[14] Although private banks accounted for less than 10 percent of total lending as of September 1990, it seems unlikely that specialized bank lending to cooperatives was substantially higher than that of the private banks, given the greater flexibility the private banks had to offer. It also seems likely that if the specialized banks wished to support the cooperative of one of its shareholders, the best way to do so would have been through a cooperative bank owned by a specialized bank.

[15] The majority of funding was personal savings. Bank loans accounted for 10 percent; this figure should be understood in the context that banks typically do

The final chapter of the perestroika stage, and one that marks the conclusive burial of the Soviet banking system, was ushered in by Yeltsin as part of his strategy to wrest control from the Soviet authorities. Following Russia's declaration of sovereignty in June 1990, the Soviet authorities moved defensively to protect Soviet assets. These steps included a decree reorganizing Zhilsotzbank and Agroprombank, two of the specialized banks, into joint stock companies owned by thousands of shareholders, in order to prevent their takeover by Yeltsin. In what became known as the "war of the banks," Yeltsin responded with a resolution claiming ownership by the Russian Republic of all of the specialized banks (except their all-union headquarters) on Russian territory. The resolution also converted the Russian branch of Gosbank into the Central Bank of Russia (CBR).

Although the Soviet authorities responded with a range of countermeasures, Yeltsin had won the battle by early August and was able to create a Russian central bank. Yeltsin's success in this particular struggle was a significant step in the ultimate demise of the Soviet Union, because it demonstrated that a republic could challenge the Soviet authorities and win. (A number of other republics, led by Ukraine, quickly followed Yeltsin's lead in claiming more authority over the banking assets on their territory.)

Yeltsin's success led to a remarkable seventeen-month period, dating from the creation of the CBR until the collapse of the USSR in December 1991, during which the Soviet central bank and the Russian central bank coexisted and struggled to assert authority over the banks on Russian territory. One of the tools in this struggle was trying to create more attractive—that is, less restrictive—regulatory environments for the banks, so that they would choose to incorporate themselves in the more appealing environment. This aggressive courting of the banks helped lay the groundwork for the rise of Russia's oligarchs and for a shift in the balance of the mutual dependence relationship from the regulator to the regulated.

---

not finance start-up operations. OPORA and VITsOM, "Usloviya i factory razvitiya malogo predprinimatel'stva v regionakh RF," Moscow 2005, http://www.opora.ru (accessed August 1, 2006).

The Rise of the Oligarchs, December 1991–August 1998

The new Central Bank of Russia moved quickly to make it impossible for the Soviet authorities to regain control of the state-owned banks on Russian territory.[16] The banks' branches were given the right to transform themselves into commercial banks, and their headquarters and regional level offices were abolished, leaving the branches able to make independent decisions about reconstituting themselves. The operating assumption was that once hundreds of new banks had been created on the basis of Russian regulations, it would be impossible for the Soviet authorities to reclaim them one by one. As CBR banker Sergei Rodionov stated, "Our task was to destroy the old system from top to bottom."[17]

Although there was some ostensible CBR supervision of this process, the rapid pace makes it clear that the banks essentially reorganized themselves. The process started on September 3, 1990, and was completed by December 1, by which point there were 453 banks based on the former Agroprombank, 125 banks based on Zhilsotsbank, and 187 banks based on Promstroibank. At the peak of the registration process, the CBR in Moscow was issuing up to fifty licenses a day.

Sberbank and Vnesheconombank were not part of this process, because of the more complex nature of their activities. Because Sberbank had historically been the only retail savings bank, Sberbank's Russian structure was kept intact and the CBR became its largest shareholder. Vnesheconombank, which was responsible for the Soviet Union's external debt, was largely left alone, and a new Russian equivalent, Vneshtorgbank, was created. Sberbank and Vneshtorgbank would continue to make their mark on the Russian banking system.

While the process of obtaining a banking license had favored prospective bank owners over the regulators for several years, the ongoing competition between Gosbank and the CBR created new opportunities for regulatory arbitrage. One of the best examples is Mosbusinessbank, which was created on the basis of Zhilsotsbank's Moscow network. Some of the Zhilsotsbank branches had already

---

[16] Unless otherwise stated, the discussion in this section up until mid-1992 is based on Hellman, "Breaking the Bank," chapters 5 and 6.

[17] Cited in Hellman, "Breaking the Bank," 202.

created their own banks and protested widely when the former Moscow headquarters tried to force them into the Mosbusinessbank structure. When the CBR concluded that Mosbusinessbank's plans did not comply with its regulations, Mosbusinessbank simply chose to register with Gosbank of the USSR, which was still a functioning central bank. This clever step led to negotiations with the CBR that ultimately resolved all of the difficulties and ensured that Mosbusinessbank was licensed by the CBR.

The CBR's technique for commercializing the Soviet state-owned banks certainly achieved its objective of destroying the old system, but the new system that it created was financially very fragile. Almost 44 percent of the new banks had less than five million rubles in declared capital, while only 5 percent had declared capital of over fifty million.[18] Even these startlingly low figures were largely irrelevant, however, because they only reflected intended starting capital; only 10 percent of this amount had to be paid in before the banks started to do business.

A related problem was the quality of the banks' loan portfolios, since the banks had all been lending to a small circle of clients in their economic sector. The Agroprombank branch in a given location lent to all of the agricultural enterprises in that region, while the Promstroibank branch lent to all of the industrial enterprises. This had created undiversified loan portfolios that in many cases still had more of the characteristics of grants, rather than loans. Furthermore, in a number of cases, particularly in more rural areas, each branch had only one or two clients that had dominated the local economy.

To complicate matters even further, these borrowers—or "grantees"—were in many cases now the shareholders of the new banks, since the banks had nowhere else to turn when they needed to find new shareholders at short notice. Many of these shareholders were enticed to buy shares with the promise of reduced interest rates on their future borrowing. Some even borrowed from the banks to purchase their shares, thereby creating fictitious capital. About half of the new banks

---

[18] Five million rubles was the equivalent of three million dollars, according to the official exchange rate, and approximately $300,000, according to the black market rate. Therefore a bank could be started with the equivalent of $30,000.

were associated with collective farms or agricultural enterprises, both of which had a history of needing additional state support.

Therefore, the 775 newly created banks, which joined the 334 independent banks already operating in Russia (many for just a few months), were on the whole a financially weaker group. Although many of the first wave of banks represented Russia's infamous "pocket" banks, in which the banks were in the pocket of their shareholders and responded to their needs, this phenomenon was even more pronounced with the second wave, in which a number of banks were owned by only one or two of their local monopoly producers. At the other extreme, the state-owned bank commercialization process also produced a number of relative giants; eight of Russia's ten largest banks as of 1992 had been created by amalgamating a number of branches from the former state-owned banks.

Weak though many of the newly commercialized banks might have been, they enjoyed one remarkable advantage: unlimited access to CBR funding. At first this access was due to failure to amend the previous interbank settlement system, in which branches of state-owned banks could draw down funds from the CBR as needed. While this initial oversight is hard enough to believe, even more incredible is the CBR's deliberate decision, after this oversight was detected, to cover any overdrafts in the accounts of the newly commercialized banks. In other words, these banks had an open spigot at the CBR. The rationale for this policy was that the commercialized banks had inherited large nonperforming loans from their former lives as state-owned banks, many at below-market interest rates; if the CBR didn't give these banks opportunities to strengthen themselves, there was a risk of destabilizing bank bankruptcies. The CBR also selected individual banks to which it provided low-cost funding for priority projects, such as agriculture, and compensated the banks for the lower profit margins.

This extraordinary funding policy greased the wheels of the entire banking sector. The CBR had minimal monitoring capacity at this point, so the banks were largely free to use the funding as they wished. Although pocket banks were often required to pass the funding on to their founders, a more profitable use for the banks was to relend it to banks that didn't have this favored access. By year-end 1992 loans from the CBR were the equivalent of 23 percent of GDP, or more than

TABLE 3.1.
Commercial Bank Lending Relative to GDP

	1992	1993	1994	1995	1996	1997	1998	1999
Commercial bank credit to the nonfinancial sector (% of GDP)	33.6	20.4	19.6	12.0	10.4	9.6	14.1	11.3

Source: Johnson, *Fistful of Rubles*, table 1.1, p. 6.

the total lending by all Russian banks relative to GDP as of the end of 2004.[19]

This liberal allocation of funding led to the last wave of lending by Russian banks until after the 1998 crisis. In 1991, the year following the conversion of the state-owned banks, lending increased by 127 percent, followed by an increase of over 400 percent in 1992. In fact, by mid-1992 most lending was being propped up by the CBR—89 percent of all loans granted in July could be traced to CBR funding. It seems reasonable to conclude that the lending done toward the end of this period was by pocket banks with access to CBR funding; for any independent banks looking at their own bottom lines, lending had become a money loser, with banks lending at rates of only 100–160 percent when inflation exceeded 1,000 percent.

This decline in lending after 1992 is shown in table 3.1. In addition, it illustrates a major theme of this chapter, which is the low overall level of lending by Russian banks, relative to GDP, throughout this period. For context, comparable ratios in mature market economies often exceed 100 percent. Using an example from another transition economy, the ratio of loans to GDP in Poland was 14.4 percent in 1995, but it had increased to 24.7 percent by 1999.[20] By comparison, the ratios in Russia were both low and lagging.

Regardless of whether the banks used the CBR's resources for passing them on to their shareholders or for trading and investing, access to CBR funds had become an integral part of their business. Client deposits had began to decrease during 1991 as inflation began

[19] Ruben Lamdany, ed., *Russia: The Banking System during the Transition* (Washington, D.C.: World Bank, 1993), 3.

[20] National Bank of Poland, "Summary Evaluation of the Financial Situation of Polish Banks, 2001," Warsaw, May 2002.

to outstrip deposit rates, followed by accelerated withdrawals as the January 1992 shock therapy program led to escalating prices and the need for more cash. Therefore, the banks maintained constant pressure on the government and the CBR to maintain the CBR's flow of funds, threatening the specter of economic collapse as the alternative. And, when the CBR periodically tried to assert at least some control over the banking system, the bankers were outraged.

Eventually, when CBR governor Gyorgy Matyukhin refused a 1.5 trillion ruble loan to cover interenterprise arrears in the summer of 1992, this and other considerations led the Supreme Soviet to acquiesce to the banks' pressure for his removal.[21] Matyukhin's replacement was Viktor Gerashchenko, who had previously been chairman of the Soviet central bank, Gosbank. Although economist Jeffrey Sachs's characterization of Gerashchenko as "the worst central-bank governor of any major country in history" is extreme, it is true that Gerashchenko's commitment to the CBR's role as the financier of Russian growth does not correspond with typical market economy practices.[22] As Gerashchenko stated at one conference, banks that financed enterprises constituting Russia's economic "backbone" would be supported financially by the CBR, regardless of the extent of the banks' own problems.[23]

This successful lobbying for the removal of the CBR governor is one of the first clear signs of the growing political power of Russian banks, which ironically was partly due to the increased financial power that they had attained with the help of the CBR. Although banks continued to lobby for individual preferences, a number of Russian banking associations had also joined together in October 1991 to form the Association of Russian Banks (ARB), one of whose goals was to "participate in the legal and normative formation of the [Russian] banking system."[24] By 1993 the ARB was able to declare its success in ensuring the election of eight Duma members, while individual

[21] One of the other causes for dissatisfaction with Matyukhin was the CBR's failure to develop a payment system suitable for the banking sector. Johnson, *Fistful of Rubles*, 83.

[22] "The World's Worst Central Banker," *Economist*, October 16, 1993, 78.

[23] "Russian Banks Get Support," World-Wire, *Wall Street Journal*, November 20, 1994, A10.

[24] "Assembleya bankovskikh krugov," *Ekonomika i zhizn'*, Bankovskiy Byulleten' 41 (October 1991), suppl., 4–5.

banks also supported a range of candidates.[25] By the 1996 election, effective lobbying by the banks and the ARB had become an accepted fact. As CBR vice governor Khandruyev stated at that time, "It is no secret that in order to be elected to the State Duma, it is necessary to have someone finance one's program. . . . Thus quite a few lobbyists for commercial banks naturally develop among the deputies in parliament."[26]

At the same time that some government control over the CBR spigot had been achieved by the end of 1993, an attractive new source of funding was already emerging to take its place. This was the system of "authorized" banks, according to which banks provided treasury functions for federal, regional, and local governments by serving as repositories and transfer agents for budgetary funds, salary and pension payments, and customs revenues. This authorized bank system was an extremely appealing source of funding for the banks; the funds were typically held in zero interest operating accounts and provided the banks with loosely defined "float" periods before the money was withdrawn for its designated use. During this period the banks could use the funds for short-term purposes such as foreign exchange trading.

A look at the twenty largest banks as of early 1996 makes it clear that some of these banks would not even have been on this list without the budgetary funding provided by their authorized bank status. At Mosbusinessbank, for example, then Russia's sixth largest bank by assets, budgetary funding accounted for 40 percent of its assets; MosIndustrialBank, then the tenth largest bank, had 50 percent of its assets as budgetary funding; and Unikombank, the twelfth largest bank, relied on budgetary funding for 38 percent of its assets.[27]

It's hardly surprising that in return for authorized bank status banks were receptive to hints and suggestions from their key contacts about other projects that they should finance voluntarily with their own resources. Even President Yeltsin made it clear that authorized bank status was a two-way street. At a meeting with bankers in 1995,

---

[25] Johnson, *Fistful of Rubles*, 117.

[26] Quoted in Virgis Pikturna, "Steering Russia's Banking System toward Stability," *Transition* 2, no. 10 (May 17, 1996): 12.

[27] *Finansovye Izvestiya*, February 9, 1996, p. 3.

Yeltsin noted that any bank interested in developing an authorized bank relationship at the federal level would be required to provide some of its own funding to state projects.[28]

One profitable use of the funds acquired by the authorized banks was investing in the Russian government debt obligations that were issued beginning in 1993. Although the government ultimately issued three different types of debt obligations, the largest in volume were GKOs, "government short-term obligations."[29] These notes, typically of three- to six-month maturities, were initially issued to help cover the federal government's budget deficit. By year-end 1994 the $3 billion in outstanding GKOs covered three-quarters of the deficit. However, the GKOs eventually transformed themselves into somewhat of a narcotic, both for the government and for the investors; 91 percent of the new GKOs issued in 1997 ($64.7 billion) were used to refinance GKOs that were maturing.

For the government, high demand for the GKOs meant that it could continue to run deficits and avoid serious budget cutting. For the banks, GKOs were a hassle-free way to make more money than by the time-consuming process of lending; in 1998, for example, GKOs were providing a 50 percent annual yield, tax free, compared to an average lending rate of 42 percent. Furthermore, the annual average GKO rates don't provide a full sense of their profitability, because their yields often jumped in response to political events. A list of the fifteen banks with the largest holdings of ruble-denominated government securities illustrates the magnitude of the banks' government securities business (table 3.2).

Foreign currency trading also continued to be a profitable activity for the banks, with fifty-seven banks having licenses to conduct foreign currency operations domestically and internationally by the early 1990s, while almost four hundred banks had licenses for domestic foreign-currency operations.[30] Furthermore, with CBR monitoring capacity still very limited, even banks without licenses often found ways to operate in these markets.

---

[28] "Kak prezident s bankirami vstrechalsya," *Ekonomika i Zhizn'*, Bankovskiy Byuletten' 36 (September 1995), 4.

[29] GKO is an acronym for *gosudarstvennaya kratkosrochnaya obligatsiya*.

[30] Hellman, "Breaking the Bank," 246, n. 21.

TABLE 3.2.
Banks with the Largest Holdings of Ruble-denominated Government Securities,
July 1997

Bank	Government securities ($ million)	Percent of assets in government securities
Sberbank	$16,819.2	57.80
Bank of Moscow	589.0	45.16
Avtobank	560.9	35.01
Vneshtorgbank	512.1	13.12
Inkombank	463.6	13.53
Mosbiznesbank	432.8	26.63
Rossiyskiy Kredit	270.3	15.42
National Reserve Bank	269.8	13.43
Oneksimbank	228.6	6.36
Mezhprombank	185.5	12.33
Mezhkombank	181.6	45.57
International Moscow Bank	148.6	11.43
Promstroibank St. Petersburg	147.8	20.04
Menatep	147.0	7.73
Copf	122.7	34.09

Source: Russia Review, 1997, reproduced in Johnson, Fistful of Rules, table 7.1, p. 209. The figures
for government securities include GKOs and another security called the OFZ, official federal debt
(ofitsialniy federal' niy zaym). It does not include the domestic dollar-denominated securities, OVVZs
(ofitsialniy vnutrenniy valyutniy zaym).

Another impetus to the growth of the foreign currency market was
the introduction of foreign currency forward contracts that Russian
banks sold to foreign investors who wanted protection for their ruble-
denominated GKOs. After the crisis it became clear that one reason
some banks made so much money on foreign currency operations was
that they did not manage the potential risk relative to their capacity.[31]
Inkombank, for example, had committed itself to $1.9 billion in for-
ward contracts with foreign counterparties, compared to its year-end
1997 capital of $1.1 billion.[32] Fulfilling these contracts with the rapidly
depreciating postcrisis ruble was clearly beyond the bank's financial
capacity. As it turned out, a number of banks became insolvent during

[31] The banks reported to the CBR that they had hedged their foreign currency
positions, but the CBR's reviews did not reveal that the hedging counterparts were
sometimes undercapitalized entities related to the banks.
[32] The bank had additional forward contracts with domestic banks that were
intended to offset the forward contracts, but the domestic contracts proved to be
unenforceable when the foreign currency market collapsed. The main point is that
Inkombank was taking inappropriate risks in this market relative to its capital.

the crisis even without redeeming these forward contracts, which in most cases elapsed without payment.[33]

A final important source of profits during this period was the voucher privatization process, which lasted from 1991 until October 1994. The primary means of privatizing larger enterprises, used in about 75 percent of all cases, allowed an enterprise's management and employees to acquire 61 percent of the company's common stock for 1.7 times the nominal price.[34] In many cases the employees then sold their shares to the management or outside buyers; some investors posted buyers outside a company's gates to make offers to employees who were on their way home.

Voucher privatization offered many opportunities to banks. Some banks traded vouchers on Russia's developing markets, some created voucher funds, some helped managers buy vouchers, and some helped their own shareholders finance the purchase of their firms. Banks were particularly active purchasers of vouchers as long-term investments; one banker summarized the approach of Russia's large banks as "we will own Russia."[35] In fact, in some cases it became difficult to ascertain whether the banks controlled the enterprises or the enterprises controlled the banks, as financial-industrial groups (conglomerates) known as FIGs became an increasingly common structure among Russia's largest banks.

It is not difficult to understand how the ties of mutual dependence continued to grow during this period. The CBR came into being with a mandate to woo banks to settle under its wing, which it did with a menu of goodies. These included legalizing the giveaway of state-owned banks and the allocation of funding. Regulatory forbearance also played an important role; even by mid-1992 the CBR had not developed the capacity to conduct annual examinations of all of Russia's banks. The fact that the CBR's various favors were

---

[33] Total forward contracts for the banking sector were approximately six billion dollars. "West Owed $6Bln in Forwards," *Moscow Times*, October 23, 1998. Some of the few banks that did agree with their counterparties on paying their forward obligations were Vneshtorgbank, Sberbank, International Moscow Bank, and Alfa Bank.

[34] This was a different part of the privatization program than the small-scale privatization program noted in chapter 2.

[35] Senior staff member, International Moscow Bank, interview with author, Moscow, September, 1996.

granted in a nontransparent manner during a period of such minimal accountability, together with the bribe-taking environment, makes it reasonable to assume that the favored banks devised ways to ensure their status.

This period also witnessed a broadening in the playing field beyond the CBR, most notably with the development of the authorized bank system and the government debt auctions. Now it was no longer just the CBR that had largesse to dispose but a range of government entities with the authority to allocate funds and confer trading access. Whereas the key relationship since perestroika had been between the newly created banks and the CBR, by the end of 1993 the CBR had less to offer the banks; the licenses had already been issued, and the CBR had considerably less funding at its disposal. The CBR continued to be an important player, particularly because of its ability to bend the rules for particular banks, but the primary lobbying efforts of the banks shifted as the government proved to be a growing source of funding and other business.

It is also not difficult to understand why lending held little appeal for the banks. Not only were the financial returns on lending inferior to what the banks could make on other activities but the banks were experiencing increasing difficulties with the loans that they had made. Financial information provided by borrowers was often unreliable, collateral was difficult to obtain, bankers often had no training, and the economy was unpredictable. As a result, as of December 1995, past-due loans accounted for 40 percent of loans outstanding. By 1997, the banking sector's losses from lending were the equivalent of 0.10 percent of GDP, compared to profits of 1.86 percent of GDP in net trading income and 0.15 percent of GDP in foreign currency operations.[36]

Despite the accuracy of the preceding statement about the banks' low interest in lending from the perspective of the banking sector as a whole, it is useful to differentiate broadly between the large Moscow-based banks and the smaller regional and local banks. My discussion

---

[36] Ursula Beyreuther, senior credit analyst, Deutsche Bank, "Comparative Analysis of the Russian and Eastern European Banking Systems," presentation at Russian Banking Forum, London, December 7–8, 2000. Losses are defined in this presentation as net interest income.

in this section focuses primarily on the large Moscow-based banks, because many of them epitomized two of the points stressed in this section—their access to many more lucrative opportunities than lending and the close ties between the banks, the CBR, and, later, the government. Furthermore, with Russia's twenty largest banks accounting for about 60 percent of banking-sector assets for the several years preceding the 1998 financial crisis, these are the banks that defined the system's trends.[37]

Nevertheless, there are several observations to make about regional and local banks to put their operations into context. It's intuitively appealing to believe that regional banks and local banks were more focused on lending as the true business of banking than their more easily corruptible big city brothers. In fact, a study undertaken by economist Ono Shigeki shows that regional banks (and smaller Moscow former state banks) did have a higher share of loans relative to assets than large Moscow banks in 1994 and 1995. However, there are no data to indicate what kind of lending was entailed—to what extent these banks were lending to small entrepreneurs or to support their shareholders.

In any case, the higher level of lending by non-Moscow banks decreased beginning in 1996, as many regional banks cut back on lending while the Moscow-based banks increased their lending (see table 3.3).

A variety of factors conspired to reduce regional lending during 1996 and 1997, including a growing tendency of local and regional governments to centralize budgetary funding and a mini banking crisis that peaked in the fall of 1995 and tightened interbank lending conditions. An accumulating burden of problem loans served as an additional deterrent, with the net result that the profits of regional banks fell by 27 percent in 1996.[38] The notable increase in lending by Moscow-based banks in 1996 is largely the result of the loans-for-shares program discussed below.

[37] Whereas nineteen of these banks were based in Moscow or St. Petersburg in 1996, by 1998 all twenty were located in these two cities.

[38] By contrast, the profits of the large Moscow-based banks increased by 75 percent. Lana Simkina, "Banking in Russia's Regions," *BISNIS,* July 1997.

TABLE 3.3.
Patterns of Lending to Enterprises and Individuals by Region (as percentage of total assets)

Location of bank	1994	1995	1996	1997
Moscow city and region	26.7	29.0	43.3	37.7
North	63.0	65.3	37.6	22.7
Northeast	44.5	50.9	42.1	28.7
Central (excluding Moscow city and region)	44.8	57.5	31.8	49.5
Volga	59.5	67.4	51.6	45.2
North Caucasus	58.4	56.3	56.5	39.4
Urals	42.6	48.6	52.7	38.7
West Siberia	43.7	47.1	55.3	35.7
East Siberia	67.5	57.8	61.6	48.9
Far East	60.0	55.9	50.6	22.7

Source: Shigeki Ono, "Lending and Investing Activities of Russian Banks from 1992 to the Beginning of 1998," *Slavic Studies*, no. 47, 2000. I am grateful to Dr. Ono for translating this table for my use. This data is based on information provided in *Ekonomika i Zhizn'* on up to 100 banks (depending on the year). Sberbank is not included.

Another perspective on the activities of local and regional banks compared to the Moscow-based banks is provided by the MSE lending programs introduced by several foreign organizations in the early and mid-1990s. The first microfinance program in Russia was introduced in Nizhny Novgorod in 1994 by Opportunity International (OI), a U.S. development organization founded in the early 1970s. OI's loans had an average size of about $3,000 and were made to groups of three to five people. By early 1998 OI was lending to 480 borrowers, 82 percent of whom were women, and had a total loan portfolio of $1.2 million.[39]

The EBRD began a $10 million pilot small-business lending project during the summer of 1993 and expanded to microfinance (defined as loans under $20,000) in the spring of 1995. By August 1998, the program, which is discussed in more detail in chapter 4, had grown to include thirteen banks from Moscow and the regions, a loan portfolio of almost $100 million, and about 6,500 borrowers.[40]

[39] Stacie Schrader, original OI project manager and now chairman of the board of FORUS Bank (to which the OI program converted), telephone interview with author, September 21, 2006, and subsequent correspondence.

[40] Elizabeth Wallace, "EBRD's Micro and Small Enterprise Lending Programmes: Downscaling Commercial Banks and Starting Greenfield Banks," in *The Development of the Financial Sector in Southeast Europe: Innovative Approaches in Volatile Environments*, ed. Ingrid Matthaus-Maier and J. D. von Pischke (Berlin: Springer-Verlag, 2004).

TUSRIF, created with funding allocated by the U.S. Congress, initiated a small business lending program in 1995, followed by micro-lending (loans under $10,000) in 1996. By August 1998, this program had grown to a loan portfolio of $14.7 million, twenty-five partner banks on a cumulative basis, and 364 loans or loan tranches on a cumulative basis. (The cumulative loan amount was $25.5 million.)[41]

Unfortunately, the experience of these programs provides incon-clusive evidence about the lending strategies of the local and regional bank participants. Stacie Schrader, the project manager for OI, recalled that the local banks in Nizhny Novgorod, which were already beginning to cut back on lending, thought the program was "crazy."[42] The incentives of the participants in the EBRD's program were complicated by a precondition for participation—acceptance into a better-known and very prestigious program initiated by the World Bank. Perhaps the most accurate assessment of the participants' lend-ing strategies is provided by James Cook, director of TUSRIF's Small Business Program, who concluded that "it didn't really matter where the banks were located." Some embraced the MSE lending programs while others were more interested in the public relations value.[43]

Certain cases do stand out, such as Bank Center-Invest of Rostov-on-Don. Founded in 1993 to serve large privatized enterprises and retail clients, in 1997 the bank initiated its own small business lending pro-gram.[44] Another example is NBD Bank of Nizhny Novgorod, founded to finance the military plants in the region that were converting to produce civilian products. As early as 1994 the bank's management realized that these clients could not provide the funding the bank needed to finance such large projects and therefore turned its atten-tion to SMEs. NBD Bank's change in strategy occurred independently of any offers of donor assistance; instead, it led to a search for training

[41] Author correspondence, Ekaterina Panteliushina, director, Corporate Commu-nications and Investor Relations, Delta Private Equity, September 27, 2006.

[42] However, although the banks were largely skeptical, the head of the Nizhny Novgorod branch of the CBR was receptive and supported OI in its efforts to get es-tablished. OI originally operated as a lending window in a local bank and later lent independently as an NGO.

[43] James Cook, former director of TUSRIF Small Business Program, 1997–2004, telephone interview with author, September 19, 2006.

[44] Author correspondence, Vasiliy Vysokov, chairman of the board of directors, Bank Center-Invest, July 17, 2006.

that resulted in the bank's joining the EBRD's Russia Small Business Fund (RSBF) program.[45]

Although we will never know how these trends would have evolved without the crisis, we can conclude that there was not a significant cluster of local or regional banks lending to small entrepreneurs before the crisis. One element of these early programs that did endure, however, was the absence of the antipoverty "label" that characterizes many microfinance programs elsewhere in the world. Instead, according to James Cook, microfinance in Russia was seen as a way "to get businesses started and to graduate to larger loan sizes." This attitude toward microfinance as a standard lending product, combined with the fact that many of the first microfinance lenders in Russia were banks, not NGOs, has contributed to Russia's progress in creating an inclusive financial sector in which microfinance is an important participant.

Returning to Russia's largest banks, although the term *oligarch* was not applied to the Russian financial elite until early 1996, Russia's wealthiest bankers had begun to achieve oligarch status by the middle of the decade.[46] An imprecise term, it referred to the wealthy businessmen who orbited around Yeltsin and who had largely amassed their initial wealth through banking and banking conglomerates. By the time the term came into use, these banking businesses had in many cases expanded into FIGs. A few oligarchs, such as Boris Berezovsky, had a business network that included a bank but in which the non-bank business—in Berezovsky's case, the automobile business—was more prominent. Berezovsky also owned one of Russia's three largest television networks; one of the other two was owned by fellow oligarch Vladimir Gusinsky. Six of eight of Russia's best-known oligarchs had majority ownership or control of a bank that was ranked as one of the twenty largest banks in Russia(see table 3.4, which lists their primary assets in 1995, prior to the loans-for-shares program).

There were two iconic events in the evolution of the oligarchs, the first of which was the loans-for-shares program of 1995. Designed as

[45] Alexander Sharonov, president, NBD Bank, telephone interview with author, January 30, 2006.

[46] The first use of the term "oligarch" is usually attributed to Russian sociologist Olga Kryshtanovskaya, who entitled a January 1996 essay in *Izvestiya*, "The Financial Oligarchy in Russia."

TABLE 3.4.
Russian Oligarchs

Name of oligarch	Primary asset[a]	Bank size rank, top 20[b]
Alexander Smolensky	SBS Agro	3
Vladimir Vinogradov	Inkombank	4
Vladimir Potanin	Oneksimbank	5
Mikhail Khodorkovsky	Bank Menatep	10
Rem Vyakhirev	Gazprom (Bank Imperial, Gazprombank, National Reserve Bank)	12 (Bank Imperial); 13 (National Reserve Bank)
Mikhail Friedman, Petr Aven	Alfa Bank	17
Vladimir Gusinsky	Media Most (Most Bank)	NA
Boris Berezovsky	LogoVAZ (Ob"edenennyi Bank, AvtoVAZbank)	NA

[a] In cases where the primary asset as of early 1995 was not a bank, the bank associated with the oligarch is in parentheses.
[b] Ranking is as of July 1, 1996, *Finansovye Izvestiya*, August 13, 1996.

a controlled method of privatization, the program initially appeared to be a form of collateralized lending by the banks to the increasingly cash-strapped government, against which the banks would receive—and manage—blocks of shares in government–owned companies. If the loans were not repaid—and ultimately none were—the banks were required to sell the shares and return 70 percent of the proceeds to the government.

Although much purple prose has been written about the loans-for-shares program, the transparent nature of its insider deals is genuinely startling. The banks that had made the original loans and organized the tenders typically won them, and at prices only slightly higher than the minimum bid. Even though all of these companies required significant investment by the buyers, the acquisition prices were still notably low. Some of the most significant acquisitions of the loans-for-shares program were Oneksimbank's acquisition of 38 percent of Norilsk Nickel for $170.1 million, its acquisition of 51 percent of the oil company Sidanco, of which it sold just 10 percent to British Petroleum two years later for a profit of approximately $475 million; Menatep's purchase of 85 percent of Yukos Oil for $309.1 million; and LogoVAZ's assumption of 51 percent control over the oil company Sibneft, with the help of SBS-Agro Bank, for $100.1 million.[47]

[47] Johnson, *Fistful of Rubles*, table 6.2, p. 186.

The loans-for-shares program was followed by the second iconic event of the oligarch period: the 1996 presidential elections. These brought the oligarchs out from individual conversations in the corridors of power, in which each oligarch looked after his own interest, to concerted public efforts to ensure the reelection of President Yeltsin.

Due to the ill health and consequent inattention of President Yeltsin, combined with the seemingly endless uncertainty of almost everyone's daily life, Yeltsin's poll ratings had fallen into the single digits by early 1996. In noteworthy contrast, Communist Party candidate Gennady Zyuganov was earning the highest ratings of all of the candidates, while his party had won the largest share—35 percent—of the votes in the December Duma elections. Zyuganov was therefore received as Russia's potential next president at the Davos World Economic Forum in February 1996, where he both impressed the participants and alarmed the Russian oligarchs who observed his favorable reception. According to Berezovsky, who has been the most forthcoming raconteur of the events at Davos and subsequently, he and Gusinsky agreed on the spot to join forces with other oligarchs—creating the "Davos pact" to ensure that Yeltsin was reelected.[48]

Although the intricacies of President Yeltsin's reelection may never be publicly known, the support of the oligarchs was critical. They understood the gravity of the situation and helped convince Yeltsin to change his campaign style; they made substantial funding available for the campaign; and Berezovsky and Gusinsky used their media networks to support Yeltsin. Anatoly Chubais, who had managed Russia's privatization program and was hired as Yeltsin's campaign manager, described the effect of their participation as follows: "The fact that big capital turned to Yeltsin had a very serious impact on . . . all of the political elite of the country, a psychological impact."[49]

Although Berezovsky's self-confidence often makes his proclamations extreme, his oft-cited comment to the *Financial Times* following Yeltsin's successful reelection that "we have the right to occupy

[48] David E. Hoffman, *The Oligarchs: Wealth and Power in the New Russia* (New York: Public Affairs, 2002), 325–58.

[49] Hoffman observes that the oligarchs may have provided funding on the basis of discounted government bonds that were made available to them; they used the profits from selling the bonds to finance Yeltsin's campaign. The Anatoly Chubais comment from an interview with Hoffman is cited on p. 329.

government posts and enjoy the fruits of our victory" does convey the atmosphere of that time. And, as if confirming Berezovsky's statement, President Yeltsin named Oneksimbank president Vladimir Potanin as the new deputy prime minister responsible for economic affairs, while Berezovsky became a member of Russia's Security Council.

Clearly, a generalized retelling of these events cannot do justice to the more intricate relationships underlying these larger develop-ments. However, the relationship between the oligarchs and the gov-ernment had some fissures even at its height. The oligarchs' wallets were hurt by the 1996 decision to allow foreigners to participate in the ruble government debt market, which lowered interest rates by making the market more competitive. They were also negatively affected by the 1997 decision to bring the authorized bank system under control and to eventually abolish it entirely. Oneksimbank alone lost an esti-mated \$862 million in funding when it lost the account of the State Customs Committee.[50] The loans-for-shares program also contributed to changes in the relationship between the oligarchs and the govern-ment, because it led the oligarchs to turn not only their attention but also their financial resources to their new assets.

Despite these underlying developments, it was not clear at the time when or how the relationship that had evolved between Russia's banks, the government, and the CBR would ever significantly change course. At least not until 1998.

The Financial Crisis, August 1998 to 2000

More than eight years after the August 1998 financial crisis, as this chapter is being written, it is impossible to construct a complete picture of what actually took place. This difficulty applies both to the financial impact of the crisis and to the actions taken by the banks, the CBR, and the government in the wake of the crisis. This lack of transparency is consistent with the mutual dependence relationship,

[50] Stephanie Baker-Said, "Uneximbank to Lose State Customs Funds," August 8, 1997, Moscow Times.com, http://www.moscowtimes.ru (accessed September 14, 2006).

because it provided all concerned with cover for their actions pre- and postcrisis.

One example of this lack of transparency is provided by comparing the results of a World Bank postcrisis review of eighteen large Russian banks with the data provided by these same banks at the same time to the CBR. Whereas the World Bank review concluded that fifteen of the eighteen banks were insolvent,[51] only eight were insolvent according to the CBR data.[52]

Because of the unreliability of the systemwide CBR data for this period, this discussion will focus on the eighteen privately owned banks that were reviewed by the World Bank. Although these banks accounted for only 8 percent of total bank lending as of year-end 1997, they provide a particularly telling perspective of the condition of Russia's banking sector. Most of these banks had participated in a banking-sector project designed by the World Bank, and, at least when originally accredited to the program, they were considered to be among Russia's most promising banks.[53] Therefore, the losses realized by this group could actually underrepresent the losses of the banking system; other, less promising banks could have had greater losses. On the other hand, because most of these banks were large, Moscow based, and well known to major international banks, the losses of this group could overrepresent the losses to the banking sector overall; this group had the largest exposure to Russian government investments and to foreign currency borrowings from foreign banks.

Regardless of these caveats, the crucial point is that the impact of the crisis on this bank sample is breathtaking. Most shocking, the combined capital of this group fell from $5.96 billion as of the end of 1997 to a negative $9.8 billion immediately following the crisis. Even if

[51] The World Bank report was based on bank data of September 1 and October 1, 1998. There was some debate regarding whether the World Bank's review applied standards that were stricter than those required by IAS . Whether or not that was the case, the difference in overall conclusions is merely a matter of degree. John van Schaik, "The Newly-Wed and the Nearly Dead," *Euromoney* 362 (June 1999), 254–63.

[52] One factor contributing to this difference is that banks reported to the CBR according to Russian accounting standards, which at the time differed significantly from IAS. Furthermore, because of the weak supervisory system and underdeveloped audit profession, there was no way to be certain that the reporting was accurate.

[53] The accreditation process began at the end of 1994.

the year-end 1997 capital figure is adjusted for the postcrisis exchange rate, the decline in capital is almost 800 percent.[54]

The sources of the losses read like a catalog of mismanagement by the banks and the superficial supervision by the CBR that had evolved over the preceding years. As the World Bank report stated, "Some of the bigger Russian banks are so deficient in capital, and have so compromised their reputation with creditors, both foreign and domestic, that their situation is beyond repair."

The largest contributor was loan losses, which accounted for 34 percent of total losses and represented over two times bank capital at year-end 1997.[55] Although this is an extraordinarily high level of loan losses, it is readily explained by the incentive structure of the oligarch period. Because lending was not a primary source of earnings, insufficient attention was paid to following sound lending principles. Instead, banks had high concentrations of loans to shareholders and related parties, many of whom either could not—or would not—repay their loans after the crisis.

For those who could not repay their loans, one frequent factor was a currency mismatch; they had borrowed in dollars, because interest rates were lower, but their revenue was in rubles. The decline of the ruble from 5.96/$1 at year-end 1997 to 16/$1 immediately after the crisis (and 20.7/$1 by year-end 1998) saddled these borrowers with almost three times the effective debt level. And, given the overall weakened state of the economy, achieving any earnings had become substantially more difficult.

However, many shareholders and related parties also chose not to repay their loans, because these payments would only have been used to repay lenders and depositors; a shareholder was better off letting his bank go bankrupt than returning borrowed money that would then be distributed to his creditors.

Foreign currency losses accounted for another 28 percent of the banks' losses. These losses included the forward contracts that have already been noted, as well as the same currency mismatch between

---

[54] Applying the September 1998 exchange rate of 16 rubles/$1, year-end 1997 capital for this group of banks was $1.7 billion.

[55] Loan losses totaled 64 billion rubles, compared to year-end capital of 27.8 billion rubles.

dollar funding and ruble lending that characterized many corporate borrowers. Large banks had found it much simpler to take loans from foreign sources, including international banks and donor organizations, than to raise funding domestically. Even for those banks seeking ruble funding, the most cost-effective approach had been to focus on winning tenders to manage budgetary funds. An exception was two large banks, SBS-Agro and Inkombank, which had begun to target consumer deposits as a funding source and were estimated to have accumulated a market share of 10 percent each. For most banks, however, the concept of creating a stable base of ruble deposits from a diversified client base was largely as irrelevant as developing a diversified loan portfolio.

Estimated losses on government securities accounted for an additional 13 percent of the losses, as a result of the government's announcement of a debt moratorium.

In addition to destroying the banks' solvency, the crisis froze all market activity. Whether they were shareholders, lenders, depositors, or borrowers, all wanted to protect themselves and get money out of the banks as quickly as possible. This understandable response created a domino effect in the market, as even some regional banks that might have been relatively unaffected by the crisis—those that had no government securities and whose shareholders and other borrowers were largely involved in local businesses—found nervous clients withdrawing deposits.

This cascading decline in banking activity was exacerbated by the actions of the CBR and government. Although their response is of particular interest to us because it corresponds with the mutual dependence relationship, it was deeply distressing to all those who lost their savings in the banks.

There were three elements in the response—or nonresponse—of the CBR and the government to the crisis. First, the CBR and the government engaged in a game of good cop/bad cop regarding the CBR's failures to withdraw banking licenses. Although the CBR sometimes seemed passively aggressive in the aftermath of the crisis, its claim that it did not have sufficient legal grounds to take appropriate steps was often accurate. Bankruptcy legislation, for example, gave bank owners the right to challenge CBR delicensing decisions, thus opening the door to years of court challenges during which a bank's shareholders could easily remove anything of value from the bank. Therefore, although the CBR put both Inkombank and SBS-Agro under temporary CBR administration, both banks managed to ignore the CBR after these decisions were suspended by regional courts.[56] Another example is provided by Imperial Bank, which lost its license several days after the crisis and then fought the CBR in the courts for years before finally going out of business in 2004. The Russian government readily blamed the CBR for its inaction but failed to introduce the appropriate legislative changes.

The CBR's failure to cease the activity of insolvent banks fed the asset stripping that was particularly noticeable at some of the larger Moscow-based banks. It was clear to the banks' owners that there were no reasonable prospects of recovery—at least not on terms acceptable to them. They therefore took advantage of the CBR's inactivity to protect themselves from the claims of lenders and depositors by taking any valuable assets from their banks. The most egregious form of this asset stripping consisted of opening a new bank—a "bridge" bank—and transferring to it the clients of the old, virtually bankrupt bank. As if this weren't painful enough for those who had lost money in the original bank, few efforts were made to conceal these activities. Alexander Smolensky, the chairman of SBS-Agro, stated memorably after the crisis that individuals should "think twice before putting money in a bank with high deposit rates," while foreign creditors deserved "dead donkey ears" for the money they had lent to SBS-Agro.[57]

As Smolensky's statements demonstrate, the owners of these banks were confident they would not be held responsible for their actions. And, largely speaking, they weren't. Oneksimbank's shareholders, to cite one example, repaid its lenders about ten cents per dollar owed to them, while at the same time opening another bank that essentially resumed the business of the now defunct bank.[58]

To be fair I should note that this cataloguing of postcrisis horrors does not apply equally to all Russian banks. I'm emphasizing the

---

[56] Yevgenia Borisova, "Big Banks Shrug Off Regulators," *Moscow Times*, September 15, 1998.

[57] Quotations cited in Victoria Lavrentieva, "Largest Pre-1988 Private Retail Bank— Finally Laid to Rest," *St. Petersburg Times*, January 31, 2003.

[58] Lenders were also given a note whose future value would depend on the new bank's earnings.

actions of the oligarch banks because these banks were the most prominent and therefore their actions the best documented. They were also the ones with whom the dominant, Moscow-based mutual dependence relationship was created. In some cases this relationship was mirrored at regional and local levels, and in other cases it was not. Certainly the losses of regional and local banks were lessened because they did not have the same access as the Moscow-based banks to the government securities market or to foreign funding. However, those with close government ties and predominantly "pocket bank" loan portfolios did suffer from the drying up of government funds. In any case, although this discussion of postcrisis events inevitably generalizes, it would be unfair to imply that every Russian bank used the crisis to defraud its lenders and depositors.

In addition, the challenges of this period were horrific and could not be resolved solely by closing insolvent banks. The CBR consistently emphasized the need to achieve stability; the experience of anxious crowds forming outside bank offices raised the specter of a complete social meltdown. The withdrawal of hundreds and hundreds of banking licenses would have been more destabilizing than stabilizing in the short term. Therefore, the more legitimate criticism of the behavior of the CBR and the Russian government is the nontransparent manner in which they made decisions.

This nontransparency can be seen in the second official response to the crisis, which was to provide a number of large banks with emergency funding. The CBR announced in November 1998 that since August it had issued $3.5 billion in funding to SBS-Agro, Inkombank, Bank of Moscow, Mosbusinessbank, Most Bank, Bank Vozrozhdenie, and "several regional banks." On what basis these particular banks were chosen was never made clear, particularly since the CBR subsequently attempted to withdraw the licenses of SBS-Agro and Inkombank.[59]

Demonstrating that the government could take action when it chose to do so, the Agency for Restructuring of Credit Organizations (ARCO) was established by decree in November 1998. ARCO's mandate was to provide financing, governance, and an organizational umbrella under which banks could be restructured. However, although

[59] Katy Daigle, "Banks Bailed Out with State Loans," *Moscow Times*, November 4, 1998.

ARCO was created relatively quickly, the weakness of its mandate can be seen in its initial funding, which was the equivalent of $330 million—compared to the $9.8 billion negative equity of only eighteen banks that I noted earlier.

In addition, ARCO's political independence was almost immediately called into question by its decision to provide emergency funding on favorable terms to Alfa Bank and Bank Vozrozhdenie. The line of those requesting ARCO funding was long and desperate, and it was never clear how Alfa Bank and Bank Vozrozhdenie managed to get to the front. As a World Bank study stated, "There is a perception that the assistance provided to these [two] banks represents another instance of the state bailing out well-connected oligarchs, and ARCO's continued involvement with them tends to undermine the agency's credibility."[60]

Finally, looking for a lever to influence activity in the moribund banking sector, the CBR and the government turned to Sberbank, the majority state-owned savings bank. Sberbank's relative importance to the banking sector had gradually been declining during the oligarch period, as other banks began to provide more and better services. At the outset of the perestroika period Sberbank had had an account for the vast majority of Soviet citizens, because it was the only bank authorized to serve individuals. This monopoly on the limited consumer-banking services available at the outset of perestroika had gradually attenuated as Russians took advantage of competitive services. Although I have been largely dismissive of the genuine banking activity undertaken by the banks during the oligarch period, Inkombank and SBS-Agro had started courting Russian citizens with higher interest rates on deposits and friendlier service. As a result, Sberbank's share of the consumer deposit market had declined to about 60 percent by January 1995, after which several banking failures during the summer of 1995 and the ensuing nervousness brought the figure back to 72.5 percent as of September 1996.[61]

Sberbank's market share took another upward spike following the crisis, largely as a result of a decision by the CBR and the Duma to

---

[60] World Bank, *Building Trust: Developing the Russian Financial Sector* (Washington, D.C.: World Bank, 2002), 294.

[61] Johnson, *Fistful of Rubles*, 108.

allow individual depositors in eight of Russia's largest banks to transfer their funds to Sberbank accounts. Although the ultimate payout entailed a loss of about 50 percent, the message was clear: for small depositors who have lost money in private banks, the state-owned bank is the only savior.[62] Sberbank's share of the consumer deposit market climbed back to the 85 percent range.

It is difficult to trace the effect of the crisis on bank lending in the official figures. Because most banks did not write off their bad loans as international accounting standards would require, the CBR's year-end 1998 data do not show any noteworthy changes in lending levels relative to banking-sector assets. What is evident, however, is that after 1998 Sberbank started to take up the lending slack. Whereas Sberbank accounted for 11 percent of all lending in 1998, this amount had jumped to 24 percent by 1999 and 26 percent by 2000. Hence, although the ratio of total lending in Russia relative to banking-sector assets remained relatively stable during this period (and actually increased relative to GDP), this is largely due to increased lending by Sberbank.[63] Given Sberbank's majority state ownership, this lending increase was inevitably the result of official instructions—a return of political influence to the banking sector in another guise.

The crisis left three major marks on Russia's banking sector. First, the relationship of mutual dependence between the privately owned banks, the CBR, and the government ceased to be the sector's defining characteristic. The free-flowing money and ability to grant political favors that had held this relationship together were significantly curtailed. The government no longer had budgetary funds to place with the banks or high-yielding securities in which the banks could invest. The banks in turn had significantly less money to invest in the pet projects of government agencies or government officials. The CBR and the government both helped the banks by their inaction after the crisis, because this gave the banks' owners time to protect their individual wealth.[64] However, once this favor had been provided,

---

[62] As it turned out, U.S. dollar depositors at Inkombank who chose to wait out the bankruptcy process ultimately received 100 percent of their deposits, albeit without interest. I am grateful to Ilkka Salonen for this observation.

[63] World Bank, *Building Trust*, 167.

[64] Although this is just conjecture, it seems possible that this delay may also have allowed the banks to protect the assets of some government officials.

there was little else to offer. The oligarchs that retained their visibility moved on to other activities, while others disappeared from the scene. Of the seven oligarch banks on the top-twenty list prior to the loans-for-shares program, only three remained on this list immediately after the crisis. And, even though several oligarchs had reconstituted themselves by the early 2000s, few of their banks remained prominent.

Second, the crisis marked the point at which the power of Russia's state-owned banks began to reemerge. This began with Sberbank's reconfiguration as a safe haven for depositors and as an increasingly useful tool for the government and CBR to influence the banking sector, particularly in light of their now-defunct relationships with the oligarch banks. As I discuss in the following section, this trend has been taken further by Vneshtorgbank, the state-owned former trade-finance bank, which has positioned itself as a counterweight to Sberbank's dominance.

Finally, the crisis left the surviving banks largely on their own to pick up the pieces and figure out what to do next.

A New Start, 2000–2006

The "new start" period for Russia's financial sector, which began in early 2000, is characterized by two developments. For the first time since banking reform began during perestroika, Russian banks were forced by the lack of other profitable activities to turn their attention to lending. Although the effect on MSE lending is not yet pronounced, there are indications that the domino effect of an increasingly competitive banking market looking for new opportunities will eventually lead to a notable increase in MSE lending.

The new start period has also witnessed the weaving together of the different strands of the tapestry required to create an inclusive financial system in which microfinance providers and borrowers are fully incorporated. Not only have Russian nonbank financial institutions that serve microborrowers achieved notable progress but the legal and regulatory environment to support these MFIs and to link them with the financial system is in the final stages of development.

Nevertheless, Russia's new start period also provides a cautionary note about the risks associated with creating an inclusive financial system. Inevitably this process takes a long time, during which policymakers and legislators could lose patience or even confidence that the reforms will ultimately bear fruit. Therefore, Russia faces the risk that official efforts to accelerate MSE growth could derail the system's ability to develop naturally according to the framework that has so painstakingly been put into place.

Beginning with the first development, the increase in bank lending, several factors coalesced to create this marked change in focus. The key impetus was that the previous profit-making opportunities had either disappeared or at least decreased: the ruble had stabilized so that there was little room for currency speculation; government debt instruments no longer offered astronomical yields; and the authorized bank system was discontinued.

In addition, although the business of eluding various taxes continued, from capital export schemes to salary schemes, these became less prevalent. As banks struggled to build relationships with domestic and foreign partners, many realized that these gray area or even criminal activities were not sustainable over the longer term. A multibillion dollar Russian money-laundering scandal at the U.S. bank, Bank of New York, burst into the news in 1999 and tangibly demonstrated the risks of these activities. International pressure against money laundering received an additional impetus after the terrorist attacks on the United States in 2001 and created an additional complicating factor for those banks still involved in capital export. Finally, a decrease in tax rates on personal income and bank profits reduced incentives for both individuals and banks to underreport income.[65] As central bank governor Sergei Ignatiev stated in a speech as the end of 2005, tax evasion continued but on a smaller scale: "Unfortunately, some banks, *mostly small ones*, are involved in questionable money laundering schemes and provide services to avoid taxation and customs duty" (emphasis added).[66]

The resulting shift in attention to lending is marked. From 1999 to 2005 lending by Russian banks increased by over ten times, from

[65] The personal income tax rate was reduced to 13 percent, and the tax rate on bank profits was reduced to 34 percent.

[66] "Central Bank Calls for Greater Transparency in Banking," *Interfax Russia and CIS Banking and Finance Weekly* 13, no. 50 (750), December 10–16, 2005.

507 billion rubles at year-end 1999 to 5.5 trillion rubles by year-end 2005.[67] Although GDP increased by over four times during this period, the even more rapid growth of lending is a signature development. The ratio of bank lending to banking assets grew from 32 percent to 56 percent over this same period, providing further evidence that banks had turned their attention to using their balance sheets to make loans.[68]

Impressive as these figures are, Russian banks still have a considerable distance to go before reaching the lending levels typical of mature market economies. As one example, while lending as a proportion of Russian GDP grew from 8.5 percent in July 1998, on the eve of the crisis, to 25.3 percent at the end of 2005, this ratio often exceeds 100 percent in mature market economies. It is also common for banks in these economies to have loan portfolios that account for 60–70 percent of their assets.

A related development during this period has been an increase in competition. Not only did many banks begin to adopt similar lending-based strategies but the large capital-depleted banks could no longer provide the funding—let alone the financial sophistication—needed by Russia's largest companies. The long-term borrowing of Gazprom, for example, which is Russia's largest company, exceeded the capital of Sberbank, Russia's largest bank, by over two and a half times as of year-end 2005.[69] Large companies such as Gazprom therefore increasingly turned to major international banks for financing and advisory services. Ironically, although the activity of foreign banks physically located in Russia had been limited by official and unofficial means, their impact was ultimately felt as they began to provide services to Russian companies offshore.[70] As a result, the large banks, including

[67] The figures cited are for loans to enterprises and individuals; loans to other banks are excluded.

[68] Central Bank of Russia, "Obzor Bankovskogo Sektora Rossiyskoy Federatsii," Internet version, no. 45, July 2006, http://www.cbr.ru (accessed September 6, 2006).

[69] As of December 31, 2005, Gazprom's long-term borrowing totaled 615 billion rubles, compared to Sberbank's year-end 2005 capital of 231 billion rubles. http://www.gazprom.com and http://www.sberbank.com (accessed September 23, 2006). The Russian central bank limits a bank's total lending to a single client to 25 percent of the bank's capital.

[70] The official limit on foreign bank investment in Russia was 25 percent of banking-sector capital. Although central bank officials argued that this limit did not create

those that were part of an industrial group, began to look for other clients.

In addition, several of the banks that were related to large industrial or natural resource groups began seeking to diversify their shareholder structure as the banks became increasingly irrelevant to the financial needs of their founders. Gazprombank, for example, has announced its plans to issue new shares in 2007; these will dilute Gazprom's ownership share from 100 percent to 66 percent.[71]

Another striking development in the new start phase was the emergence of three new banks created specifically to tap new markets: Bank Russky Standart, created to provide consumer finance through consumer goods stores; DeltaCredit, a mortgage bank created by the U.S.-Russia Investment Fund; and KMB Bank, the bank for lending to microenterprises and small businesses that was created by the EBRD and other donors. All three banks showed the Russian banking sector how much potential banking business was still untouched; they also introduced tailor-made methodologies and technology to ensure their success.

The bank Russky Standart burst onto the scene in 2000 as the brainchild of Russian entrepreneur Roustam Tariko. Tariko had already built an extensive spirits importing business, followed by the launch of what became one of Russia's premier vodka brands, Russky Standart. Having had considerable hands-on experience with Russia's consumer market and distribution network, Tariko recognized the potential for providing consumer finance through sales outlets. Even more impressive than what was then a novel idea, Tariko was willing to stake part of his own fortune on this project only two years after Russia's financial crisis.

Russky Standart's business, which was backed by a proprietary credit scoring model that generated lending decisions within fifteen minutes of application, took off quickly. Total loans had soared to

---

a disincentive for foreign investors, because the limit was far from being reached, it could also be argued that it created a psychological barrier to those banks potentially interested in the market. Unofficial obstacles faced by foreign banks included the opaque and time-consuming process of obtaining (1) a bank license and (2) permission to expand into Russia's regions.

[71] Arkady Ostrovsky and Patrick Jenkins, "Dresdner to Handle Share Issue for Gazprombank," *Financial Times,* December 8, 2005.

$3.5 billion by the end of 2005, making Russky Standart the second largest consumer lender in Russia after Sberbank and one of Russia's twenty largest banks.[72] Both domestic and foreign bankers quickly took note, leading to a wide range of other consumer-finance initiatives, both at point of sale and through more traditional bank lending.[73] Just one example of the attractiveness of Russky Standart's business was provided by the attempt of the French bank BNP Paribas to buy 50 percent of the bank in 2004.

DeltaCredit provides a similar story of an entrepreneurial organization developing a tailor-made methodology for lending to a previously untapped market sector—consumer mortgages. DeltaCredit faced challenges that were even more severe than those of Russky Standart; mortgage loans are considerably larger and longer term than consumer loans and the legal framework for mortgage lending was incomplete. By addressing these issues systematically and by adjusting U.S. mortgage practices to the Russian market, DeltaCredit was able to both build a mortgage portfolio of about $200 million by mid-2005 and to demonstrate to other banks that this was a viable market. Furthermore, DeltaCredit estimates that the market will grow from its current size of approximately $1 billion to $10–20 billion by 2010. Once again, both Russian and foreign lenders took note, with Société Générale buying DeltaCredit in the fall of 2005 for 2.5 times book value.[74]

The story of KMB Bank is recounted in detail in chapter 4. Like Russky Standart and DeltaCredit, it created a methodology for lending to an untapped market—in this case MSEs—and in doing so introduced this market to other lenders as well. During 2005 Banca Intesa acquired the majority stake in KMB Bank for almost four times book value.

The successful creation of these new banks coincided with increased foreign interest and investment in Russia's banking sector.

[72] *Interfax Russia and CIS Banking and Finance Weekly* 14, no. 5 (757), January 28–February 3, 2006.

[73] It should also be noted for context that Citibank and Raiffeisenbank, two of the largest foreign-owned banks in Russia, had already been providing limited consumer financial services, such as account services and credit cards, to top-tier Russian clients, such as those with secure employment with foreign multinationals.

[74] "French Seal DeltaCredit Deal," *Moscow Times*, August 15, 2007, p. 7.

This trend is still under way and is therefore not fully reflected in the available data. Although the number of banks with foreign ownership increased from 126 at year-end 2001 to 136 at year-end 2005, their lending share increased only slightly from 7.2 percent to 8.1 percent as of April 2006.

Nevertheless, the best sense of the competitive impetus that foreign banks can provide is already visible in Russia's consumer-banking market. This is the most rapidly growing banking sector in Russia, with consumer loans/GDP having grown from 6 percent of GDP in 2000 to 13.7 percent in 2005, against the mouthwatering backdrop of ratios of 50 percent and more in mature market economies. Despite this highly competitive environment and the relatively small overall market share of foreign-owned banks, the foreign banks successfully increased their share of the consumer lending market from 5.76 percent at year-end 2003 to 8.4 at year-end 2005, in a market in which consumer lending increased 2.1 times in 2004 and 1.8 times in 2005.[75]

An important caveat regarding this information is that CBR data do not differentiate between loans made to individuals for consumer goods purposes and loans made for business purposes. The growth of banks such as Russky Standart makes it clear that much of the increase is in consumer lending, but it also masks what would be very useful information about lending to small unincorporated businesses.

The consumer-lending growth trend is likely to continue, with essentially all of Russia's largest banks, domestic and foreign-owned, having developed strategies to expand in this market. One example is Raiffeisenbank, one of Austria's largest banks, whose $550 million purchase of Impexbank in early 2006 (with a consumer-loan portfolio of $430 million) represents the largest foreign bank investment to date by absolute size.[76]

Although the sharp increase in consumer lending is the most noticeable outcome of the increasingly competitive Russian banking market, bankers expect that a future trend will be in lending to smaller businesses. According to Ilkka Salonen, president of International

[75] Central Bank of Russia, "Otchet o razvitii bankovskogo sektora i bankovskogo nadzora v 2004 godu," 20–21. Data from the 2005 report is on p. 28. http:// www.cbr .ru, (accessed December 20, 2005).

[76] *Interfax Russia*, January 28–February 3, 2006.

Moscow Bank (one of Russia's ten largest banks), the SME market will eventually become "as attractive as the consumer finance market," and the jump in SME lending will mirror that in consumer lending, once banks work out the appropriate methodology. Microborrowers are of interest as well, according to Salonen, because they are "much more loyal customers" that can grow together with the bank.[77] Another perspective on microfinance and banking was expressed by Garegin Tosyunyan, president of the Association of Russian Banks, who noted the importance of microfinance in ensuring a constant flow of new clients to the banking sector. Tosyunyan also created a memorable comparison of the financial sector with the human body: microfinance plays the role of the smallest blood vessels and capillaries, without which the arteries and veins, and the body as a whole, cannot function. The relevance of Tosyunyan's remarks was underscored by the event at which he made them: the press conference announcing the creation of the Russian National Partnership of Microfinance Market Stakeholders, of which the Association of Russian Banks is a founding member.[78]

MAP corroborated this evolving interest in smaller borrowers when it reported to the Sixth All-Russian Conference of Representatives of Small Enterprises in 2005 that "lending to small business is of real interest for banks."[79] By contrast, MAP had reported as recently as 2003 that "the banking sector is for the most part oriented toward serving large companies, which significantly raises the costs of small companies and leads to higher interest rates."[80]

The manner in which Russian banks have turned their attention toward lending in the new start period provides an unusual perspective on the mechanisms of banking-sector development. No significant regulatory changes encouraged these shifts in behavior. In fact,

[77] Ilkka Salonen, president, International Moscow Bank, telephone interview with author, January 26, 2006.

[78] Press release, "Vedushchie uchastiniki rynka obedinyayut svoi usiliya po razvitiyu sistemy mikrofinansirovaniya malogo biznesa," February 13, 2006, http://www.rmcenter.ru (accessed August 2, 2006).

[79] VI Vserossiyskaya Konferentsiya Predstaviteley Malykh Predpriyatiy, "Informatsiya o konferentsii," p. 1, http://www.siora.ru (accessed July 1, 2005).

[80] "Doklad Ministerstva Rossiykoy Federatsii po antimonopol'noy politike i poderzhke predprinimatel'stva na III Vserossiyskoy konferentsii predstaviteley malykh predpriyatiy," p. 5, http://www.siora,ru (accessed July 1, 2005).

when bankers interviewed for this book were asked which banking regulations have had the greatest impact since their bank was founded, the only consistently cited regulation was the introduction of deposit insurance in 2004.

Startling as this response first seems, it corresponds with the gradual rehabilitation of the CBR's role, from the inappropriate blurring of its functions during the 1990s to its becoming a more even-handed professional regulator in the years following the crisis. Regulations did not play an important role before the crisis; even the creation of a specialized department in 1996 as an effort to enforce regulations on the largest banks did not succeed. There were simply too many banks for the CBR to supervise; many regulations could be circumvented either by inaccurate reporting or by special arrangements with the CBR; and the CBR's incentive structure was not conducive to enforcing regulations.

During and immediately after the crisis the CBR was too preoccupied with responding to problems to be able to address longer-term regulatory issues. The CBR did continue and even strengthen its monitoring of bank compliance with legal and regulatory requirements, including suspending and withdrawing some bank licenses. Furthermore, as early as 2000 and 2001 it turned its attention to fictitious capital and put banks on notice that their inflated capital schemes were well understood.[81] These actions did not significantly affect bank behavior, however. Instead, the stripped-down postcrisis financial environment served as a form of de facto regulatory system by not providing the banks with opportunities to take on risky activities. Furthermore, the surviving banks had altered their own risk appetite, having in many cases depleted their capital to such an extent that they could ill afford to make any more mistakes.

Now that Russia has had a number of years of financial stability, and the banks have focused their activities in areas that the CBR is qualified to regulate, the CBR has gradually been able to assert its role. The successful use of deposit insurance as a tool for the CBR to

---

[81] At a banking conference in September 2002, CBR deputy chairman Andrei Kozlov noted that "no less than half" of Russia's banks had used various methods to inflate their capital during the previous ten years. Igor Moiseev, "Dva capital," *Vedemosti*, September 9, 2002.

authorize banks for participation in the program marks the high point of the CBR's professionalism since its creation. Of the 1,270 banks that applied for the program, 343 were rejected, indicating that the authorization process was taken seriously. The most tragic indication of the effectiveness of the CBR's assertion of authority can be seen in the fatal shooting in September 2006 of Andrei Kozlov, the first deputy CBR governor who led the CBR's campaign. It is assumed that Kozlov's death was arranged by a banker or bankers whose activities were threatened by his efforts to enforce the CBR's regulations.[82]

Moving from banks to nonbank lenders, the second important development during the new start period has been the creation of a legal and regulatory environment that not only includes but accommodates other financial institutions that provide services to MSEs. The approximately 1,200 of such nonbank lenders as of year-end 2005 had microfinance loans outstanding of over $500 million to about 400,000 borrowers, which is approximately the same dollar amount of microfinance lending by commercial banks. (A microfinance loan is defined as a loan of up to 300,000 rubles, or approximately $10,700.)[83]

A detailed 2004 survey by the Russian Microfinance Center covered 171 nonbank microfinance lenders with a total loan portfolio of $140 million.[84] The breakdown of the types of lenders in the survey, which was designed to be representative of the field as a whole, can be seen in table 3.5.

Looking at these lenders by type of group, Russia's credit cooperative movement has an impressive history as a grassroots undertaking, having been initiated in 1991 by a group of Moscow State University economists who were seeking ways to help families survive the wrenching changes in the Russian economy. The Law on Credit Cooperatives was adopted in 1992, following which Russia's first credit cooperative

[82] Guy Chazan, "Blood Money: Murdered Regulator in Russia Made Plenty of Enemies," *Wall Street Journal*, September 22, 2006, A1.

[83] Anna Akhmedova, "Malen'kie kredity na ogromnye summy," *Vedemosti*, June 28, 2006, http://www.rmcenter.ru (accessed August 2, 2006).

[84] Russian Microfinance Center and Resource Center of Small Entrepreneurship, "Tendentsii razvitiya rynka nebankovskogo microfinansirovaniya v Rossii, 2003–2004," Moscow, 2006, http://www.rmcenter.ru (accessed August 2, 2006).

TABLE 3.5.
Survey of Nonbank Microfinance Lenders

Type of lender[a]	Percent of market	Number of lenders
Citizen cooperatives[b]	26	62
Government funds	24	37
Private funds	21	15
Consumer cooperatives[c]	15	27
Private MFIs	8	3
Agricultural consumer credit cooperatives[d]	6	23
Other	0.3	4

Source: This table is derived from information in diagram 9, p. 22, of the 2003–4 study.

[a] A summary of the laws governing the different types of cooperatives is in FINCA International, Russian Microfinance Center, and Resource Center of Small Entrepreneurship, "Analiz razvitiya mikrofinansirovaniya v Rossii," part 2, Moscow, 2004.

[b] These organizations are governed by the Law on Citizen Consumer Credit Cooperatives, which limits membership to 2,000 individuals per cooperative and allows the cooperatives to lend to members and take deposits from them. Up to 50 percent of a cooperative's loan portfolio can consist of business loans. Citizen cooperatives are allowed to accept funding, including loans, from other organizations but cannot take deposits from nonmember individuals. Cooperatives governed by this law are allowed to make payments on behalf of their clients.

[c] These organizations are governed by the Law on Credit Cooperatives (Consumer Societies and Their Unions). Both individuals and legal entities can be members of credit cooperatives and the cooperatives can take deposits from individual members and nonmembers. They can also accept funding and loans from other organizations. All loans must be given to members. These cooperatives cannot undertake payments for their clients.

[d] These organizations are governed by the Law on Agricultural Consumer Cooperatives. This law allows both individuals and legal entities to be members, although the majority of members must be agricultural producers. Only members can place deposits and take loans; funding, including loans, can be accepted from other organizations but not from nonmember individuals. Cooperatives governed by this law cannot make payments on behalf of their clients.

was founded in the ancient city of Suzdal.[85] By the end of 2005 the movement had grown to include more than 550 agricultural credit cooperatives, which had more than 32,000 members, and approximately 600 consumer credit cooperatives.[86]

The second-largest type of lender in this table is the government funds that are largely the legacy of the Federal Fund for the Support of Small Business. Having lost access to federal funding in 2004 (the fund was closed down in 2005), the fate of these funds will now be determined individually, with some closing and some re-creating themselves with different forms of organizational structure and financial

[85] Anna Baitenova, legal adviser, Russian Microfinance Center, interview with author, Moscow, July 28, 2005.

[86] Mikhail Mamuta, "Nebankovskie mikrokredity: Kto ikh daet?" *Natsional'nyy Bankovskiy Zhurnal* 7, no. 30, July 2006, http://www.rmcenter.ru (accessed July 31, 2006).

support. As a group, these funds had the weakest loan portfolios as of year-end 2004. Although 50 percent of the lenders in the survey did not have past- due loans over thirty days of over 1.9 percent of total loans, for the state funds the past-due-loans figure was 4.9 percent.

Private funds and MFIs constitute a dynamic part of Russia's non-bank lenders, as can be seen by looking at the three largest lenders in these combined categories, two of which began operations after 1998. One such program was initiated by the Foundation for International Community Assistance (FINCA), whose programs in Samara and Tomsk had achieved combined loans outstanding of $14.8 million as of April 2006, an average loan size of $2,675, and past-due loans of under 1 percent.[87]

A second example is provided by the Russian Women's Microfinance Network, which provides funding and technical assistance to MFIs located in five locations in Russia. As of year-end 2005 the combined loan portfolios of the network's affiliates totaled $8.3 million, had an average loan size of $1,388, and past-due loans of 1 percent.[88] During 2005 the network became the first organization in Russia to receive a nonbank deposit-and-lending license from the CBR. This newly created type of license provides these organizations with the credibility of CBR supervision in the context of a lower-capital requirement (€500,000 instead of the minimum €5 million required for newly created banks) and less stringent reporting requirements. Correspondingly, organizations with this type of license are not authorized to take retail deposits.[89]

The third example, and a third direction of development, is provided by OI's program, which consolidated its five regional organizations to create FORA in 2001. FORA continued to expand in an essentially untapped market until 2004, when some of its larger borrowers began to turn to other lenders who could provide larger loans and more products and services. Seeing this as the beginning of a longer-term trend, as the interest of banks in smaller borrowers was also growing, FORA's board concluded that converting its operations

[87] http://www.villagebanking.org (accessed September 14, 2006).

[88] Anna Gincherman, Relationship Manager for Eastern Europe and the Middle East, Women's World Banking, correspondence with author, September 19, 2006.

[89] Mikhail Mamuta, director, Russian Microfinance Center, telephone interview with author, September 14, 2006.

into a bank would enhance its ability to help its borrowers continue to grow. A bank license would also enable FORA to expand its funding sources and create a more solid legal foundation for its operations, which until then had been operating according to unclear provisions of the civil code and the banking law.[90]

FORA converted to FORUS Bank during 2005, making history in Russia by being the first microfinance lender to convert to banking operations. As of year-end 2005 the FORA Fund, which was in the process of transferring its operations to the bank, had loans outstanding of over $27 million, an average loan size of $1,950, and past-due loans of under 1 percent.[91]

Complementing the growth of Russia's nonbank lenders have been efforts to incorporate them more closely into the financial system and to improve the legal and regulatory environment in which they function. The developments I outline below represent critical steps in finalizing a genuinely inclusive financial sector in Russia.

Efforts to strengthen the linkages between MFIs and banks include the CBR's agreement to revise a regulation that requires significant loan-loss provisioning by banks lending to MFIs and has therefore served as a deterrent to such lending.[92] In addition, the CBR's authorization of a new type of license for non–deposit-taking lending organizations, the first of which was granted to the Russian Women's World Banking Finance Network, brings these organizations under CBR supervision.

A further step, which is potentially more controversial, is a government program that provides partial guarantees (up to 50 percent) for lending to MFIs and SMEs. This program was designed to enable MFIs and new businesses that do not have sufficient collateral to obtain bank funding. The intention is to help these borrowers establish a track record so that they can subsequently borrow without a guarantee.[93]

---

[90] Schrader interview.

[91] http://www.forafund.ru (accessed September 14, 2006).

[92] Summary of remarks by G. Petrova, deputy sector head of the CBR Department of Regulation and Supervision, at the February 21, 2006, meeting of the Subcommittee on Microfinance of the Russian Chamber of Commerce and Trade and the Committee for the Development of Microfinance of the Association of Russian Banks, http://www.rmcenter.ru (accessed August 6, 2006).

[93] Alliance Media, "Moskva: Opredeleny 10 bankov dlya realizatsii programmy kreditovaniya MB," August 28, 2006, http://www.opora.ru (accessed September 14, 2006).

Although this program contradicts microfinance best practices, the fact that borrowers can access the program only once is an important feature that could help it realize its objectives.

Progress has also been made in improving the environment for Russia's cooperatives, which have operated without supervision and in an unclear legal and regulatory environment created by the overlapping of the three laws that address credit cooperative activities.[94] These two issues represent the biggest unclosed gap in the inclusive financial system framework. As of the third quarter of 2006 the Ministry of Finance was seriously evaluating alternatives for supervising the cooperatives, and a second draft of a revised law on cooperatives was under active discussion.[95]

The revised Law on State Support for Small Entrepreneurship, which I discussed in chapter 2, as well as the proposed new Law on Microfinance Organizations, will also play important roles by resolving gaps and contradictions in the legal and regulatory environment. A further development that will help small borrowers, regardless of the type of lender, is the creation of credit bureaus that began in 2005. Good borrowers will be able to create an independently documented track record that can be used in all of their loan applications.

A critical factor underpinning this progress in building an inclusive financial system is that throughout its over ten-year history in Russia, microfinance has retained its image as a lending methodology designed for small borrowers without a formal borrowing history and minimal collateral. It was not introduced to Russia as a poverty-alleviation mechanism, and it has never acquired that label. Mikhail Mamuta, the director of the Russian Microfinance Center, summarized this viewpoint with his observation that microfinance is a business development tool, albeit one that can play a role in poverty reduction by providing business opportunities.[96] Although Russia's unusual social and economic circumstances in the early 1990s account for the way in which microfinance was introduced in Russia, the fact that it has been embraced so broadly by bankers, regulators,

---

[94] The Law on Agricultural Cooperation (1995), the Law on Consumer Cooperation (1997), and the Law on Consumer Cooperatives of Citizens (2001).

[95] Mamuta interview.

[96] Mamuta interview.

legislators, and policymakers provides a useful perspective on maximizing microfinance's audience.

It makes intuitive sense that a more competitive and inclusive lending market will lead to more MSE lending as an undertapped market, and anecdotal evidence supports this assessment, but it is not yet possible to demonstrate that this is actually the case. Part of the inability is due to data shortcomings, but it's clear nonetheless that MSE lending in Russia remains at low levels. Loans to microenterprises (loans up to approximately $10,700) are estimated to be $1 billion, compared with demand of $5–$7 billion, while loans to small enterprises are estimated to be $5 billion, compared with demand of $30 billion.[97] An OPORA survey of small businesses and individual entrepreneurs yielded similar results. It found that only 15.8 percent of the respondents were using bank loans; another 22.4 percent had wanted bank funding but had either not received it or had found the terms unacceptable.[98]

"We wouldn't have been able to take advantage of the market potential without financing."

Café Inc. opened for business in October 1998, two months into Russia's financial crisis.[99] The business, which was founded by three partners, provides cafeteria services for companies that offer their employees an opportunity to eat on the premises. Café Inc. was able to break into the business because it knew the supply market better than some of its foreign competitors and was able to offer less expensive services. This advantage turned out to be particularly relevant in the midst of the crisis.

Although Café Inc.'s start-up costs were not high, because it is largely a service business, its ability to borrow money to get started was key. As the company's marketing manager put it, "We wouldn't have

---

[97] Russian Microfinance Center, "Mikrofinansirovaniye v Rossii," June 29, 2006, presentation. The small business estimates are from the journal *Ekspert* and are cited in the RMC presentation.

[98] OPORA and VITsOM, "Usloviya i factory," 62–64.

[99] The names of the company and interviewee are pseudonyms.

been able to take advantage of the market potential without financing." Café Inc. is now one of the three biggest players in its market and finds that the strongest competition is from smaller companies that are able to undercut their prices. So, buying them out—and growing further—is the only way to succeed. The market's potential continues to be enormous, including expanding to other cities as well as to other types of institutions, such as schools, hospitals, and prisons.

The Russian government's program to reduce the administrative burden on small businesses has actually made business more complicated for Café Inc. Whereas previously the myriad food inspectors could be bribed to avoid the need to comply with outdated regulations, the increased scrutiny of the behavior of inspectors and regulators has made this shortcut much more difficult.

It's important to recall for context that small entrepreneurs surveyed in the 2004 CEFIR–World Bank study rated access to finance as only their sixth most serious constraint, out of nine potential constraints.[100] On the other hand, 50.1 percent of the entrepreneurs in the OPORA survey noted above stated that they had sufficient financing to continue their businesses at the current level but not to grow; only 24.1 percent were confident that they had sufficient financing to grow.[101] Russian policymakers, like their counterparts all over the world, understandably see room for improvement in these financing figures and search for ways to help. It's unfortunate that some of these efforts inadvertently pose the biggest risk to the natural growth of MSE finance. One program targeted at MSEs deserves note, as does the broader issue of banking-sector competitiveness.

The Federal Fund for the Support of Small Business was the government's primary vehicle for providing financial support for small business from its creation in 1995 until it was closed down in 2005 following a survey revealing that only 5 percent of Russian entrepreneurs

[100] This was a slight improvement over the 2001 survey, when access to finance had been ranked fifth.
[101] OPORA and VITsOM, "Usloviya i factory," 55.

even knew of its existence.[102] The fund's mandate was to support small business development through a variety of activities, including improving the enabling environment, facilitating investment, providing guarantees to small business support programs, and providing direct loans at subsidized interest rates to small businesses.[103] Although the fund was consistently hobbled by inadequate funding, all of the entrepreneurs interviewed for this book who were asked about their experience with the fund simply rolled their eyes. As one entrepreneur explained, "These programs are for the Halliburtons"—in other words, the well connected.[104]

Given the fund's failure, it is perplexing that a similar program was introduced by the Russian Development Bank, a state-owned bank created in 1999. As in the case of the fund, the Russian Development Bank's support for small business consists largely of making loans to regional banks for them to lend in amounts of up to $360,000 to small businesses. The federal government's 2004 budget included a $90 million allocation for the bank to raise funds against a state guarantee. The bank has also raised funding without a state guarantee and by the end of 2005 had concluded loan agreements totaling $360 million with sixty-four regional governments.[105]

The primary shortcoming of the Russian Development Bank's program is the subsidized interest rates provided to borrowers; as of the end of 2005, the maximum ruble interest rate was 15 percent, compared to a market rate of 20 percent and higher. One problem with such subsidies is that they run the risk of creating unsustainable lending programs; once the donor can no longer provide a subsidy, there is usually no program.

[102] Peter Rutland, "Russian Small Business: Staying Small," *Jamestown Foundation Eurasia Daily Monitor*, March 15, 2005, reprinted in Johnson's Russia List, http://www.cdi.org/russia/johnson.

[103] The fund was positioned at the apex of a three-tier network of 75 regional and 170 municipal funds that it helped to create.

[104] The fund was hampered throughout its existence by insufficient financial resources; its sole source of funding was the federal budget, which provided no allocations during the difficult years of 1998 and 1999. The fund was further crippled by the loss of 400 million rubles held in Russian banks that failed during the crisis. Sylvie K. Bossoutrot, "Microfinance in Russia: Finance for Micro and Small Entrepreneurs," World Bank Working Paper, October 2005.

[105] "Nachali s malogo," *Profil*, September 9, 2005, reproduced on the website of the Russian Development Bank, http://www.rosbr.ru (accessed December 23, 2005).

In addition, interest-rate subsidies are unlikely to generate independent interest in microbusiness or small business lending by the participating banks, for whom the allowable margin, in this case 3–4 percent, is relatively low. As I discussed in chapter 1, lending to MSEs is a staff-intensive and expensive process that is only of genuine interest to banks when they can charge interest rates and fees that ensure them an attractive profit. A related consideration is that the scope of the Russian Development Bank's program is so broad that none of the participating banks will be able to create the economies of scale necessary for a sustainable MSE program.

Finally, because MSEs are able to pay market rates, subsidizing the rate can create a vicious cycle by giving the impression that the funding is more of a grant than a loan, therefore reducing the borrower's incentive to repay the loan—and sometimes creating the impression that MSE borrowers have so many problems that they need even more financial support. Instead, as Vneshtorgbank vice president Sergey Suchkov stated at the Sixth All-Russian Conference of Representatives of Small Enterprises, the main problem for Russian small business today is not the *cost* of a loan but the difficulty of getting a loan.[106]

"Why does the state make loans to small businesses when we can get loans from banks?"

Andrei Berezovsky is a former physicist with the serious but modest air of a person confident in his ability to solve problems. Berezovsky's first private venture in the 1990s was developing banking software. This led him to explore starting a specialized journal, which he ultimately concluded would not be a profitable venture. Berezovsky's research into journal publication, however, led him to the world of offset printing. Because most high-quality printing in the mid-1990s was being imported from Western Europe, Berezovsky saw the opportunity to develop domestic capacity. The fact that offset printing had a technical component was also important, because his scientific background gave him an upper hand in mastering the technology. In addition, according to

[106] VI Vserossiyskaya Konferentsiya, "Informatsiya o konferentsii," p. 8, http://www .siora.ru (accessed July 1, 2005).

Berezovsky, criminal groups were less interested in technically complex businesses because they were too difficult to monitor.

Berezovsky started the business, Fabrika Ofsetnoy Pechati, with his own savings and ingenuity. His first printer, which he bought second-hand and refurbished himself, now looks forlorn amid the shiny German and Japanese equipment that dominate his shop. Looking back, Berezovsky says the first four years were the most difficult. It took a year to master the technology of the business and then several more to learn how to deal effectively with equipment suppliers. He has concluded that it is more important to purchase equipment with good service contracts than to purchase top-of-the-line equipment. Another challenge at the beginning was theft by employees; Berezovsky was not able to control this problem until he was able to implement a comprehensive accounting system. Although Berezovsky was accustomed to being self-reliant, external financing made an important difference in his ability to grow. Never even having considered the possibility of approaching a bank, Berezovsky said that "when SBS-Agro Bank contacted me and offered me a loan, I couldn't believe it."[107]

Berezovsky has the same matter-of-fact attitude toward the 1998 crisis as the other entrepreneurs interviewed for this book. One of the biggest problems was his SBS-Agro loan, which, because it was denominated in dollars, became substantially more expensive with the decline of the ruble. Demand for advertising increased substantially after the crisis, as Russian companies couldn't afford foreign printing and wanted to take advantage of the dearth of imported goods. But they had no money with which to pay for the advertising. Berezovsky managed to negotiate acceptable terms with everyone and emerged from the crisis with a much stronger business.

As of the end of 2005, Berezovsky's issues are those of success. His business has grown so much that he needs to move outside of Moscow, with considerable costs entailed in moving heavy printing equipment. He is thinking of diversifying into a manufacturing business. He's interested in leasing products but is also able to get delayed payment terms

[107] SBS-Agro was a participant in the EBRD MSE-lending program discussed in chapter 4.

from equipment suppliers—an unusual accomplishment for a Russian businessman. Has he ever thought of taking advantage of Russian government small business support programs? His answer: "Why does the state make loans to small businesses when we can get loans from banks?"

This discussion brings us to the state-owned banks Sberbank and Vneshtorgbank, whose combined loan portfolios at year-end 2005 exceeded 41 percent of the banking sector's loans. The case of Vneshtorgbank is important because it demonstrates the state's ongoing concern about MSE finance and its levers for addressing that concern. The impetus for Vneshtorgbank's program was a meeting in January 2004 between President Putin and Andrei Kostin, the chairman of Vneshtorgbank. Following the meeting Kostin announced that Vneshtorgbank, which had previously focused on large financings, often with an international component, would lend $1 billion to smaller businesses that year.[108] Although it soon became clear that creating a creditworthy loan portfolio of $1 billion in MSE loans would take longer than a year, Vneshtorgbank started its program within six months, and had accumulated an MSE loan portfolio of $34.5 million in its first year of operation.[109] By the third quarter of 2006 the portfolio exceeded $400 million.[110]

It is exactly this kind of relationship between state-owned banks and the state, in which one conversation with the president or a senior state official can lead to a complete change in direction, that creates concern. Vneshtorgbank and Sberbank are both large enough that they could easily make the market unattractive for commercial lenders if they followed the example of the Russian Development Bank and introduced nonmarket conditions into their MSE programs. It's

[108] Bossoutrot, "Microfinance in Russia," 31.

[109] "VTB-22 to Build Small Business Loan Portfolio to 5 bln Rubles," *Interfax*, September 9, 2005. Vneshtorgbank defines microloans as loans up to $30,000; medium loans are up to $1 million. http://www.vneshtorgbank.ru (accessed December 22, 2005).

[110] Sergey Suchkov, vice president, VTB-24, telephone interview with author, September 13, 2006.

important to stress that currently both programs operate according to market principles. Furthermore, the rapid growth of Vneshtorgbank's subsidiary responsible for the micro- and SME program, VTB-24, has created a positive demonstration effect in the market. In fact, far from dominating the market, Suchkov noted that his biggest challenge is expanding staff quickly enough to meet market demand.[111] Nevertheless, a change in direction could be readily implemented.

Looking at the impact of the state-owned banks more generally, there is also the risk that their dominance of the market could prevent the increasing competitiveness in the market from reaching its full potential. This could happen simply as a result of their size, with recent research indicating that bank concentration increases the difficulty of obtaining financing in countries with low levels of economic and institutional development. Moreover, this effect is increased by a larger share of state-owned banks. This research also concludes that the negative effect of concentration is felt more strongly by SMEs than by large companies.[112]

The Russian government has not indicated any concern about the dominant role of Sberbank and Vneshtorgbank. Russia's case is particularly unusual because rather than following the worldwide trend to reduce the role of state banks the Russian government is supporting the growth of Vneshtorgbank, which has been much smaller than Sberbank since the breakup of the Soviet Union. According to the joint Russian government–central bank strategy for the banking sector, the central bank will maintain its controlling share of Sberbank for the "near future," while the government intends to maintain a sufficient share ownership of Vneshtorgbank "to enable it to influence its policies."[113] Plans are also underway to create a new Russian Bank of Development that would merge the current Russian Bank of Development and two smaller state-owned banks. It can only be hoped that the two themes in this section—the market-generated increase in lending by Russian banks and progress in finalizing an

[111] Suchkov interview.

[112] Thorsten Beck, Asli Demirguc-Kunt, and Vojislav Maksimov, "Bank Competition and Access to Finance," draft dated May 2003.

[113] Pravitel'stvo Rossiyskoy Federatsii i Tsentral'nogo Banka Rossiyskoy Federatsii, "O Strategii razvitii bankovskogo sektora Rossiyskoy federatsii na period do 2008 goda," April 4, 2005, http://www.cbr.ru (accessed December 20, 2005).

inclusive financial system—will continue regardless of developments in the state-owned banks.

The changes in Russia's banking sector since the beginning of perestroika are as striking as the changes in the MSE sector discussed in chapter 2, with banks aggressively seeking opportunities in a market that barely existed when perestroika began. The extent and ongoing impact of these changes makes it clear that analyzing financing for MSEs requires a bigger picture perspective than that of the MSE market alone. The historical disinterest in lending to Russian MSEs had less to do with the MSEs themselves than with the availability of other opportunities. Once the incentive structure changed, lending in general, including lending to MSEs, has become of more interest to banks. Although the concept of an inclusive financial sector typically entails educating established financial market players about the relevance of microfinance, the concept can also be applied in another way: the successful creation of an inclusive financial system requires understanding the financial system and its development as a whole.

This broader and historical approach also helps put market developments into perspective. Although MSE lending levels in Russia are currently low, they appear to be at the beginning of an upward trend. It is ironic that the full realization of this trend, which has been achieved with the help of sound policy and regulatory decisions, could face the greatest risk—inadvertently—from Russian policymakers. One such risk is posed by the mere dominance of Sberbank and Vneshtorgbank—their market power alone could prevent Russia's banking sector from reaching its full competitive potential. Even more damaging would be large-scale programs, implemented through these banks or other vehicles, to use subsidized interest rates or guarantee programs to increase MSE lending.

The danger of such programs is the havoc that they wreak in markets that are independently developing their own interest and skills in MSE lending. In chapter 2 I argued that the resilience of Russia's entrepreneurs demonstrates that they don't need government handouts to survive. In this chapter I have shown that interest in MSE lending is increasing, albeit gradually, as banking-sector competitiveness has grown and as the legal and regulatory environment for such lending, including by NBFIs, has been strengthened.

Chapter 4, which recounts the story of KMB Bank, a bank founded to serve MSE clients, illustrates the commercial sustainability of this business. Russia's experience provides an example of how to involve commercial lenders in closing the global microfinance gap. We would all lose if well-intended state efforts to accelerate this process derail the progress that has been made.

Chapter 4

KMB BANK, THE RUSSIAN SMALL BUSINESS CREDIT BANK

This book's three themes of microfinance, the emergence of Russian entrepreneurs, and banking-sector development intersect at KMB Bank, the bank founded in 1999 by the EBRD to lend to micro- and small entrepreneurs.[1] KMB contributes to our evolving understanding of microfinance because it has always treated micro- and small entrepreneurs as closely related, even overlapping, groups. The fact that 59 percent of KMB's clients more than doubled their loan size over five years is evidence that this approach can be successful in helping clients grow. KMB's own growth deserves note as well; at the end of 2005 its loan portfolio of $415 million made it one of the largest non-state-owned MSE banks in the world. In addition, KMB's experience demonstrates that MSE finance can be attractive to commercial banks, with Banca Intesa, the second largest bank in Italy, having acquired majority ownership at the end of 2005.

KMB also provides another vantage point for looking at the development of Russian entrepreneurs, for whom lack of finance is frequently a stumbling block. Although not every Russian who wants to borrow money will be a successful borrower and businessperson, KMB's case study shows that, with the right methodology, there are substantially more good borrowers out there than most of us would

---

[1] The acronym is based on the bank's Russian name, which is Bank Kreditovaniya Malogo Biznesa.

have expected. This experience casts serious doubt on the assumption that the key to helping entrepreneurs raise more financing is reducing the risk to the lenders.

KMB's story is also a microexample of a bank operating in the macroenvironment of Russia's banking sector. The early chaos of Russia's banking sector never actually prevented Russian banks from lending; instead, it created incentives that made other activities more attractive than lending. When KMB and other banks started lending more actively after the 1998 crisis, the environment was sufficiently conducive for them to do so. Borrowers were certainly available and the regulatory environment, although in disarray, was not prohibitive. Therefore banks such as KMB that had well-honed lending methodologies were able to grow as quickly as their funding and infrastructure allowed and to develop sound loan portfolios that minimized the need to resort to the problem-ridden court system. In the process, KMB has contributed to the postcrisis evolution of Russia's banking sector by demonstrating that entrepreneurs can be good clients.

In this chapter I devote considerable detail to the range of challenges encountered by KMB, in order to give readers a hands-on feel for the ups and downs of KMB's daily existence. Furthermore, although every problem or challenge is unique in its details, many of KMB's challenges more generally are characteristic of those facing MSE lenders founded by donors and socially committed investors: managing growth, ensuring sound corporate governance, operating in the vicissitudes of a developing economy, finding the balance between profitability and mission, and ensuring the continuation of MSE lending after the exit of the original founders. This microlevel discussion provides a counterpoint to the more macro discussion of financial-sector and MSE development of the previous chapters.

The chapter is organized according to the five chronological stages of KMB's growth. First, I describe the EBRD's Russia Small Business Fund (RSBF) program that preceded KMB and whose crisis, brought on by the Russian financial crisis of 1998, led to the creation of KMB. KMB was founded in 1999; this second stage through the end of 2001 encompassed the "getting started" years. KMB evolved during this period from an EBRD program into a bank, while achieving a loan portfolio of almost $100 million. The third stage is the "turning point" years of 2002 through mid-2003. The challenges of growth caught up with KMB during this period, both in managing a rapidly growing bank—the first serious fraud occurred in 2002—and expanding the capital base, which precipitated a shareholder debate about KMB's future direction. The fourth or "maturity" stage began in mid-2003, following agreement among the shareholders about how to balance KMB's social and profit motives. The maturing of KMB can be seen in the nature of the bank's products and business, the market's growing recognition of KMB, and the evolution of the bank's loan portfolio. This fourth stage overlaps with the fifth, which began in the fall of 2004 and consisted of the search for a strategic investor to further expand KMB's capital and bring in additional technical expertise.

Throughout these phases, three themes have been critical to KMB's successful development. First, KMB was led from the beginning by an outstanding chief executive officer, Reiner Mueller-Hanke, who had played a major role in building up the Russia Small Business Fund for the EBRD and had also had previous management roles in MFIs in South America. Mueller-Hanke's ability to manage and motivate an ever-growing staff and adapt to the changing demands of the Russian banking market was invaluable to KMB's survival. Furthermore, for its first four years, KMB was run under a management contract by IPC, an experienced micro- and small business finance consulting company that put an effective management team in place and trained KMB's staff.[2] Finally, KMB's shareholders successfully addressed the issue that eventually faces all MFIs: how to balance the social mission with the need for financial sustainability. Although this issue can be emotional and divisive, the key to success in KMB's case was that the final resolution was accepted by all of the shareholders: it was not a lingering source of dissent.

The Russia Small Business Fund, 1993–1998

The EBRD's RSBF program began modestly as one of a gamut of programs designed in the early 1990s to assist the crisis-ridden Russian economy. These programs ranged from participating in the privatization of large state-owned enterprises to encouraging foreign investment,

---

[2] IPC is discussed in chapter 1.

from efforts to strengthen the banking sector to programs to encourage the growth of small business. Although the successful development of small business and microlending has since become a hallmark of the EBRD's activities, this outcome was certainly not predictable in the early 1990s.

The RSBF program was initiated in April 1993 by the Group of 7 (G-7), which requested the EBRD to create a $300 million small-business-lending program for Russia. Half of the program was to be financed by the G-7 and half by the EBRD. Reflecting the untested nature of this type of project, the EBRD began with a $10 million pilot project, approved by the EBRD's board of directors in June 1993, followed by a $45.5 million extended pilot project, approved in March 1995. A key aspect of the extended pilot project was that it expanded the product range from small business loans to microloans. The success of the pilot programs led to approval of the full $300 million program by the EBRD's board of directors in August 1995. Although other donor efforts were also under way to develop micro- and small business lending programs in Russia, most notably the TUSRIF program, none was on the enormous scale envisaged by the G-7.

To understand the pioneering nature of the RSBF program, we should recall the political and financial environment discussed in chapters 2 and 3. The EBRD's pilot program was approved during President Yeltsin's stand-off with the Russian Congress of People's Deputies; EBRD board approval was obtained in June 1993; and President Yeltsin dissolved Congress and the Supreme Soviet in September. GDP was also continuing to decline, with a drop of 12 percent in 1993, while inflation for the year was 847 percent. The 1991–93 period was an active one for small enterprise growth, augmented by the small-scale privatization program that ended in 1994. On the lending side, however, much of the lending in 1992 was funded by the CBR and funneled to shareholders of pocket banks, while by 1993 other ways of making money had turned the heads of Russian bankers. By 1995 the situation had stabilized enough so that lawmakers could turn their attention to adopting the Law on State Support for Small Entrepreneurship. However, as 1995 was also the year of the loans-for-shares program, which enshrined big business as the partner of the government, the EBRD clearly faced an uphill struggle in generating support for lending to small businesses.

The EBRD staff member responsible for the RSBF program, Elizabeth Wallace, was particularly well suited for this assignment. As a self-described "nonbanker" and driven by a strong social conscience, Wallace was both undaunted by challenges that would have unnerved most bankers and motivated to make a significant contribution to Russia's economic development. In this quest she was well matched by IPC, one of the initial group of consulting firms that helped the EBRD establish the two pilot projects.

IPC had already made a name for itself and established considerable expertise in running successful microlending programs in South America. Although most observers focused on the daunting—and potentially insurmountable—differences between the MSE markets in South America and Russia, IPC adopted a "can-do" attitude and applied its South American experience to Russia when appropriate and adapted it as necessary. Although the EBRD worked with several consulting firms in the first years of the RSBF program, IPC proved to be the most successful in its ability to continually meet the EBRD's demands for growth and maintain a high-quality loan portfolio. IPC's success was due to five factors.

First, IPC developed a borrower analysis methodology that used the information available without sacrificing analytical rigor. Most borrowers did not have accurate financial records, and even those that did would not consider providing them to an outsider such as the EBRD. IPC worked around that information shortfall by creating its own sources of information. Borrowers with kiosk operations, for example, had an IPC-trained banker track the cash coming into and going out of the business in order to create a cash flow analysis. Bankers were also sent to each borrower's home to get a sense of the borrower's standard of living and whether a borrower might take too much money out of the business for personal expenses to be able to repay a loan. Home visits also provided an opportunity to assess the potential for additional collateral, such as television sets and other personal belongings.

A second and related aspect of IPC's success was that it encouraged RSBF partner banks to quickly take 100 percent risk on their small business loan portfolios. The RSBF program was initially designed to require banks to take a gradually increasing share of the credit risk, as their level of comfort with small business lending increased. However, IPC's experience in South America had shown that bank management took on greater ownership of similar lending projects when the risks were their own responsibility. IPC therefore insisted on applying this lesson in Russia as well.

Although hands-on analysis takes time and can therefore be expensive, a third element of IPC's success was an incentive structure that effectively balanced efficiency and loan quality. Successful bankers could earn up to an additional 50 percent of their salary in incentive pay, depending on the size and quality of their loan portfolios. Furthermore, the incentives were paid monthly, thereby creating an immediate link between performance and reward.

The incentive structure was well complemented by the management style of IPC's charismatic founder, Claus-Peter Zeitinger, which constituted the fourth element of its success. Zeitinger had an unusual ability to select promising employees: both young foreigners, many of whom were German, and young Russians. The IPC staff was young, bright, and eager to prove themselves; this created a healthy competitive atmosphere among them as they strove to test their abilities and justify Zeitinger's confidence in them. In addition, IPC's staff adopted Zeitinger's commitment to pushing MSE finance to its limits of outreach and efficiency. This commitment led to the sometimes superhuman work effort that individuals can summon when they believe in the inherent value of their work.

Finally, as the only RSBF consulting firm with microlending experience, IPC took on the development of the RSBF's microloan portfolio when it was added as a new product in March 1995. Although the small business lending program had been progressing well, the RSBF took off when microloans were added. In less than two years the microloan portfolio accounted for over $10 million in microloans and almost two thousand borrowers. This was the equivalent of almost one-third of the total loan portfolio in dollar amount outstanding and over 75 percent of borrowers.

The initial RSBF microloans were defined as loans up to $20,000 to borrowers with up to twenty employees, with exceptions for "large" microloans of up to $30,000. Small loans were defined as loans up to $50,000, an amount that was increased to $75,000 and then $100,000—with occasional exceptions to $125,000—to borrowers with up to fifty employees; subsequently the number of employees was increased to 100.

The size contrast between the RSBF's microloans and those in South America and Asia is quite marked. It is therefore useful to recall the argument made in chapter 1 that the key point about microfinance loans in Russia—and some other transition economies—is *not* that they are larger than typical microfinance loans in South America and Asia and that this larger size makes them somehow different or not "really" microfinance loans. The key point is that regardless of the size, the characteristics of the borrowers are the same: they are struggling entrepreneurs in the informal economy who are not being served by the formal financial sector.

IPC's initial successes were important in ensuring that the EBRD was able to expand the program according to the G-7's—and now the EBRD's—ambitious vision. Even by the mid-1990s international financial organizations were struggling to create successful projects in Russia—in any field. A Russian program with a growing track record, particularly one as counterintuitive as micro- and small business finance, attracted both attention and funding.

Russian banks were active participants in the RSBF, although the degree of their commitment varied. As I discussed in chapter 3, the Russian banking sector did not make a full-scale shift toward genuine banking activity—intermediating on an arm's-length basis between savers and borrowers—until after the 1998 crisis. There was simply too much money to be made from other activities and no serious regulatory efforts to prevent banks from doing so.

Donor-sponsored lending programs, however, did interest Russian banks, particularly if they had two characteristics. First, programs sponsored by a prestigious organization, such as the World Bank or the EBRD, were attractive because they provided credibility to the banks chosen to participate. Second, programs that provided funding were particularly appealing, because the Russian markets were still so volatile that they could not provide long-term funding to the banks.

It is difficult to disentangle the motives that encouraged Russian banks to join the RSBF program, which offered both a prestigious sponsor and long-term funding. Furthermore, a precondition for RSBF participation was acceptance into an even better-known program, the Financial Institutions Development Program (FIDP), known more commonly as the "twinning" program. This program, which was initiated by the World Bank with EBRD participation, quickly became the international "seal of approval" for Russian banks.[3]

The EBRD's rationale for requiring FIDP participation as a precondition for RSBF approval was well justified. Not only was there was no point in duplicating the due diligence process but FIDP participation would provide complementary institutional strengthening of the participating banks. Nevertheless, this requirement did muddy the waters for ascertaining a bank's motives for participating in the RSBF. Looked at from the vantage point of a Russian bank, having passed the hurdles for participating in the twinning program, why wouldn't one reap the full benefits and participate in the RSBF program as well?

It must be stressed that the RSBF program was not a "free ride"; RSBF partner banks were required to take 100 percent of the risk for their microloan portfolio and an increasing share of the risk for their small business loan portfolio. Furthermore, partner banks were required to lend at market rates of interest; there were no opportunities to provide subsidized lending to favored clients. Nevertheless, a bank would not need a strong prior commitment to micro- and small business lending to see the advantages of participating in a program that also had a prestigious sponsor and provided funding and training.

In fact, there was nothing wrong with a bank deciding to participate in the RSBF with a "why not" attitude. One of the premises of the program was that its results would essentially sell themselves; once a bank could see from its own operations how successfully it could lend to micro- and small borrowers, the bank would become a convinced champion of the business.

Unfortunately, Russia's financial crisis prevented a full test of this assumption. The ultimate test would be whether banks "graduated" from the RSBF program and continued to do micro- and small business

---

[3] The FIDP program provided funding for foreign banks to "twin" or "partner" with Russian banks. Modeled after a successful program in Poland, FIDP was intended to facilitate knowledge transfer between foreign and Russian banks, develop strong institutional relationships, and potentially create relationships in which a foreign bank would eventually invest in its Russian partner. No Russian bank of any size could afford not to be in the twinning program: the World Bank enjoyed considerable prestige in Russia; the program's extensive vetting process seemed to promise to identify Russia's strongest banks; the $500 million program was by far the largest banking program in Russia; and a companion program, the Enterprise Support Program, gave FIDP banks access to technical assistance and long-term funding for lending.

lending on their own, without donor funding and without technical assistance. However, the crisis occurred before the RSBF had reached a stage at which the test could be implemented.[4]

Regardless of the underlying motivations of the participating banks, the RSBF program was a clear success in generating lending to Russia's new entrepreneurs. After beginning as a $10 million pilot program in 1993, the program had expanded to achieve loan outstandings of almost $100 million by the August 1998 financial crisis, representing loans to approximately 6,500 borrowers. Thirteen banks participated in the program, there were over five hundred trained loan officers, and problem loans accounted for under 2 percent of the entire loan portfolio.[5] The EBRD seemed to have discovered an almost magical lever for contributing to Russia's economic future. Although MSE lending represented under 1 percent of bank lending in Russia—and most of it was done through the RSBF program—the growth potential seemed boundless.

The 1998 financial crisis, however, brought this growth to a rapid halt. Those banks that did not create bridge banks found themselves holding defaulted government obligations, dollar liabilities that had ballooned in size compared to their ruble-denominated assets, and borrowers who were in an equally distressed financial state. It is a testament to the value of the RSBF program that the EBRD partner banks that survived the crisis—particularly small regional banks for whom micro- and small business clients represented a significant part of their business—worked closely with the EBRD to restructure their obligations and rebuild their RSBF business.

The impetus for the creation of KMB came from this crisis. The RSBF program had demonstrated that micro- and small business lending was a viable business in Russia, as well as one with tantalizing potential for helping to build a class of independent, small-scale entrepreneurs. In some ways the program became even more important for these entrepreneurs after the crisis, as they struggled to put their businesses back together. Therefore, from an economic development perspective, this

---

[4] The EBRD replicated the RSBF program in a number of other countries, such as Ukraine and Kazakhstan, where graduations did occur successfully, albeit in environments where banks were actively interested in expanding their loan portfolios.

[5] Wallace, "EBRD's Micro and Small Enterprise Lending Programmes."

was an appropriate time to expand the program, despite the new risks created by the crisis. However, the few surviving RSBF partner banks were small and could not take on new borrowing from the EBRD to expand their lending. More fundamentally, the crisis had shaken the EBRD's willingness to work with partner banks as intermediaries, because of the program's inevitable vulnerability to each partner bank's financial condition.

Although this was an extraordinarily counterintuitive solution in the postcrisis atmosphere in Russian banking, one possible solution to these challenges was for the EBRD to create its own micro- and small business bank. Such a bank would resolve three issues simultaneously. First, the EBRD would have its own focused micro- and small business lending vehicle and not be subject to the changing strategies of its partner banks. Second, such a bank would enable the EBRD to preserve and build on the human capital that had been developed by the RSBF program, by providing employment to the bankers who had been trained by the RSBF but whose employers had closed their doors. Third, the bank would serve as a home for the RSBF loans that the EBRD had taken over from its failed partner banks and which had served as collateral for the EBRD's funding. Hence the creation of KMB Bank.

Getting Started, 1999–2001

KMB's "getting started" years span the period from 1999 to 2001. The key development during this period was KMB's successful transition from being an EBRD project, supervised by EBRD staff and focusing on lending outreach, to becoming a bank, answerable to its shareholders and operating the full range of banking activities, from deposit taking to lending to funds transfers to treasury operations.

Within the larger Russian context, this was the period in which Russian entrepreneurs snapped back quickly from the financial crisis and were seeking to expand, while many Russian banks were still grappling with depleted capital and large problem-loan portfolios. The starting conditions were auspicious for KMB's expansion.

There were four initial challenges in the creation of KMB: getting the approval of the EBRD, obtaining commitments for funding and training from donors, securing a banking license, and attracting other investors.

Although the EBRD approval process seemed interminable at the time—with several revised proposals required by the Operations Committee (the EBRD's credit committee)—the more impressive fact is that the EBRD was even willing to contemplate creating a new bank in the wake of Russia's financial crisis. Not only were most influential bankers and donors trying to protect the money that they had already invested in Russia—not put new money in—but dedicated micro- and small business banks were still a relatively new phenomenon anywhere in the world. Prodem, the Bolivian microfinance NGO that became the cover story for the microfinance industry when it converted into BancoSol, had taken this step only in 1992. The EBRD did have the encouraging example of its investment in the Micro Enterprise Bank of Bosnia-Herzegovina, which had begun operations in November 1997, but this bank was also too new and operating in circumstances too different from those in Russia to serve as a definitive model. The creation of KMB Bank, which was approved by the EBRD's board of directors in February 1999, was a step into the unknown.

As important as the board's approval was the agreement of the G-7 and EU to support KMB's development by providing funding for KMB's operations on a cofunding basis with the EBRD (as in the RSBF program); financing the initial training of KMB personnel; and supplementing the salaries of the bank's senior management during the first two years of operations. This support from both the G-7 and the EU was critical in ensuring KMB's successful start up.[6]

The third challenge, obtaining a Russian banking license, was renowned for its Byzantine opacity. Obtaining a new banking license in Russia was so difficult that investors were often forced to acquire licenses from banks that were going out of business. The EBRD circumvented this painful process because in 1992 it had invested with several Russian partners to create the Russian Project Finance Bank (RPFB), which had been designed to address the project financing gap that existed in the early years of Russia's economic transition. Given the collapse of the project finance market following the crisis, the RPFB's shareholders agreed that the EBRD and the new

---

[6] KMB also benefited indirectly from earlier donor-funded training provided to RSBF partner banks because, as I noted, some of the employees of partner banks that failed during the crisis subsequently joined KMB.

investors in KMB would take over the RPFB license. Even so, just getting the necessary CBR approvals for this change required about a year.

The fourth step, bringing in other investors, was not as difficult as might have been anticipated, once the EBRD approval was in place. The opportunity to do something positive in postcrisis Russia by working with the EBRD as an experienced partner was appealing to organizations that had not given up on Russia. The EBRD's challenge was to identify potential partners that shared its commitment to KMB's social mission and also believed that this mission could be achieved by creating a commercial bank.

KMB's shareholder structure, finalized at the end of 2000, consisted of four investors. The EBRD's share of 35.2 percent was matched by the 35.2 percent share of the Soros Economic Development Fund (SEDF). SEDF added its credibility as an equal shareholder to the EBRD in addition to buying out the shares of the RPFB's existing shareholders. Because investors in emerging economies typically prefer the security of newly issued shares, in order to avoid the risk that selling shareholders may be passing on undisclosed liabilities, SEDF's willingness to purchase these shares, and its implementation by Dennis Vinokourov, was irreplaceable. The fact that SEDF's president and chief executive officer Stewart Paperin reported directly to George Soros facilitated this and other important decisions throughout SEDF's role as a KMB shareholder. The commercial background that Paperin, as well as SEDF's first board nominee, Sophie Pompea, brought to KMB also ensured that a wide range of perspectives was always on the table.

Second in the size of its investment was Deutsche Investitions- und Entwicklungsgesellschaft mbh (DEG), now an investment arm of the German development agency, KfW Bankengruppe. DEG also had a commitment to MSE development, in addition to positive experiences with IPC. DEG's initial ownership share in KMB was 21.9 percent.

Finally, Stichting Triodos-Doen (Triodos), an investment fund managed by a privately owned Dutch development bank, although a relatively small investor with a 7.7 percent share, brought impressive credentials with its track record of supporting micro- and small business development initiatives all over the world. DEG and Triodos each had three board nominees during KMB's first six years, each of whom was a senior staff member.[7]

The initial agreement between KMB's shareholders focused on KMB's mission, its growth targets, its management, and its governance structure. It was agreed that KMB's mission was to expand financial services to the financially underserved entrepreneurial sector in Russia and to do so on a profitable basis. It was anticipated that the mission would be operationalized over a five-year period, at the end of which KMB's loan portfolio would reach $180 million in a five-branch-base-case scenario, or $350 million in a fifteen-branch-base-case scenario. There was also a general understanding that none of the initial investors intended to be a long-term investor in KMB; they all saw their roles as development organizations that would help KMB get started and demonstrate the financial sustainability of its business model. It was assumed that after five to seven years the market would recognize KMB's value and that the initial investors could exit by selling to a long-term strategic investor or through an initial public offering (IPO).

Reflecting the pivotal role that IPC had played in the expansion of the RSBF program, it was agreed that IPC would manage KMB under a management contract. This contract required IPC to provide KMB's management team: the chief executive officer, the chief financial officer, and the chief operating officer. It was anticipated that IPC's fee would be paid in the form of shares in KMB.[8]

Finally, the shareholder agreement established a five-person board of directors.[9] Each shareholder had the right to nominate one individual to the board, while the EBRD, given its role in creating the

[7] Triodos's final board nominee was Peter Blom, the president, CEO, and chairman of the board of management of the Triodos Bank Group.

[8] IPC also held the management contract for the Micro Enterprise Bank of Bosnia-Herzegovina.

[9] Russia follows the German model in which a bank is managed by a supervisory board, roughly equivalent to a board of directors in the United States, and a management board, which is the senior management team. The primary practical difference between a supervisory board and a board of directors is that the supervisory board is not involved in the daily activities of the bank, whereas it is common in the United States for the board of directors to include members of the bank's management. For the sake of simplicity, since most readers are more familiar with the board of directors terminology, that is the terminology used in this book.

bank, had the right to nominate two. An interim board for the period pending completion of the share transfers from the RPFB investors consisted of three EBRD employees (of which I was one) and one SEDF nominee.

The primary theme during KMB's "getting started" period was corporate governance, both board-management relations and staffing. Regarding board-management relations, one of the corporate governance challenges in any financial institution is to define the boundary of risk-taking responsibilities between the board of directors and the management. Although the board of directors is responsible for establishing risk parameters, such as the maximum loan size to be approved by management and acceptable leverage and liquidity levels, there often remains a gray area concerning what actually constitutes risk activities. It is not uncommon, particularly in newly created organizations, for there to be some initial miscommunication between the management team and the board of directors regarding the responsibilities of each.

This typical start-up situation was further complicated at KMB because the management team was responsible to three sources of supervision and instruction: the newly created board of directors; Zeitinger at IPC, who had to ensure that the management team fulfilled the contract terms; and the Group for Small Business team at the EBRD, which was responsible for the EBRD's relationship with KMB, including the considerable financial resources the EBRD had provided to KMB. Furthermore, while KMB's management team already had longstanding relations with IPC and the EBRD, relationships with the board had to be created from scratch.

A good example of the resulting corporate governance challenges is KMB's funding policy. KMB's interim board of directors initially focused its attention on the quality of KMB's loan portfolio. The directors were not familiar with IPC's methodology and therefore wanted to assure themselves that the lending part of the business was well controlled. Because the RSBF program had been a lending program and the reporting to the EBRD and IPC was very well developed, the board's information requests were easily addressed.

Not sufficiently addressed, however, was KMB's funding policy. The board of directors, for whom working with KMB was a new experience, did not initially realize that funding required its immediate attention.

KMB's management team, never having been responsible for funding before, reported on funding to the board but did not realize that this was an important topic to which to draw the board's attention. Although this unperceived misunderstanding lasted for only a few weeks, it is an example of a common corporate governance challenge. The issue also underscores a funding issue that is common to donor-created banks in countries where there is not a well-developed local currency market.

Funding was a particularly critical issue in KMB's early days and posed both a major source of profits and risks. As I noted earlier, KMB's primary source of initial funding was the EBRD. As was to be expected, no outsiders were willing to take the risk of lending to a newly created bank, especially one operating in the wake of Russia's financial crisis. Although the long-term maturity of the EBRD funding was an enormous advantage, the EBRD could only lend to KMB in dollars, not rubles. The EBRD had no deposit-taking operations of its own in Russia with which to obtain rubles, and regulations in the Russian capital markets did not allow the EBRD, which was not a Russian-incorporated legal entity, to borrow rubles. As a result, KMB had to devise its own means to obtain rubles to lend to its clients, about one-third of whom requested ruble-denominated loans.

Extensive deposit-taking operations were also not an option. The EBRD's board of directors had stipulated that KMB would not market deposit services in its early days of operations. Although KMB's borrowers would maintain accounts at KMB, the EBRD's board considered it inappropriate to expose the general public to the risks of a newly created bank. Furthermore, even without this constraint, the Russian public was still too shell-shocked from the financial crisis to be interested in making, or even able to make, new deposits.

KMB's only option for obtaining rubles was to borrow them on the Russian interbank market. This market had also been badly hurt by the financial crisis and operated with very short-term maturities; thirty days was considered unusually long, with the more standard borrowing period in the one- to five-day range. KMB therefore had to borrow rubles in this very short-term market and lend them to clients for much longer periods of six to twelve months.

Although the difference in interest rates between the short-term and longer-term market was very profitable for KMB, it also created high risks. The operating assumption was that the short-term deposits would continually be renewed; however, if that proved not to be possible for some reason, then KMB would not have the money to repay its depositors, having used the funds to make loans of longer maturities.[10] Once the board of directors understood these risks, it was obliged to limit the use of short-term ruble funding.

It is important to stress that no one was concealing KMB's ruble-funding operations; once the interim board fully understood the riskiness of these activities, it was a simple process to establish limits and reporting procedures. The main point of the example is to illustrate the challenge of establishing appropriate corporate governance procedures in a new organization.[11]

A second important enhancement of KMB's corporate governance during the "getting started" period concerned KMB's staffing. KMB's rapid expansion required constant review of its personnel structure, in order to ensure that the bank's employees were sufficiently qualified to manage the challenges of a growing bank. Furthermore, because KMB's core management and staff had been trained by IPC as small business and microfinance lenders, it was necessary to hire outsiders with expertise in other areas of banking.[12]

This understandably caused some anxiety; it was not clear how individuals with purely commercial backgrounds would merge with the IPC team, all of whom had made a career commitment to development finance. Furthermore, not only was it important for the management to have genuinely shared objectives but KMB could not afford to provide the same compensation package as a big Russian bank. Its employees

[10] Although this "maturity mismatch" is a standard source of profitability for banks worldwide, there are several risk mitigants in developed economies that were not available to KMB. One mitigant is extensive historical data regarding client behavior, on the basis of which a bank can estimate what proportion of its current account balances and short-term deposits can realistically be assumed to "behave" like longer term deposits, in the sense that the clients are likely to keep the money in the bank for a longer period. Banks in developed markets can also create liquidity reserves by holding a portfolio of government securities that can be readily sold.

[11] The risks of this funding method were realized at the end of 2001, when short-term ruble interest rates rose so sharply that KMB lost an average of 5 percent on its ruble loan portfolio during December alone—even after the limits had been implemented. These losses essentially erased the funding gains that had been achieved earlier in the year.

[12] A few members of the RPFB staff, such as the head of treasury, did continue to work for KMB.

had to be satisfied with a degree of psychological compensation from their work.

One of the bank's first senior-level management members to be hired from "outside" was a bank auditor from PricewaterhouseCoopers (PWC), with a mandate to expand the bank's internal controls and audit capacity. While inevitably over the years some of the bank's new outside staff fit in well and some did not, this first new senior team member did make a successful transition. In doing so, she helped build the management's and board's confidence in bringing in outside expertise.

The strengthening of KMB's audit and controls function was further consolidated by the board's decision to create a board audit committee. Russian banks were required by law to have audit commissions, but these were often rubber-stamp structures that in any case could not include board members. Although KMB was performing according to plan, its ambitious expansion plans entailed considerable risk, and the audit committee would be positioned to determine whether there were risks below the surface that needed to be resolved so that KMB could meet its growth targets. As I discuss in the next section, the timing of these two audit and control enhancements proved to be propitious.

KMB opened its doors for business with nine employees, an inherited RSBF loan portfolio of $8 million, and customer accounts of about $4 million, most related to a transaction inherited from the RPFB. Although KMB would ultimately receive $12.5 million in new capital from its new shareholders, this process had not yet been completed; the bank's equity at the start of its operations was about $3 million.

KMB quickly energized its lending activities and achieved new loans outstanding of over $13 million by year-end 1999, almost $44 million by year-end 2000, and just short of $100 million by year-end 2001. KMB also expanded geographically, reaching the end of 2001 with five branches, eleven representative offices, and twenty-eight credit centers. KMB was able to reach monthly profitability several months ahead of schedule in August 2001, thus marking a key turning point in its "getting started" period. (KMB achieved its first full-year profit of $1.4 million in 2002.)

Particularly noteworthy was KMB's loan quality, with loans past due for more than thirty days relative to total loans maintained at under

1 percent. So unusual were these results that in 2001 its external auditor, PricewaterhouseCoopers, obtained an exceptional approval from its ratings committee to reduce KMB's loan-loss provisions below the minimum that the committee had mandated for all Russian banks. The PWC audit partner for KMB characterized the committee's decision as "extraordinary."

KMB achieved these results by following the microfinance lending principles that I outlined in chapter 1, with continued fine-tuning based on evolving experience. The process starts with the borrower completing a standardized loan application that requires information about the history of the business, the ownership structure, the professional background of the owners, current and historical financial information, the proposed collateral, and the purpose of the loan. KMB requires that any business to be financed have at least a three-month history, in order to create some sense of its viability. (Although some supporters of new-business development consider this type of requirement an unreasonable impediment to growth, it is one of KMB's most liberal requirements. Imagine your reaction if one of your acquaintances asked you for a loan to support a business that had been operating for such a short period of time.)

The loan officer uses the application as the basis for preparing a proposal to the bank's credit committee, again using a standardized format. The proposal process includes a visit to the premises and home of first-time borrowers, as well as determining the borrower's "true" financial condition and the degree to which it may vary from the borrower's official financial statements.

Although assessment of the borrower's character is an integral part of the loan officer's evaluation, and activities such as home visits provide important insights, KMB's security service also evaluates the borrower's reputation and history by using its own contacts in the local government and other security services. This use of security services is not typical in developed economies, where borrowers have documented borrowing histories to which lenders have ready access. However, it is a standard operating feature of banks throughout the countries of the former Soviet Union, which have had to develop their own sources of information. The development of credit bureaus, which were introduced in Russia in 2005, should lead to increasing use of this more formalized source of borrower information.

Identifying appropriate collateral is an important part of the loan proposal process, particularly for first-time borrowers for whom creating the appropriate repayment discipline—and therefore a realistic risk of losing its collateral—is critical. As a result, KMB makes considerable effort to diversify the value of the collateral. For example, if a $5,000 loan is collateralized by an automobile with a value of $7,000, the borrower can realistically assume that KMB would probably not take the car if the borrower delays in making its first $500 principal repayment. However, if the borrower has provided a television set as collateral as well, the chances are much greater that KMB would take the television set following a first nonpayment. Not only is a television set simpler for KMB to sell but KMB's response would be more commensurate with the scale of the borrower's failure.

Although collateral registration procedures in Russia have many shortcomings, including the time and cost of registration, these have never been significant impediments for KMB. One way in which KMB addresses the challenges is by structuring loans so that the collateral is not automatically released when the loan is repaid; repeat borrowers have to go through the collateral registration process only one time. This approach is particularly useful for real estate collateral, for which registration is particularly tedious. For smaller collateral items, such as television sets, and particularly for first-time borrowers, KMB sometimes avoids the registration process entirely by taking the collateral and holding it on its premises. The agreement with the borrower stipulates that KMB has the right to the collateral, but KMB goes through the steps of registering that right only if the borrower defaults. KMB also has an Express Micro loan product, for amounts up to $10,000, for which it does not require collateral.

Personal guarantees are another important form of loan support, particularly because of the often overlapping nature of a small entrepreneur's business and personal affairs. In addition to requiring the personal guarantee of the borrower, KMB also requires the guarantee of the borrower's spouse. This requirement ensures that a borrower cannot avoid repayment by transferring assets to the spouse, as well as avoiding situations in which a spouse is not informed of the financial commitments being made by his wife or her husband.

Loans are approved by a tiered set of credit committees, primarily according to the total amount of borrowing by the client. Smaller loans are approved in the local representative office or branch, while larger amounts are approved by the credit committee at the head office. Although at one point KMB decentralized decision making to the point that two individuals constituted a "committee" for the bank's smallest loans, this procedure was discontinued when it proved to be vulnerable to fraud. Currently all of the bank's credit committees consist at a minimum of a legal expert, the business manager (such as the branch manager), and a credit specialist.

The credit committees typically play an active role not only in approving or turning down a loan proposal but in evaluating other aspects of the proposal, such as the collateral, interest rate, and repayment schedule. In addition, the committee defines the frequency with which the borrower has to be formally monitored by the banker managing its relationship. Formal monitoring consists of a visit to the borrower and a written analysis of the borrower's most recent financial information. (Borrowers are required to provide monthly financial information.) Loans with a maturity of more than one year typically require formal monitoring every six months, while shorter-term loans often do not have formal monitoring requirements, given the built-in monitoring function played by the monthly loan repayments. Typically, lenders are in frequent contact with their borrowers in the normal course of business—for example, most borrowers come to the bank to make their loan repayments—so an experienced lender can also use these informal contacts and the monthly financial reporting to keep an eye on the borrower's business.

The most common causes of serious payment problems are disputes between partners, loss of a major market or client, or the borrower having concealed other financial obligations from KMB. Almost all of the problems are resolved out of court, typically through some restructuring of the repayment schedule or selling some of the collateral or both. KMB usually has to resort to court procedures only when a client has acted in bad faith. Most clients have payment delays because of genuinely unforeseen problems and, because they want to maintain an ongoing relationship with KMB, they are motivated to work with the bank to resolve their problems. In 2002, for example, KMB used the court system for only 14 percent of its problem loans. With sixty-four loans past due for over thirty days as of year-end 2002, many of which were not yet at the "problem loan" stage, KMB used the court system fewer than ten times throughout the year.

To conclude this discussion of KMB's "getting started" years, it is important to be clear about the contribution of donors to KMB's results; observers sometimes exaggerate the amount of donor support and therefore disregard the relevance of KMB's results for commercial banks. As I noted, the G-7 and other donors contributed generously to help cover KMB's start-up costs. By the end of 2001, however, the training was largely completed and the salary supplements to KMB's senior management came to an end.

There were two main sources of donor funding going forward. One source was motivated by the European Union's interest in accelerating KMB's geographic outreach. This funding typically consisted of the salary of one trainer per new location for two years, the salary of one lending officer per location for six months, and funding for some training, advertising, travel, and equipment. KMB covered all of the other expansion costs.

The other source was the funding provided by the EBRD and other donors. Not only was long-term funding not available to any Russian banks in this postcrisis period, but the EBRD's lending rate of LIBOR + 2.5 was also favorable for KMB, particularly during 1999 and 2000 when LIBOR was in the range of 5 percent and KMB could make dollar loans at rates approaching 20 percent.[13] However, other foreign-owned banks operating in Russia enjoyed a similar funding advantage, because their parent banks could fund them at lower cost than if the banks raised their own funding on the Russian market. Therefore KMB had an initial funding advantage compared to domestically owned banks, but not to foreign-owned banks. Its advantage relative to foreign-owned banks lay in the fact that foreign-owned banks were hesitant to resume lending in Russia immediately after the crisis.

It should also be noted that the RSBF program forbade KMB and any other RSBF banks from providing below-market rates to their borrowers. Furthermore, all of the banks in the RSBF program were able to

[13] LIBOR is the acronym for London Interbank Offer Rate, which is a daily reference rate based on the interest rates at which banks offer to lend unsecured funds to other banks in the London wholesale money market.

borrow from the EBRD at the same interest rate; there was no favoritism shown to KMB.

Once the start-up period was completed, the primary donor support for KMB's operations was long-term funding. This funding is gradually being replaced by commercial sources of funding, as was intended by the donors.

Turning Points, 2002–Mid-2003

While the getting started years of 1999–2001 witnessed KMB's transformation into a bank, the turning point years of 2002 through the middle of 2003 were critical for defining KMB's future direction. Two major issues arose during this period. The first was KMB's first serious fraud, which required a thorough reevaluation of KMB's policies and procedures, in addition to incurring the associated increased costs. The second was the need to expand KMB's capital base to ensure its ongoing growth, a process that raised fundamental issues concerning KMB's future strategy and, correspondingly, its shareholder structure.

The year 2002 started out well for KMB. Not only had 2001 been a success but KMB's newly established leasing business was developing well and a new one-day-approval $1,000 "Express Micro" loan was enjoying strong demand. There was every reason to expect that KMB would meet its aggressive year-end loan target of $130 million and achieve its first full year of profitability.

This aura of confidence collapsed abruptly in July, with the discovery that an employee had committed fraud in one of the bank's branches. This banker had arranged to provide loans to acquaintances, who in turn returned the money to him for his own use. No sooner had KMB absorbed the shock of this fraud and started to implement corrective measures, when a second large fraud, based on the creation of shell companies, was discovered in November at one of KMB's representative offices.

These two frauds were a painful blow for KMB. The bank's management had prided itself on its well-trained staff and carefully honed lending methodology. Furthermore, KMB's management had worked hard to imbue the staff with the same commitment to the MSE business that they had inherited from IPC: a fervent belief that, by providing financial services to the underserved, they were contributing to Russia's future. This belief was the basis for a strong esprit de corps that was further bolstered by the staff's confidence in their technical skills and pride in the substantial responsibilities that had been entrusted to them. The frauds represented a personal betrayal as well as a loss of money for KMB.

One of the major organizational changes introduced as a result of the frauds was the creation of a "middle office" to increase the segregation of responsibilities between those working with clients in the "front office" and those processing and recording transactions in the "back office." The middle office was designed to reduce the risk of collusion between front and back office employees as well as to streamline the bank's operations.

KMB's management also grappled with the question of how to maintain a strong corporate culture over its many locations and time zones, particularly with a rapidly expanding staff that was often hired in small local offices and therefore harder to immerse in the bank's corporate culture than the staff in larger offices. One silver lining of the fraud cases is the positive contribution they made to KMB's corporate culture. Rather than withholding information about the fraud from bank staff, the bank's management decided to share the information in an effort to reduce the risk of future frauds. This approach, which differed so dramatically from the "mind your own business" corporate culture of the Soviet era, encouraged KMB staff to value open communication.

Of course the costs associated with the response to the frauds were significant. Not only was more staff required to implement the enhanced separation of activities but the bank's drive to decentralize lending decisions also had to be revised, with an inevitable impact on productivity levels. A decision was also made not to pursue further rapid geographic expansion; because of the increased cost per location resulting from the increased controls, it made more sense to maximize the use of the existing locations, including the development of sub-branch offices. At its maximum size during the time frame discussed in this chapter, KMB had seven branches and over fifty smaller offices.

Finally, although it had always been understood that KMB would eventually have to upgrade its information technology and management information systems to keep pace with its growth, these upgrades now became a more immediate priority. Although the costs did not increase immediately, it was clear that a substantial investment was needed.

There are two points regarding the fraud episodes to emphasize in conclusion. First, despite the frauds, KMB was able to keep the proportion of problem loans at the same low levels it had achieved in the past; the frauds were onetime events that did not have a systemic impact on loan quality. Second, fraud is the "dirty secret" of microfinance, to cite the title of a discussion group at the 2002 Microfinance Summit. Given the imperative for MFIs to decentralize their lending to the maximum extent possible, in addition to the largely cash nature of MFI operations, we should not be surprised to learn that fraud is a common occurrence. Furthermore, because controlling fraud does raise important issues related to financial sustainability, it is more useful to be open about the occurrence of fraud than to ignore it.

This first turning point in KMB's development coincided with the second development: KMB's rapid growth rate could only be sustained if it obtained additional capital by mid-2003. The need for such an increase raised two interrelated issues for the shareholders: the new shareholder structure and KMB's future strategy.

The pivotal issue concerning the new shareholder structure was the possible expansion of the shareholder group to include IPC. As a complement to IPC's micro- and small business consulting services, the company had created an investment arm, ProCredit, to invest in MSE banks.[14] The group's ability to invest in the banks it was managing presented several advantages for the other shareholders. ProCredit/IPC's expertise and involvement in a number of banks in the region potentially helped to create economies of scale; the cost and effort to develop an appropriate information technology system, for example, could be spread over all of the ProCredit investee banks. In addition, some shareholders perceived a positive alignment of interests between ProCredit's position as an investor and IPC's role as manager of the investee banks.

A ProCredit investment also addressed one of the most troublesome questions for founders of MFIs: how to ensure the continuation of the

---

[14] The original name of IPC's investment arm was Internationale Micro Investitionen Aktiengesellschaft, known as IMI. For simplicity, I use its newer name, ProCredit.

MFI's mission after the founders had exited. Because microfinance is often thought of as a poverty-alleviating, sometimes charitable undertaking, microfinance specialists sometimes assume that commercial investors in an MFI would not be genuinely interested in the microfinance business and would use the MFI as a platform for doing other business. As Elisabeth Rhyne of ACCION noted, "Many in the microfinance community, both advocates and critics of commercialization, are nervous about handing over their beloved institutions to the private sector. They wonder whether to trust purely private investors to maintain the social mission."[15]

ProCredit proposed to address this potential risk by creating a holding company to hold its own shares in the MSE banks; other investors in these MSE banks could exchange their individual bank shares for holding company shares, and, if the holding company went public, they would then have the ability to exit completely. ProCredit would ensure the continued MSE commitment throughout this process, because of its own commitment to MSE lending and because any public issuance of the holding company shares would be aimed at socially conscious investors.

As I noted, the original management agreement with IPC had envisaged compensating IPC in KMB shares; therefore, there had always been the expectation that IPC would become an active shareholder. However, there was a significant difference between ProCredit's joining the KMB shareholder group as a minority investor and its taking on the strategic investor role. In particular, a strategic investment by ProCredit posed two potential concerns to KMB's shareholders.

First, not all of the shareholders were prepared to commit KMB to ProCredit's development model. The assumption that no commercial investor would make a commitment to KMB's mission did not seem to be fully tested in the still relatively early days of global microfinance. Small business finance was clearly of interest to commercial investors all over the world. And, even more important, KMB's experience was showing that microfinance lending could be profitable; although KMB's smallest loans did not cover their costs,

---

[15] Elisabeth Rhyne, "Maintaining the Bottom Line in Investor-Owned Microfinance Organizations," *MicroBanking Bulletin*, August 2005.

the bank's microfinance portfolio as a whole was its most profitable loan category.

As a result, it seemed possible that a commercial investor might be interested in KMB's ability to serve both markets and in exploring possible synergies between the two. Furthermore, such an investor might be able to create the best of both worlds by marrying world-class banking technology with KMB's social mission. Therefore, although the accomplishments of IPC and ProCredit were highly respected, there was a sense that there could be more than one potential model for a young MSE bank and a desire among some shareholders to explore what those other models might be.

A second and related issue with a ProCredit investment concerned the exit options for the existing shareholders. As I noted, the assumption that the shareholders could exit through a ProCredit holding company hinged on ProCredit's ability to take that company public. However, if for some reason this did not prove to be possible, the shareholders might find their ability to exit to other investors blocked as well, since new investors might not wish to invest in a bank in which another investor already had substantial control. Furthermore, if ProCredit were able to raise the funds to buy out the existing shareholders, the exit price was expected to be lower than that offered by a fully commercial investor, because ProCredit would be raising funding among socially oriented investors and therefore at lower multiples. Although it was too early to assess possible exit prices, some shareholders also were not willing to limit their upside potential at this relatively early stage of KMB's development.

As in any discussion regarding an organization's strategy and the need to reconcile a variety of interests and beliefs concerning both moral and financial objectives, the debate regarding KMB's future shareholder structure was fraught and sometimes painful. The discussion was made more difficult because KMB's shareholders had to weigh a specific proposal from ProCredit against uncertain other options. Furthermore, the shareholders were not only risking their own financial and development commitments; they also felt a moral responsibility as the steward of funds that had been provided by donors.

After intense discussions that lasted almost a year, the shareholders decided to keep their options open regarding KMB's future strategic investor.[16] All of the shareholders participated in the capital increase and the shareholder group was not changed, although SEDF and the EBRD each raised their stake to 37.5 percent, while DEG reduced its stake slightly. As a condition of participating in the capital increase, the shareholders agreed on a set of principles that defined the characteristics of a future strategic investor in KMB, and in particular ensuring that investor's commitment to KMB's social mission.

An outstanding characteristic of KMB's shareholder group is that, once the conclusion was reached, there was no looking back; everyone signed the agreement in good faith and proceeded to act accordingly. Although good faith alone is not always sufficient to ensure a positive outcome, in the case of KMB's shareholders this relationship was forged over a difficult period in which every shareholder had to grapple with the implications of a failure to reach agreement: KMB would not be able to increase its capital and a successful and important venture would not be able to grow to its full potential. The fact that some of the board member seats changed during this period contributed to this outcome, because it brought in new people with a new outlook. However, the positive outcome should be attributed more fundamentally to the shareholders themselves and to KMB's management. The EBRD, SEDF, DEG, and Triodos all believed in KMB's future and worked together at senior levels to create an agreement that was acceptable to all. KMB's management in turn created an organization in which everyone could believe. There was never any question about whether KMB would be successful in realizing its social and financial objectives; the question was how best to maximize this success.

KMB's management completed 2002 by demonstrating that it deserved this confidence; even though the uncertainties related to the capital increase persisted into 2003, the bank achieved the budgeted loan growth of 34 percent and exceeded the profit target. Year-end results showed a loan portfolio of $130 million, average loan size of slightly over $6,000, net profit after tax of $1.37 million, and a return on average equity of 12.3 percent.

---

[16] KMB's capital needs were addressed on an interim basis by issuing subordinated debt. It was agreed that IPC would be paid on a flat fee basis, because the plan to compensate IPC in shares had become complicated with difficulties about possible tax consequences.

Maturity Period, Mid-2003–2005

Although KMB continued to grow and mature during its "turning point" years, it is appropriate to characterize the post-turning point period as the bank's "maturity period," because so many of the ingredients of change that had been introduced in earlier periods began to come to fruition. This maturing of KMB can be seen in the nature of the bank's products and business, the market's growing recognition of KMB, and the evolution of the bank's loan portfolio.

KMB's credit products evolved during this period in response to three stimuli: growth in competition, particularly with the introduction of consumer finance; an increased focus on profitability; and changes in the client base.

Looking first at competition, KMB had always competed for clients with other banks in the EBRD's RSBF program. Furthermore, when KMB first started to open branches outside of Moscow, it sometimes did so in locations where the RSBF program was already operating with other partner banks. Not only had these locations already proven to have an attractive client base but one factor that KMB considered in choosing new locations was the size of the loan portfolio it had inherited from failed RSBF partner banks. Having a branch in cities with large inherited portfolios would make the loans easier to monitor and provide a base for expansion. KMB also expanded to locations that had not been served by the RSBF, but starting in some cities that were already known to the staff helped to create a positive beginning to the branch expansion program.

A particularly good example is provided by KMB's first branch opened outside Moscow, in Nizhny Novgorod, which had been the closed military city of Gorky to which Andrei Sakharov was sent for internal exile during the Soviet period. Because of a progressive local administration and a particularly well-educated population from its military days, Nizhny Novgorod quickly established a reputation in the early 1990s for being hospitable to entrepreneurs. Russia's first microfinance program, undertaken by Opportunity International, started in Nizhny Novgorod in 1994.

The EBRD RSBF program in Nizhny Novgorod had also been quite strong before the crisis, in the number of partner banks and the quality of their bankers. Competition for small business borrowers continued after the crisis; Sberbank had an active lending program in Nizhny Novgorod as did NBD Bank, a locally owned bank that was one of the few RSBF partner banks that survived the 1998 financial crisis, and in which the EBRD became a shareholder in 2000. Although neither bank welcomed the new competition, the market proved to be large enough for all of them.

Over the 2001–02 period KMB's competition began to expand beyond other banks in the RSBF program. Most notably, consumer finance became more widely available, spurred on in particular by the creation of Russky Standart Bank. Although Russky Standart's loans were for different purposes than KMB's—a typical Russky Standart client borrowed to buy a television or a refrigerator—a family business could conserve cash by buying a television on credit and then using the cash for its business. Even more threateningly for KMB, Russky Standart, DeltaCredit, and the other consumer-focused banks that emerged during this period could build a client base to which they could then offer products that competed directly with KMB's. How long would clients keep going to KMB for business loans and services only if other banks could offer financing for their business as well as personal needs? KMB might even risk going out of business if it continued to offer a limited range of products while other banks expanded their products into what had previously been KMB's niche.

This expansion of the consumer finance market coincided with the second major influence on KMB's operations during this period, which was its ongoing efforts to enhance its profitability. KMB had exceeded its profitability targets in all of its years of operation, but the discussions related to its capital increase had occasioned a renewed focus on how KMB could maximize its profitability while fulfilling its social mission. KMB had established an extensive geographic network with newly enhanced controls and infrastructure; the more that this network could be used to generate new business, the higher would be the returns on the existing investment. Furthermore, the more products that KMB could offer its existing client base, the less likely KMB would be to lose these clients to other banks. As a result, KMB introduced a line of consumer finance products in 2004.

Adapting to changes in its client base was the third stimulus for changes in KMB's credit products. KMB had first redefined its microloan product in early 2002, when the microloan category was expanded from loans of up to $5,000 to loans of up to $10,000. Small loans, which had been defined as loans up to $100,000, were redefined as loans up to $50,000. KMB's evolving experience showed that borrower characteristics shifted most notably at around the $10,000 borrowing level and at about the $50,000 borrowing level. As I noted, KMB also introduced an Express Micro loan in 2002; this was a $1,000 loan (since increased to $10,000) with same-day turnaround and no collateral requirement. This product reflected KMB's confidence in its ability to streamline its decision-making process without sacrificing credit quality, as well as its recognition that there was potential market demand for such a product.

Responding to the continuing evolution of the Russian economy, KMB redefined its client categories again in the fall of 2004. As the economy grew and the costs of doing business rose, it took higher borrowing levels than before for borrowers to begin to change the way that they did business and to shift from one borrower category to another. Microloans were defined upward as loans up to $20,000, and small loans were redefined as those up to $100,000. In addition, the Express Micro product was increased to $5,000.

Providing more products and services to clients coincided with another direction that KMB had already been pursuing for several years: the need to expand its client funding base. Not only did clients increasingly expect a competitive range of deposit products but, as KMB continued to develop, it had become clear that client deposits would have to become a key part of the bank's funding strategy. KMB could not rely on donor funding forever; in any case this funding was in dollars, while more than slightly over half of KMB's loan portfolio was now ruble denominated. Even though the domestic interbank market had become more stable than at the time of KMB's creation, it would not be prudent to rely on it too heavily for funding. Therefore, KMB's management and board of directors reached the same conclusion that banks share all over the world; although the cost of raising client funding can be expensive, there is usually no alternative. On the positive side, client funding is typically highly diversified; once clients have opened their accounts with a bank, they often prove to be less interest-rate sensitive than the interbank market.

Once KMB's capital increase enabled the bank to raise more client funding, the amounts grew rapidly, with customer accounts increasing from 19 percent of funding at year-end 2003 to 34 percent at year-end 2004, representing a ruble increase of almost 100 percent. The appropriateness of this funding strategy was clearly demonstrated during the "mini–banking crisis" that Russia experienced during the summer of 2004. While the interbank market collapsed and some banks experienced client withdrawals of over 20 percent, KMB's client withdrawals were limited to 6 percent. KMB's deposit base also began to grow again after the crisis.

The second characteristic of KMB's maturity period was increased recognition by the market. In the first years of KMB's operations there was a certain market skepticism about its business model. Banks were having a hard enough time doing what was considered the more standard business of lending to large companies: How could a bank lend successfully to MSEs? Perhaps not surprisingly, I met this skepticism more often among foreigners with backgrounds similar to my own, rather than among Russian policymakers and bankers. Foreign bankers and advisers sometimes seemed to think that KMB's success could not last because its decentralized decision making would eventually lead to massive problem loans. Others discounted KMB's experience because its start-up costs had been funded by donors. A third, more negative, attitude toward microfinance in general was that it doesn't make a positive contribution to the economy because it is only financing consumer goods traders. Russian policymakers and bankers who did not have preconceived notions about what was and was not possible in the banking world were more receptive to learning from KMB's experience.

KMB inevitably developed its reputation gradually, particularly as it established good relations with its counterparties in the interbank market and continually achieved strong financial results. But the first major breakthrough in changing market perceptions occurred with the issuance of KMB's ruble-denominated bond in October 2002, slightly before the beginning of the time period discussed in this section.

A ruble debt market had begun to develop in Russia in the 2000–2001 period, fueled by a large increase in ruble liquidity caused primarily by high oil prices. KMB's management took the initiative to tap this market and identified Raiffeisenbank as the most appropriate investment bank to arrange and underwrite KMB's first debt issue. Not only was Raiffeisen one of the most experienced arrangers of ruble bonds but it recognized the potential for KMB's future growth, even though this first bond issue was relatively small for the Russian market.[17] Raiffeisen and KMB agreed that the bond issue would be the ruble equivalent of about $10 million, with a three-year maturity with six-month put options for the investors, and a fixed coupon of 15 percent.[18]

This first ruble bond issue for KMB was a success. Demand was even higher than expected, and the yield on the initial placement was 18 percent, compared to the 18–21 percent then typical for similar issues.[19] Equally important, there were no problems with redemptions at the six-month put date. There was even sufficient demand to increase the size of the issue, although the size of KMB's capital made this impossible. In any case, the positive reception for the bonds encouraged Raiffeisen to lengthen the put period to one year.

KMB followed this successful experience in December 2003 with a syndicated loan that had both a dollar and a ruble tranche. This loan was arranged by Raiffeisen, and several other international banks participated, including Citibank. Clearly KMB had "arrived" in terms of other banks recognizing the soundness of its banking operations.

A second important development in expanding KMB's visibility was its decision to hire a rating agency to evaluate KMB's performance. In December 2003 Moody's assigned KMB's foreign currency deposits a rating of Ba3/NP, the highest rating available for non–state-owned Russian banks. Although KMB is a micro- and small business bank, not solely a microfinance bank, this was one of the first such ratings in the world by a major rating agency.

Perhaps the sweetest accolade of all, however, came from the Association of Russian Banks: in the spring of 2004 the association recognized KMB as the foreign-owned bank that had made the most significant contribution to Russia's economy. Since KMB had increased its lending during 2003 by a net amount of almost 8,500 loans, the rationale for the award was clear.

KMB's successes also increased its leverage in contributing to the policy environment for SME lending. One example can be seen in

---

[17] Russian regulations prevented the bond issue from exceeding the size of KMB's capital.

[18] This put-option structure was characteristic of the ruble bond market at that time.

[19] To put these figures in perspective, the ruble inflation forecast for the year was 14 percent and KMB's ruble lending rate was in the 24 percent range.

the outcome of a loan proposal that the World Bank had made to the Russian government to encourage the further development of SME lending. As is the standard structure for such loans, the Russian government would be the borrower and it would on-lend the funds to selected Russian banks that would in turn lend to SMEs. Although this loan was discussed with the Russian government for several years, and was officially approved by the World Bank's board of directors, the Russian government ultimately decided not to accept the loan. According to a participant in the discussions, one senior Russian decision maker concluded that SME lending would increase without government assistance, as the example of KMB demonstrated.

Another example was the CBR's decision, in the spring of 2004, to liberalize its policy of allowing only branch offices to issue loans. KMB had been discussing this issue with the CBR for over two years: the policy was inconvenient for borrowers who had relationships with KMB's representative offices, because they sometimes had to travel two or more hours to a KMB branch location to receive their loans. The policy also reduced the efficiency of KMB's operations, because it prevented the bank from fully using its network. KMB was in the forefront of banks debating this issue with the CBR because, unlike the majority of Russian banks, it recognized the importance of decentralizing lending and other decisions as much as possible.

Finally, KMB's maturity period is characterized by the evolution of its loan portfolio. By mid-2005 it had more than doubled over the preceding three years, reaching $285 million compared to $127 million in mid-2002. The number of loans grew accordingly, from over seventeen thousand to over thirty-four thousand.

Although by mid-2005 a smaller proportion of the loan portfolio consisted of borrowers new to KMB than previously, the absolute number of new borrowers increased over this period. In mid-2002, 64 percent of the bank's clients were new, based on the number of loans and 54 percent were new, based on loan volume. By mid-2005, the proportion of new clients had declined but was still relatively high, with new clients accounting for 41 percent of loans and the loan portfolio. In absolute terms there were over eleven thousand new clients in mid-2002 and almost fourteen thousand new clients in mid-2005. KMB's management estimates that 40 percent of its clients by number have never previously borrowed from a bank.

With only one exception, the purpose of the bank's loans did not change noticeably over this period. As of mid-2005, 57 percent of the loans outstanding were for the broad category of trade, which is typically some type of sales activity, such as a store (54 percent in mid-2002); 24 percent were for services other than transport, such as restaurants, beauty parlors, and business services (18 percent in mid-2002); and 16 percent was for industry and other production (21 percent in mid-2002).[20] The most significant change in the purpose of the loans was that agriculture and food processing grew from zero in mid-2002 to 10 percent of the loan portfolio as of mid-2005. This shift reflects a trend toward agricultural production in Russia and a corresponding strategy by KMB to target this sector.

Although the high proportion of sales activity among KMB's borrowers might seem to support the criticism of some development specialists that microfinance is merely a mechanism for sustaining non–value-added activities, I consider this a surprisingly short-term view. The microfinance client base by definition does not have the resources to create value-added businesses; retail sales are often their only hope of survival, let alone of accumulating capital. Furthermore, after decades of Soviet rule, Russia continues to offer mouth-watering opportunities for consumer goods providers. With the Swedish furniture multinational IKEA continuing to open stores in Russia, it is hard to criticize Russians who also want to tap the consumer market. Finally, the OPORA surveys that I noted in chapter 2 revealed that local and regional administrations often force small entrepreneurs into retail businesses by restricting their access to other businesses in favor of those with better connections.

This three-year period was also characterized by an improvement in the geographic diversification of the loan portfolio, with Moscow's share of the portfolio shrinking from 24 percent to 15 percent. The dispersion among other locations did not change significantly, with the next five locations accounting for about 44 percent of the loan portfolio in both periods. There were two shifts within this group, with Barnaul (in Siberia) expanding from 6 percent to 8 percent of the

---

[20] The comparison between the two periods is not precise, because a category of "mixed," which accounted for 7 percent of the mid-2002 loan portfolio, was no longer used by mid-2005.

TABLE 4.1.
Loan Sizes

	Mid-2002	Mid-2005
Loans up to $10,000	24%	22%
Loans between $10,001 and $50,000	33%	33%
Loans over $50,000	43%	45%
Number of loans over $100,000	710	510
Total number of loans	17,231	33,680
Average loan size, year-end	$7,580	$9,096

portfolio and Nizhny Novgorod falling from 9 percent to 7 percent. The other top five non-Moscow locations, Yekaterinburg, St. Petersburg, and Novosibirsk, maintained their relative positions.

Another positive development during this period was an increase in the ruble proportion of the loan portfolio to 58 percent in mid-2005 from 40 percent in mid-2002. Not only did KMB have greater access to ruble funding but borrowers were increasingly realizing that it made more sense for them to borrow in their domestic currency, rather than taking the exchange-rate risk of borrowing in dollars.

Information about borrower loan size during this period provides a useful perspective on the potential risk of "mission drift" that I noted in chapter 1. The portfolio allocation between loan sizes remained approximately the same during this period, although the absolute number of loans over $100,000 dropped from 710 loans to 510 loans. Average loan size growth of 20 percent over this period was substantially under the inflation rate and does not incorporate the fact that the average loan size at year-end 2001 was $10,620—higher than the average four years later. Certainly, an important part of the reason for the lack of mission drift was the commitment of KMB's shareholders and supporting donor agencies to serve small borrowers. However, serving smaller clients also made good sense: this was the bank's most profitable client segment.

KMB's accumulated performance also demonstrates the value of its products in helping its clients grow. As can be seen in table 4.2, 59 percent of the clients who had a five-year relationship with KMB more than doubled the size of their borrowing over this period, while an additional 11 percent increased their borrowing size by at least 50 percent. This data clearly illustrates the positive contribution that

TABLE 4.2.
KMB Client Growth

Average loan growth rate, June 1, 2000–June 1, 2005 (%)	Proportion of 948 borrowers with five-year history at KMB (%)
Over 100	59
50–100	11
25–50	4
1–25	4
No changes	14
Reduction in loan size	8

MSE lending can make to economic growth. It also provides an example of the synergies available when one institution provides both micro- and small business loans, because this enables the lender to accommodate borrower growth.

The dynamics of KMB's development from 2001 through 2005 are shown in table 4.3. Two points are particularly important to note. One is the growth of the loan portfolio to almost $416 million. Another is the leveling off and then the decline in profitability in 2005. This was largely due to the costs of upgrading KMB's computer system and is expected to be recouped in future years; the magnitude of these types of expansion costs underscores the contribution that a commercial investor can make to an MSE-focused bank.

TABLE 4.3.
Key Financial Indicators, KMB

	2001	2002	2003	2004	2005
Net loans $000	$96,980	$130,183	$192,613	$241,934	$415,760
Customer accounts $000	$10,178	$30,704	$47,516	$101,202	$137,072
Shareholders' equity $000	$9,991	$12,273	$16,157	$32,351	$33,062
Net profit after tax $000	($1,076)	$1,368	$3,559	$3,699	$1,873
ROAE[a]	(10.2)	12.3	25.0	15.3	5.83
ROAA[b]	(1.1)	0.9	1.6	1.2	0.43
Average loan size	$10,620	$7,580	$6,660	$7,460	$9,096

Source: Annual audited financial reports.

[a] ROAE, the return on average equity, is calculated as the net profit after tax divided by average year-end equity.

[b] ROAA, the return on average assets, is calculated as the net profit after tax divided by average year-end assets.

The Strategic Investor Search

KMB's shareholders had agreed during the discussion of the capital increase that a search for a strategic investor would be initiated once the capital increase was fully under way and after the signing of a new shareholders' agreement that reflected the understanding concerning the characteristics of such a shareholder.

Discussions regarding the process for identifying a new investor began in the fall of 2003 and led to the creation of a three-person investment committee in March 2004. The committee concluded that the most appropriate way to undertake the search was to hire an investment bank to manage the process. Individual board members as well as the shareholders and KMB's CEO had already received a number of inquiries from potential investors, and the board and the committee wanted to ensure that these and other potential investors were carefully reviewed by an experienced party to ensure the optimal outcome.

Despite KMB's relatively small size and the corresponding limit on any investment-banking fees that were linked to the dollar amount of a new investment, a significant number of well-known investment banks competed actively for the mandate. Part of the interest was generated by two significant foreign investments in the banking sector that had taken place in the weeks preceding the awarding of the mandate: GE Capital acquired majority ownership of Delta Bank, a small bank focused on the consumer market, and BNP Paribas had reached agreement to purchase a majority stake in Russky Standart Bank, the consumer finance bank.[21] Not only did these acquisitions demonstrate that investors were interested in the Russian banking market but the pool of potential investee banks was rapidly shrinking. KMB, with its large geographic network, well-trained staff, sound loan portfolio, and commitment to transparency, would presumably be of interest to a wide range of investors.

KMB's shareholders accepted the investment committee's recommendation to hire Renaissance Capital, a Russian investment bank with extensive experience in mergers and acquisitions in the Russian market, to manage the strategic investor search. The shareholders specified that

---

[21] The BNP Paribas purchase was ultimately not finalized.

the investor should have a sound reputation, extensive international experience, and a clear commitment to financing Russian entrepreneurs. It was agreed that all of the shareholders, except for the EBRD, would sell their shares to the new investor. The EBRD would remain a shareholder, with its holding reduced to 25 percent plus one share, in order to ensure that KMB's MSE lending was continued as agreed.

Renaissance Capital held initial discussions with a number of potential investors, both international and Russian banks, before narrowing down the candidates to a small group of major international banks. After negotiations between these banks and KMB's shareholders, it was determined that Banca Intesa, the second largest bank in Italy, had made the best offer and would become KMB's new and largest investor, with an ownership share of 75 percent less one share. Banca Intesa confirmed its intention to continue to develop KMB's MSE lending as well as to accelerate the development of retail products and services that KMB had initiated during 2004. The acquisition was approved by the CBR in September 2005.

KMB has achieved several important "firsts" in its relatively brief existence. It is the first MSE bank in the post-Soviet transition economies to have developed out of a lending program, rather than having started as a greenfield bank. KMB is also the largest MSE bank in the transition economies, as well as one of the largest non–state-owned MSE banks in the world. Finally, KMB is the first MSE bank in the former Soviet Union to attract a commercial investor.[22]

What can we learn from KMB's experience? KMB is an example of the type of positive contribution that donor organizations and socially responsible investors can make to MSE development. By absorbing the start-up and learning costs that a commercial investor would not have been able to accept in the uncertainty of Russia's postcrisis environment, KMB's founders and supporters created a bank that can now serve its MSE clientele profitably. In addition, KMB's experience has shown that small entrepreneurs can be attractive clients, thereby creating a demonstration effect that continues to influence the Russian banking market.

---

[22] The first MSE bank in the region to attract a commercial investor was the American Bank of Kosovo, which was acquired by Raiffeisen Bank in 2004.

The story of KMB also illustrates firsthand the seamlessness—and fluidity—of the relationship between micro- and small business lending that I discussed in chapter 1. Not only did the reality of the marketplace lead to KMB's changing its definition of microborrowers a number of times over the years but the fact that KMB could lend to both micro- and small business clients enabled the bank to help its clients grow—and grow alongside them.

Finally, Banca Intesa's acquisition of KMB will provide important lessons for those interested in the future of MSE finance and the potential of commercial banks to help close the global microfinance lending gap.

CONCLUSION

Russia's experience has a number of lessons with global relevance for microfinance and economic development more broadly. Despite the incredible challenges of the past two decades, Russia is finalizing the creation of the type of inclusive financial system that has become a key development objective for the microfinance field as a whole. The legal, policy, and regulatory environment in Russia is in the final stages of revisions that will strengthen the links of MFIs to the financial sector and facilitate the further growth of MSEs. As important, banks are poised to increase their MSE activity.

One of the reasons for these achievements is that Russia did not have decades of banking traditions that segregated microfinance as a charitable project to help the poor. Having been largely introduced to Russia through the banking sector, microfinance has always been accepted by policymakers, regulators, and bankers as a standard banking activity that can make an important contribution to economic growth. Because everyone is interested in growth, microfinance has broad appeal.

A related lesson from Russia's experience is that loan size can be a misleading tool for the microfinance field. Average microfinance loan sizes in Russia and many other transition countries are larger than in countries where microfinance first took hold, but the basic microfinance principles are the same. Once we rid ourselves of the loan-size perspective we can see more clearly that microfinance is part of a continuum of financial services to entrepreneurs without any clear or permanent dividing lines between microfinance and small business finance. Understanding this point is critical for ensuring that microfinance can fulfill its potential as a tool of economic growth.

Russia also provides one of the first cases of an MSE bank that was created by donor agencies and socially committed investors and then sold to a fully commercial investor. As I have stressed in this book, the microfinance lending gap is so large that it will never be breached without hundreds of billions of dollars of commercial bank investment. Therefore the case of KMB deserves our close attention as a potential model for the future. Donor and socially committed investors understandably become attached to micro- and small business banks that overcome sometimes extraordinary obstacles to grow and become profitable. However, they rarely have the financial resources or expertise to bring banks like KMB to their maximum scale.

Russia provides cautionary lessons as well about potential pitfalls in the creation of an inclusive financial system. The main challenge is that getting all of the pieces into place takes time. During that period, policymakers and legislators learn to appreciate the potential importance of MSEs. However, despite their efforts to support MSE growth, the results of their work take a long time to materialize. The risk during this period is that new programs and policies, designed to address the perceived failures of those that have been put in place, could create a self-fulfilling prophecy by causing the original framework to fail. Almost all of the conditions have been created for MSE finance to expand rapidly in Russia over the next several years, based on the sound and painstaking work that has been done. It is critical that legislators and policymakers maintain confidence in the market's ability to respond positively to these conditions.

Analyzing the history of the development of finance for Russian entrepreneurs has also provided the opportunity to look at the broader context of how Russia's banking system has developed. This approach provides several useful perspectives for understanding what does and does not work in banking-system development and its relationship to financing MSEs.

Although it is clear that the incestuous relationship between banks, the CBR, and the government before 1998 was not a recipe for banking-system development, the more interesting perspective is provided by the postcrisis environment. From a regulatory point of view the environment in the immediate postcrisis years could be described as relatively neutral. The relationships between banks, the CBR, and the government became more at arm's length after the crisis, but there were no major initiatives on the part of the CBR to gain control of a sector that had never been under its control. The first such comprehensive effort did not begin until 2004 with the introduction of deposit insurance.

During this intervening period, therefore, the banks were largely on their own. Of course they had regular CBR inspections, were levied fines for failure to comply with regulations, and in some cases even lost their licenses, but the overall environment did not change substantially. What did change was their relationship with the CBR and the government, the profit-making activities in which they could participate, and therefore their incentives. And this new incentive structure turned the attention of the banks toward lending.

Foreign-owned banks, both commercial and donor-funded, also played a role, first in creating a demonstration effect and subsequently through making investments that are continuing to heighten the competitive environment. I find Russia's experience particularly compelling because it shows how market forces have gradually built momentum once the incentive structure was re-created following the crisis.

The development of Russia's banking system also provides another perspective on building inclusive financial systems. The microfinance methodology is rooted in the basics of good lending methodology: accurate financial analysis, appropriate loan structure and collateral or collateral substitute, and comfort with the borrower's character. As the Russian banking system was evolving during the 1990s most of the bankers were completely new to the banking business. They were forced to learn on the job by trial and error and in many cases relied more on the strength of personal relationships as a guarantee of repayment than on the objective financial analysis that we take for granted. However, hundreds of bankers did receive microfinance training and, as important, reinforced this training with the daily experience of making microfinance loans and ensuring that they were repaid. These lenders used their experience to create the strong loan portfolios that can be seen today at KMB Bank, VTB-24, NBD Bank,

FORUS Bank, and others. Whether these bankers will continue in MSE finance or move on to other careers in finance, the knowledge of how to make a good loan is knowledge that they will carry with them. Therefore, the inclusiveness of Russia's financial sector has helped to strengthen the banking system.

Lending to MSEs helps Russia's banking sector in another way by providing a means for banks to diversify their loan portfolios. A failure of a small client, or even ten or twenty small clients, will not threaten a bank's solvency. More diversification of loan portfolios will also help to diversify Russia's economy, which continues to be dominated by oil and gas production.

Finally, on the theme of Russian entrepreneurs, I hope that the readers of this book have been as heartened as I am by the remarkable achievements of these millions of unsung survivors. Although it is a mistake to invest our own aspirations in people whose experiences are unimaginable, it's hard not to hope that these entrepreneurs could help form the core of a sustainable democracy in Russia. One intriguing theme of the development of entrepreneurship in Russia has been the effective use of associations for furthering their interests. Moreover, once entrepreneurs understood the limits of what the state could do for them, they reversed direction to focus instead on how less state involvement would help them more. The concept of a lobbying association that isn't focused on handouts but on letting businesses go about their business has lessons for many of us.

To conclude on this note of the relationship between entrepreneurs and political development, the results of a 2004 survey of small businesses in Samara are thought-provoking. When entrepreneurs were asked if they would pay all of their local taxes if the revenue were utilized transparently, 60 percent responded affirmatively. It's an intriguing perspective on how entrepreneurs could help Russia help itself.[1]

---

[1] Fifty-three percent of the entrepreneurs responded positively for regional taxes and 36 percent responded positively for federal taxes. The survey was conducted by the Expert Institute of the Union of Industrialists and Entrepreneurs, at the request of the administration of the Samara oblast, 2004. Information provided by Tatiana Alimova.

BIBLIOGRAPHY

Akhmedova, Anna. "Malen'kie kredity na ogromnye summy." *Vedemosti,* June 28, 2006.

Alliance Media. "Moskva: Opredeleny 10 bankov dlya realizatsii programmy kreditovaniya MB." August 28, 2006.

Anderson, James H., and Cheryl W. Gray. "Anticorruption in Transition 3: Who Is Succeeding . . . and Why?" World Bank, 2006.

Annibale, Bob. "A Commercial Strategy for Microfinance." Presentation at the Asia Microfinance Forum, Beijing, March 21–25, 2006.

Aslund, Anders. *How Russia Became a Market Economy.* Washington, D.C.: Brookings Institution, 1995.

Baker-Said, Stephanie. "Uneximbank to Lose State Customs Funds." *Moscow Times,* August 8, 1997.

Beck, Thorsten, Asli Demirguc-Kunt, and Ross Levine. "Small and Medium Enterprises, Growth, and Poverty: Cross-Country Evidence." World Bank Policy Research Working Paper 3178. December 2003.

Beck, Thorsten, Asli Demirguc-Kunt, and Vojislav Maksimov. "Bank Competition and Access to Finance." Draft dated May 2003. http://american.edu/academic.depts/ksb/finance_realestate/mrobe/Seminar/Beck.pdf.

Beyreuther, Ursula. "Comparative Analysis of the Russian and Eastern European Banking Systems." Presentation at Russian Banking Forum, London, December 7–8, 2000.

Borisova, Yevgenia. "Big Banks Shrug Off Regulators." *Moscow Times,* September 15, 1998.

Boussotrot, Sylvie K. "Microfinance in Russia: Finance for Micro and Small Entrepreneurs." World Bank Working Paper. October 2005.

Buckley, Neil. "Gunmen Claim Life of Russia's Bank Reformer." *Financial Times,* September 15, 2006.

CEFIR (Center for Economic and Financial Research) and World Bank. "Monitoring the Administrative Barriers to Small Business Development in Russia: The Fifth Round." Moscow, Summer 2002. http://www.cefir.ru.

——. "Monitoring the Administrative Barriers to Small Business Development in Russia: The First Round." Moscow, November 2005. http://www.cefir.ru.

——. "Monitoring the Administrative Barriers to Small Business Development in Russia: The Second Round." Executive Summary. Moscow, March 2003. http://www.cefir.ru.

Central Bank of Russia. "Obzor Bankovskogo Sektora Rossiyskoy Federatsii." Internet version no. 45. July 2006. http://www.cbr.ru.

——. "Otchet o razvitii bankovskogo sektora i bankovskogo nadzora v 2004 godu." http://www.cbr.ru.

——. "Otchet o razvitii bankovskogo sektora i bankovskogo nadzora v 2005 godu." http://www.cbr.ru.

Chazan, Guy. "Blood Money: Murdered Regulator in Russia Made Plenty of Enemies." *Wall Street Journal*, September 22, 2006, A1.

Cherkasova, Nadya. "Bum nachnyotsya: No cherez 2–3 goda." *Natsional'nyi Bankovskiy Zhurnal* 7, no. 30. July 2006.

Consultative Group to Assist the Poor (CGAP). "Aid Effectiveness in Microfinance: Evaluating Microcredit Projects of the World Bank and the United Nations Development Programme." Focus Note No. 35. April 2006.

——. "Commercial Banks and Microfinance: Evolving Models of Success." Focus Note No. 28. June 2005.

——. "Financial Institutions with a 'Double Bottom Line': Implications for the Future of Microfinance." Occasional Paper No. 8. July 2004.

——. "Foreign Investment in Microfinance: Debt and Equity from Quasi-Commercial Investors." Focus Note No. 25. January 2004.

Daigle, Katy. "Banks Bailed Out with State Loans." *Moscow Times*, November 4, 1998.

Daley-Harris, Sam. *State of the Microcredit Summit Campaign Report 2005*. http://www.microcreditsummit.org.

Development Alternatives. "Banking the Underserved: New Opportunities for Commercial Banks." Paper commissioned by the Financial Sector Team, Policy Division, Department for International Development, London, April 2005.

Dolgopyatova, T. G., ed. *Malyy Biznes v Rossii*. Moscow: Institute of Strategic Analysis and Development of Entrepreneurship (ISARP), n.d.

Dyer, Jay, J. Peter Morrow, and Robin Young. "The Agricultural Bank of Mongolia." In *Scaling Up Poverty Reduction: Case Studies in Microfinance*. Case study prepared for "Global Learning Process for Scaling Up Poverty Reduction" conference, sponsored by CGAP and the World Bank, Shanghai, May 25–27, 2004.

Ekonomika i zhizn'.

European Bank for Reconstruction and Development. "Transition Report 2001: Energy in Transition." 2001.

Finansovye Izvestiya.

FINCA International, Russian Microfinance Center, and Resource Center of Small Entrepreneurship. "Analiz razvitiya mikrofinansirovaniya v Rossii." Part 2. Moscow 2004.

"French Seal DeltaCredit Deal." *Moscow Times,* August 15, 2007.

Gaddy, Clifford G., and Barry W. Ickes. "Russia's Virtual Economy." *Foreign Affairs* 78, no. 5 (September–October 1998).

Garvy, George. *Money, Financial Flows, and Credit in the Soviet Union.* Cambridge, Mass.: Ballinger Publishing for the National Bureau of Economic Research, 1977.

Gonzalez, Adrian, and Richard Rosenberg. "State of the Microcredit 'Industry': Outreach, Poverty, and Profitability." Presentation at "Access to Finance: Building Inclusive Financial Systems" conference sponsored by the World Bank, Washington, D.C., May 20, 2006.

Goskomstat Rossiyskoy Federatsii. "Maloye predprinimatel'stvo v 1995 godu." Moscow. 1996.

Grossman, Gregory. "The 'Second Economy' of the USSR." *Problems of Communism* 27, no. 5 (September–October 1977).

———. "The Second Economy: Boon or Bane for the Reform of the First Economy?" In *Economic Reforms in the Socialist World,* edited by Stanislaw Gomulka, Yong-Chool Ha, and Cae-One Kim. Armonk, N.Y.: M. E. Sharpe, 1989.

Harper, Malcolm, and Sukhwinder Singh Arora, eds. *Small Customers, Big Market: Commercial Banks in Microfinance.* Warwickshire, United Kingdom: ITDG, 2005.

Hellman, Joel Scott. "Breaking the Bank: Bureaucrats and the Creation of Markets in a Transition Economy." PhD diss., Columbia University, 1993.

Helms, Brigit. *Access for All: Building Inclusive Financial Systems.* World Bank, 2006.

Hof, Robert D. "A Major Push for Microphilanthropy." *Business Week* online, November 4, 2005, http://www.businessweek.com.

Hoffman, David E. *The Oligarchs: Wealth and Power in the New Russia.* New York: Public Affairs, 2002.

Hulme, David, and Paul Mosley. *Finance against Poverty.* Vol. 1. New York: Routledge, 1996.

Institut Predprinimatel'sta i investitsii. "V Vserossiyskaya konferentsiya predstaviteley malykh predpriyatiy 'Uskorennoye razvitie malogo preprinimaltel'stva kak faktor ustoychogo rosta ekonomiki'" (Materials related to the Fifth All-Russian Conference of Representatives of Small Enterprises). 2004. http://www.rcsme.ru/libList.

Interfax Russia and CIS Banking and Finance Weekly 13, no. 50 (750), December 10–16, 2005, and 14, no. 5 (757), January 28–February 3, 2006.

"International Banks and Their Expanding Role in Microfinance Investing." *microcapital.* http://www.microcapital.org.

International Monetary Fund. "Russian Federation: Staff Report for the 2000 Article IV Consultation and Public Information Notice Following Consultation." IMF Staff Country Report No. 00/145. November 2000.

Johnson, Juliet. *A Fistful of Rubles: The Rise and Fall of the Russian Banking System.* Ithaca: Cornell University Press, 2000.

Jones, Anthony, and William Moskoff. *KO-OPS: The Rebirth of Entrepreneurship in the Soviet Union.* Bloomington: Indiana University Press, 1991.

"Kak prezident s bankirami vstrechalsya." *Ekonomika i Zhizn'.* Bankovskiy Byuletten' No. 36. September 1995.

Kaufmann, Daniel, Aart Kraay, and Massimo Mastruzzi. "Governance Matters IV: Governance Indicators for 1996–2004." Policy Research Working Paper. Report No. WPS3630. World Bank. June 1, 2005.

Kesner, Lauren. "Redefining Microfinance as a Strategy to Achieve the MDGs: International Year of Microcredit Report Advocates Shift from Poverty Alleviation to Wealth Creation." *Microfinance Matters* 16, September 2005.

Kulikowski, Hubert. "Basel II Impact on Availability and Cost of Financing for SMEs." May 11, 2004. http://www.pwcglobal.com.

Lamdany, Ruben, ed. *Russia: The Banking System during the Transition.* Washington, D.C.: World Bank, 1993.

Lavrentieva, Victoria. "Largest Pre-1988 Private Retail Bank—Finally Laid to Rest." *St. Petersburg Times,* January 31, 2003.

Liedholm, Carl, and Donald C. Mead. "Small-Scale Industries in Developing Countries: Empirical Evidence and Policy Implications." International Development Paper 9. Michigan State University Department of Agricultural Economics, East Lansing, 1987.

———. *Small Enterprises and Economic Development: The Dynamics of Micro and Small Enterprises.* New York: Routledge, 1999.

Littlefield, Elizabeth, and Richard Rosenberg. "Microfinance and the Poor: Breaking Down the Walls between Microfinance and Formal Finance." *Finance & Development* 16, no. 2. June 2004.

"Maloye predprinimatel'stvo v Rossii 2002 and 2004." Statistical handbook. Goskomstat (2002), Rosstat (2004). Moscow.

"Malyi i sredniy biznes pokazali rekordnye tempy razvitiya." *Rosbalt,* September 21, 2006. http://www.rcsme.ru/news.asp.

Mamuta, Mikhail. "Nebankovskie mikrokredity: Kto ikh daet?" *Natsional'nyy Bankovskiy Zhurnal* 7, no. 30. July 2006.

Marulanda, Beatriz, and Maria Otero. "The Profile of Microfinance in Latin America in 10 Years: Vision and Characteristics." ACCION. 2005.

Ministry of Antimonopoly Policy and Support for Entrepreneurship. "Doklad Ministerstva Rossiskoy Federatsii po antimonopol'noy politike i poderzhke predprinimatel'stva na III Vserossiyskoy konferentsii predstaviteley malykh predpriyatiy" (Materials related to the Third All-Russian Conference of Representatives of Small Enterprises). 2002. http://www.rcsme.ru/libList.

MicroBanking Bulletin no. 11. August 2005.

Moiseev, Igor. "Dva capital." *Vedemosti,* September 9, 2002.

"Nachali s malogo." *Profil',* September 9, 2005.

National Bank of Poland. "Summary Evaluation of the Financial Situation of Polish Banks, 2001." Warsaw, May 2002.

Ono, Shigeki. "Lending and Investing Activities of Russian Banks from 1992 to the Beginning of 1998." *Slavic Studies* 47. 2000.

OPORA (Obshcherossiyskaya Obshchestvennaya Organizatsiya Malogo i Srednogo Predprinimaltel'stva) and VITsOM (Vserossiyskiy Tsentr Issledovaniy Obshchego Mneniya). "Usloviya i factory razvitiya malogo predprinimatel'stva v regionakh RF." Moscow, 2005. http://www.opora.ru.

Organizing Committee of the Fourth All-Russian Conference. "Itogovye materiali, IV Vserossiyskoy konferentsii predstaviteley malykh predpriyatiy: Vzaimodeystviye malogo i krupnogo biznesa" (Materials related to the Fourth All-Russian Conference of Representatives of Small Enterprises). 2003. http://www.rcsme.ru/libList.

Organizing Committee of the Sixth Conference. VI Vserossiyskaya Konferentsiya Predstaviteley Malykh Predpriyatiy. "Informatsiya o konferentsii" (Materials related to the Sixth All-Russian Conference of Representatives of Small Enterprises). 2005. http://www.rcsme.ru/libList.

Ostrovsky, Arkady, and Patrick Jenkins. "Dresdner to Handle Share Issue for Gazprombank." *Financial Times*, December 8, 2005.

Pashchuk, A., "Much Attention to Small Credits." *Sekret Firmy* 6 (February 14–20, 2005).

Petrova, G. Summary of remarks at February 21, 2006, meeting of the Subcommittee on Microfinance of the Russian Chamber of Commerce and Trade and the Committee for the Development of Microfinance of the Association of Russian Banks. http://www.rmcenter.ru.

Pikturna, Virgis. "Steering Russia's Banking System toward Stability." *Transition* 2, no. 10. May 17, 1996.

Piontkovsky, Andrei. "Berezovsky Still Powerful despite Being Dismissed." *St. Petersburg Times*, November 17–23, 1997.

Popov, Nikolai. "A Fateful Triangle: Business, Government, and the People." *Novoe Vremya*, no. 19. May 18, 2005.

Pravitel'stvo Rossiyskoy Federatsii i Tsentral'nogo Banka Rossiyskoy Federatsii. "O Strategii razvitii bankovskogo sektora Rossiyskoy federatsii na period do 2008 goda." April 4, 2005. http://www.cbr.ru.

Rabobank Press Release. "Rabobank Consortium Acquires Interest in Tanzanian Bank." August 25, 2005. Primezone. http://www.primezone.com/newsroom/news.html?d=84571.

Research Center for Small Entrepreneurship. "Malye predpriyatiya: Posledstviya krizisa." Tacis Project SMERUS9803. 2000.

Rhyne, Elisabeth. *Mainstreaming Microfinance: How Lending Began, Grew, and Came of Age in Bolivia.* Bloomfield, Conn.: Kumarian Press, 2001.

Richardson, Dave C., "Going to the Barricades for Microsavings Mobilization: A View of the Real Costs from the Trenches." *MicroBanking Bulletin* 9. July 2003.

Robinson, Marguerite S. *The Microfinance Revolution: Sustainable Finance for the Poor.* Vol. 1. Washington, D.C.: World Bank, and New York: Open Society Institute, 2003.

Rosstat. "Maloe predprinimatel'stvo v Rossii, 2005." Moscow, 2005.

———. "Pokazateli deyatel'nosti malykh predpriyatii za 2005 g." Moscow, 2006.

"Russian Banks Get Support." World-Wire, *Wall Street Journal*, November 20, 1994.

Russian Independent Institute of Social and National Problems. "Osenniy krizis 1998 goda: Rossiyskoye obshchestvo do i posle." Moscow, 1998.

Russian Microfinance Center. "Mikrofinansirovaniye v Rossii." Presentation to the Advisory Council of the National Association of Microfinance Providers and the Council on Federations of the Russian Federation. June 29, 2006. http://www.rmcenter.ru.

Russian Microfinance Center. "Vedushchie uchastiniki rynka obedinyayut svoi usiliya po razvitiyu sistemy mikrofinansirovaniya malogo biznesa." Press release. February 13, 2006. http://www.rmcenter.ru.

Russian Microfinance Center and Resource Center of Small Entrepreneurship. "Tendentsii razvitiya rynka nebankovskogo microfinansirovaniya v Rossii, 2003–2004." Moscow, 2006. http://www.rmcenter.ru.

Rutland, Peter. "Russian Small Business: Staying Small." *Jamestown Foundation Eurasia Daily Monitor*, March 15, 2005.

Schreiner, Mark. "Scoring: The Next Breakthrough in Microcredit?" CGAP Occasional Paper No. 7. January 2003.

Shestoperov, A. M. "Dinamika razvitiya malogo predprinimatel'stva v region-akh Rossii." Report for 2004, dated May 2005; report for 2005, dated May 2006. Natsional'nyy Institut Sistemnykh Problem Prednimatel'stva. http://www.nisse.ru.

Simkina, Lana. "Banking in Russia's Regions." *BISNIS.* July 1997.

State Committee of the Russian Federation for the Support and Development of Small Entrepreneurship, the Council on Industrial Policy and Entrepreneurship under the Government of the Russian Federation, the Chamber of Commerce and Industry of the Russian Federation. "I Vserossiyskiy S"ezd Predstaviteley malykh predpriyatiy" (Materials Related to the First All-Russian Congress of Representatives of Small Enterprises). 1996. http://www.rcsme.ru/libList.

Tacis. "Russian SME Observatory Report 2001." Executive summary. Moscow. June 2002.

Tacis. Resource Center for Small Entrepreneurs. "Russian SME Observatory Report 2001." Moscow. June 2002.

United Nations. *Building Inclusive Financial Sectors for Development.* 2006.

USAID and Russian SME Resource Centre. "Analysis of the Role and Place of Small and Medium-Sized Enterprises in Russia." Moscow, 2003.

van der Putten, Frans Paul. Coordinating author. "A Billion to Gain? A Study on Global Financial Institutions and Microfinance." ING Microfinance Support. Amsterdam, February 2006.

van Schaik, John. "The Newly-Wed and the Nearly Dead." *Euromoney* 362. June 1999.

Volkov, Vadim. *Violent Entrepreneurs: The Use of Force in the Making of Russian Capitalism.* Ithaca: Cornell University Press, 2002.

"VTB-22 to Build Small Business Loan Portfolio to 5 bln Rubles." Interfax. September 9, 2005.

Wallace, Elizabeth. "EBRD's Micro and Small Enterprise Lending Programmes: Downscaling Commercial Banks and Starting Greenfield Banks." In *The Development of the Financial Sector in Southeast Europe: Innovative Approaches in Volatile Environments*, edited by Ingrid Matthaus-Maier and J. D. von Pischke. Berlin: Springer-Verlag, 2004.

Wendel, Charles B. "Ten SME Facts." *SME Weekly*. Financial Institutions Consulting. April 13, 2004. http://www.ficinc.com.

"West Owed $6Bln in Forwards." *Moscow Times*, October 23, 1998.

Wighton, David. "Citigroup Plans to Fund Microfinance Programme." *Financial Times*, September 22, 2006.

World Bank. "Russian Economic Report #7." World Bank Russian Country Department. Economics Unit. February 2004.

———. *Building Trust: Developing the Russian Financial Sector*. Washington, D.C.: World Bank, 2002.

"The World's Worst Central Banker." *Economist*. October 16, 1993.

Yasin, E. G., A. Yu. Chepurenko, V. V. Bueva, eds. "Maloye predprinimatel'stvo v Rossii: Proshloye, nastoyashchee i budushchee." Moscow: Fund "Liberal Mission," 2003.

Yermakov, V. P., and V. Sh. Kaganov. "Razvitie malogo predprinimatel'stva v Rossii: Glavnye napravleniya (po materialiam II Vserossiyskovo s"ezda malykh predpriyatiy)" (Materials related to the Second All-Russian Congress of Representatives of Small Enterprises). 2000. Moscow.

Yoffi, A. D., V. Shch. Kaganov, and A. I. Mishchin, eds. "Maloye predprinimatel'stvo v Rossii: Sostoyaniye, problemy, perspektivy." Analytical materials prepared for the Second All-Russian Congress of Entrepreneurs, Institute of Entrepreneurship and Investment, Moscow, 1999.

Yunus, Muhammad. *Banker to the Poor: Micro-Lending and the Battle against World Poverty*. New York: PublicAffairs. 1999.

INDEX

Note: Italic page numbers refer to tables.